ALIGNMENT

ALIGNMENT

USING THE BALANCED SCORECARD
TO CREATE CORPORATE SYNERGIES

Robert S. Kaplan
David P. Norton

HARVARD BUSINESS SCHOOL PRESS

BOSTON, MASSACHUSETTS

© 2006 Harvard Business School Publishing Corporation

All rights reserved.
Printed in the United States of America
10 09 08 07 06   5 4 3 2 1

Library of Congress Cataloging-in-Publication Data

Kaplan, Robert S.
  Alignment / Robert S. Kaplan, David P. Norton.
    p. cm.
  Includes index.
  ISBN 1-59139-690-5
  1. Strategic planning. 2. Industrial management. 3. Industrial organization. 4. Strategic alliances (Business) 5. Organizational effectiveness. I. Norton, David P., 1941- II. Title.
  HD30.28.K3543 2006
  658.4'012—dc22

                                                                      2005030504

CONTENTS

Preface   *vii*

1. Alignment: A Source of Economic Value   1

2. Corporate Strategy and Structure: Historical Perspective   29

3. Aligning Financial and Customer Strategies   43

4. Aligning Internal Process and Learning and   77
   Growth Strategies: Integrated Strategic Themes

5. Aligning Support Functions   119

6. Cascading: The Process   169

7. Aligning Boards and Investors   193

8. Aligning External Partners   221

9. Managing the Alignment Process   245

10. Total Strategic Alignment   259

Index   *291*
About the Authors   *301*

PREFACE

Alignment is the fourth book in our collaboration. Our initial article, "The Balanced Scorecard: Measures That Drive Performance," and first book, *The Balanced Scorecard: Translating Strategy into Action*, introduced the new approach for measuring organizational performance.[1] The article and book provided guidance and examples for selecting measures in the four Balanced Scorecard perspectives, and described the emerging system for managing strategy that early adopters of the concept had used. A subsequent article, "Using the Balanced Scorecard as a Strategic Management System," and our second book, *The Strategy-Focused Organization*, described how enterprises were now using the scorecard as the centerpiece of a sophisticated system to manage the execution of strategy.[2] These works, elaborating on the strategy management system introduced in the first book, identified five key principles for aligning an organization's measurement and management systems to strategy:

1. Mobilize change through executive leadership
2. Translate strategy into operational terms
3. Align the organization to the strategy
4. Motivate to make strategy everyone's job
5. Govern to make strategy a continual process

A third book, *Strategy Maps*, and article, "Having Trouble with Your Strategy? Then Map It," elaborated on Principle 2 of how to translate strategy into tangible objectives and measures.[3] The book and article introduced a general framework for representing strategy through specific objectives that could be linked in cause-and-effect relationships across the four Balanced Scorecard perspectives. The framework aligned processes, people, and technology to the customer value proposition and customer and shareholder objectives.

The current book extends Principle 3: align all organizational units to the strategy. Most enterprises consist of multiple business and support units. Corporations operate diverse units under a single corporate umbrella to capture economies of scale and scope. But to achieve these benefits, the corporate headquarters needs a tool to articulate a theory for how to operate the multiple units within the corporate structure to create value beyond what the individual units could achieve on their own, without central guidance and intervention. After all, a corporate headquarters may subtract more than it adds. It incurs explicit costs through the salaries and support expenses of the corporate executive team. It also could impose implicit costs through delayed decision making and onerous reporting requirements on operating and support units. The value creation that offsets these headquarters costs must arise from aligning decentralized units to create a new source of value, which we call *enterprise-derived* value.

This book introduces the role for an enterprise Strategy Map and Balanced Scorecard that clarify corporate priorities, which can then be clearly communicated to each business and support unit, and also to the board of directors and key customers, suppliers, and alliance partners. Corporate headquarters subsequently examines the Strategy Maps and scorecards developed by these units to monitor whether and how the enterprise's priorities are being implemented by each one. Used in this way, the enterprise Strategy Map and Balanced Scorecard provides corporate executives with a governance framework that helps to unlock previously unrealized value from enterprise synergies.

Beyond aligning organizational units, the primary focus of this book, the enterprise must also align employees and management processes and systems to the strategy (Principles 4 and 5 of the strategy-focused organization). For completeness purposes, we explore, in less detail, these additional two alignment processes in the final chapter of the book.

ACKNOWLEDGMENTS

This book builds upon an extensive literature on corporate-level strategy, which we summarize in Chapter 2. We are indebted to the pioneering work of the strategy scholars who educated us about the power of corporate-level strategy: Alfred Chandler, Michael Porter, Cynthia Montgomery, David Collis, Joseph Bower, Michael Goold, Andrew Campbell, Marcus Alexander, Gary Hamel, C. K. Prahalad, and Constantinos Markides. We hope that we have represented their contributions faithfully and have added to them by explicating how to design a measurement and management system that communicates and manages the capture of enterprise-derived value.

We have also benefited greatly from the experiences of the more than thirty enterprises we cite in this book. The innovations in their organizations continually stimulate and enrich our thinking. In particular, our thanks go to the following contributors:

• Aktiva	Andreja Kodrin
• Bank of Tokyo- Mitsubishi	Takehiko Nagumo, Nobuyuki Hirano
• Canon, USA	Charles Biczak
• Citizen Schools	Eric Schwarz
• DuPont	Craig Naylor
• First Commonwealth Financial Corporation	Angela Ritenour, Jerry Thomchick
• Handleman Company	Stephen Strome, Mark Albrecht, Rozanne Kokko, Gina Drewek
• Hilton	Dieter Huckestein, Dennis Koci
• IBM	Ted Hoff, Lynda Lambert
• Ingersoll-Rand	Herb Henkel, Don Rice
• KeyCorp	Henry Meyer, Michele Seyranian
• Lockheed Martin	Pamela Santiago
• Marriott	Roy Barnes
• MDS Corporation	John Rogers, Bob Harris
• Media General	Stewart Bryan, Bill McDonnell
• New Profit Inc.	Vanessa Kirsch

- RCMP   Giuliano Zacardelli, Keith Clark

- Unibanco   Marcelo Orticelli

- U.S. Army   Strategic Readiness System Team

We are also indebted to the professional staff of the Balanced Scorecard Collaborative. These talented people push the envelope of good management practices with their clients on a continuing basis. They are our fountain of knowledge. We would like to recognize the following for their specific contributions to this book: Arun Dhingra for his work on finance organization alignment, Robert Gold for his contributions to IT organization alignment, Cassandra Frangos for her leadership on human capital alignment, Mike Nagel for his pioneering work on board governance, Randy Russell for his research on management best-practices programs, and Rob Howie for leading our Balanced Scorecard Hall of Fame program.

We would like to acknowledge the work of Steve Fortini, who prepared the many complex graphics. Final acknowledgment to our assistants—Rose LaPiana and David Porter—and to the HBS Press staff, including Hollis Heimbouch, our editor for all four Balanced Scorecard books, and Jen Waring, production editor.

NOTES

1. R. S. Kaplan and D. P. Norton, "The Balanced Scorecard: Measures That Drive Performance," *Harvard Business Review* (January–February 1992): 71–79; R. S. Kaplan and D. P. Norton, *The Balanced Scorecard: Translating Strategy into Action* (Boston: Harvard Business School Press, 1996).
2. R. S. Kaplan and D. P. Norton, "Using the Balanced Scorecard as a Strategic Management System," *Harvard Business Review* (January–February 1996): 75–85; R. S. Kaplan and D. P. Norton, *The Strategy-Focused Organization: How Balanced Scorecard Companies Thrive in the New Competitive Environment* (Boston: Harvard Business School Press, 2001).
3. R. S. Kaplan and D. P. Norton, "Having Trouble with Your Strategy? Then Map It," *Harvard Business Review* (September–October 2000): 167–176; R. S. Kaplan and D. P. Norton, *Strategy Maps: Converting Intangible Assets into Tangible Outcomes* (Boston: Harvard Business School Press, 2004).

CHAPTER ONE

ALIGNMENT

A SOURCE OF ECONOMIC VALUE

ON FALL AND SPRING WEEKENDS, we often see eight-person shells racing up the Charles River separating Boston and Cambridge. Although each shell contains strong, highly motivated athletes, the key to their success is that they row in synchronism. Imagine a shell populated by eight highly conditioned and trained rowers, but with each rower having a different idea about how to achieve success: how many strokes per minute were optimal and which course the shell should follow, given wind direction and speed, water current, and a curvy course with multiple bridge underpasses. For eight exceptional rowers to devise and attempt to implement independent tactics would be disastrous. Rowing at different speeds and in different directions could cause the shell to travel in circles and perhaps capsize. The winning crew invariably rows in beautiful synchronism; each rower strokes powerfully but consistently with all the others, guided by a coxswain, who has responsibility for pacing and steering the course of action.

Many corporations are like an uncoordinated shell. They consist of wonderful business units, each populated by highly trained, experienced, and motivated executives. But the efforts of the individual business units are not coordinated. At best, the units don't interfere with each other, and the corporate performance equals the sum of the individual business units' performance minus the cost of the corporate headquarters. More likely, however, some of the business units' efforts create conflicts over shared customers or shared resources, or the units lose opportunities for even higher performance by failing to coordinate their actions. Their combined results fall considerably short of what they could have achieved had they worked better together.

The shell's coxswain is like a corporate headquarters. A passive coxswain consumes valuable space, weighs down the boat, and detracts from the crew's overall performance. A superior coxswain, in contrast, understands the strengths and weaknesses of each rower, studies the external environment, and analyzes the competition. The coxswain then determines a clear course of action for the shell and ensures its implementation by coordinating the rowers for optimal performance. The superior coxswain, like a well-led corporate headquarters, adds to the performance of the individual rowers.

ALIGNMENT MATTERS

Each year, the Balanced Scorecard Collaborative selects a few organizations for induction into the Balanced Scorecard Hall of Fame for Strategy Execution.[1] These organizations have demonstrated successful implementation of their strategies using a performance management system based on the BSC.

For example, consider Chrysler Group, the U.S. automobile division of DaimlerChrysler, which faced a forecast loss of $5.1 billion in CY 2001. The division brought in a new CEO, who used the BSC to communicate a turnaround strategy involving both cost reductions and future growth through new product development. Despite continued weakness in the U.S. automobile market, Chrysler generated $1.9 billion in profits in 2004 through a combination of great new car introductions and major production efficiencies. Media General, a regional communications company (newspapers, television, and Internet), used the scorecard to align its diverse properties to a new convergence strategy and saw its stock increase 85 percent more than that of its competitors over a four-year period. Korean conglomerate E-Land (retail apparel, hotels, furniture, and construction) doubled its revenues to $1.1 billion between 1998 and 2003 while increasing profits from $8 million to $150 million in the same period.

We have studied the specific management practices used by the Hall of Fame organizations and compared their practices with those of two other groups accessed through an online survey: high-benefit users (HBUs) report that they have achieved significant results through use of the Balanced Scorecard, and low-benefit users (LBUs) claim only limited benefits with their scorecard programs. We classified both groups' management practices along the five key management processes that we have previously identified as important for successful strategy implementation.[2]

- *Mobilization*: orchestrating change through executive leadership
- *Strategy translation*: defining Strategy Maps, Balanced Scorecards, targets, and initiatives
- *Organization alignment*: aligning corporate, business units, support units, external partners, and boards with the strategy
- *Employee motivation*: providing education, communication, goal setting, incentive compensation, and training of staff
- *Governance*: integrating strategy into planning, budgeting, reporting, and management reviews

Figure 1-1 compares the three groups in the levels of excellence they achieved in strategy management practices. The results reveal a strong ordinal ranking. The practice levels of the Hall of Fame organizations exceed those of the other two groups on each strategy management process, and the practice levels of the high-benefit users exceed those of the low-benefit users on each process as well. Higher performance of strategy management practices is associated with high levels of benefits received.

The greatest gap between the practices of Hall of Fame organizations and those of the other two groups occurs for organization alignment. Enterprises enjoying the greatest benefits from their new performance management systems are much better at aligning their corporate, business unit, and support unit strategies, and this indicates that alignment, much like the synchronism achieved by a high-performance rowing crew, produces dramatic benefits. Understanding how to create alignment in organizations is a big deal, one capable of producing significant payoffs for all types of enterprises. Our interest in this subject is natural because surveys of senior executives report that the Balanced Scorecard is one of their top tools to create organizational integration.[3]

ENTERPRISE-DERIVED VALUE

Aligning organizational units to create value at the enterprise level generally gets less attention than creating value at the business unit (BU) level. Most strategy theories focus on business units, with their distinct products, services, customers, markets, technologies, and competencies. A

Figure 1-1   Relationship Between Managerial Excellence and Level of Benefits

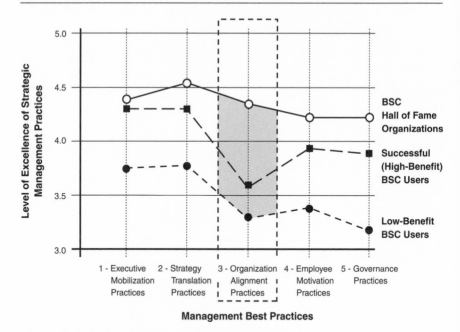

Participants rated their level of practice excellence on a 5-point scale
(1 = "We are awful at this"; 2 = "We are not good at this"; 3 = "We are okay at this";
4 = "We are good at this"; 5 = "We are best practice at this")

business unit strategy describes how the BU intends to create products and services that offer a unique, differentiated mix of benefits, called the *customer value proposition*, to potential customers. If the value proposition is sufficiently attractive, the customer makes a series of purchases that creates value for the business unit. In our previous book we discussed four value proposition archetypes around which business units typically compete.[4]

Best Total Cost	Offer products and services that are consistent, timely, and low cost
Product Leader	Offer products and services that expand existing performance boundaries
Customer Solutions	Provide a customized mix of products and services, combined with know-how, to solve customers' problems

System Platform   Provide a platform that becomes the
                                     industry standard for offering products
                                     and services

Business units develop Strategy Maps and Balanced Scorecards to help them gain consensus for the strategy among the senior executive team, communicate the strategy to employees so that they can help the organization implement the strategy, allocate resources consistent with the strategy, and monitor and guide the strategy's performance. All these activities enable the business unit to create value from its customer relationships.

Most contemporary corporations, however, are made up of portfolios of business units and shared-service units. For a corporation to add value to its collection of business units and shared-service units, it must align these operating and service units to create *synergy*. This is the domain of corporate or enterprise strategy, defining how the headquarters adds value.[5] When the enterprise aligns the activities of its disparate business units and its support units, it creates additional sources of value, which we call *enterprise-derived value.*

$$\begin{bmatrix} \text{Value} \\ \text{Creation} \end{bmatrix} = \begin{bmatrix} \text{Customer-} \\ \text{Derived} \\ \text{Value} \end{bmatrix} + \begin{bmatrix} \text{Enterprise-} \\ \text{Derived} \\ \text{Value} \end{bmatrix}$$

$$\begin{bmatrix} \text{Value} \\ \text{Creation} \\ \text{Strategy} \end{bmatrix} = \begin{bmatrix} \text{Customer} \\ \text{Value} \\ \text{Proposition} \end{bmatrix} + \begin{bmatrix} \text{Enterprise} \\ \text{Value} \\ \text{Proposition} \end{bmatrix}$$

For example, a corporation might establish a new sales channel that promotes the cross-selling of products and services offered by its various business units. It might gain economies of scale by sharing an expensive and critical resource, such as a manufacturing plant, a common information system, or a research and development group. Synergies will not occur unless the corporate level plays an active role to identify and coordinate opportunities for integrating the behavior of its decentralized business units. If, however, the corporate headquarters does not create such synergy—or, worse, subtracts from the value created by its collection of operating and service units—investors can rightfully question why the various units are bundled together. Shareholders would receive higher value if the anergystic (opposite of synergistic) corporation would dissolve, leaving them with proportional ownership in the individual operating companies and avoiding the cost and bureaucracy of operating the corporate headquarters.

Corporate strategy describes how an enterprise avoids this fate by creating value greater than that achieved if its individual units were operating autonomously. We refer to the set of specific cross-business objectives intended to create enterprise-derived value as the *enterprise value proposition*.

Public-sector and nonprofit organizations face similar issues. The Department of Defense must integrate the efforts of large, powerful units (such as the Army, Navy, Air Force, Marines, and Defense Logistics Agency) that are well funded and have years of autonomous operation and tradition. The Royal Canadian Mounted Police must align its diverse functional and regional units, including national police units dealing with international crime and terrorism, remote units that promote health and safety in aboriginal communities, and contract policing units that provide provinces and municipalities with localized traditional police services. The American Diabetes Association and the Red Cross must unite a multinational network of decentralized units under a common brand and philosophy. Each requires a methodology, such as the Balanced Scorecard and Strategy Map, to clarify, communicate, and facilitate its enterprise role.

The Enterprise Value Proposition

The four-perspective framework of a business unit's Balanced Scorecard describes how the unit creates shareholder value through enhanced customer relationships driven by excellence in internal processes. These processes are continually improved by aligning people, systems, and culture. The four perspectives are as follows:

Financial	What are our shareholder expectations for financial performance?
Customer	To reach our financial objectives, how do we create value for our customers?
Internal Process	What processes must we excel at to satisfy our customers and shareholders?
Learning and Growth	How do we align our intangible assets— people, systems, and culture—to improve the critical processes?

Each of these four perspectives is linked in a chain of cause-and-effect relationships. For example, a training program to improve employee skills (the learning and growth perspective) improves customer service (internal process), which, in turn, leads to greater customer satisfaction and loyalty (customer) and, eventually, increased revenues and margins (financial).

The four-perspective framework for business unit strategies turns out to extend naturally for developing an enterprise Balanced Scorecard (see Figure 1-2). The corporate headquarters does not have customers, nor does it operate processes that make products or services. Customers and operating processes are within the domain of the business units. The corporate headquarters aligns the value-creating activities of its business units—enabling them to create more benefits to their customers or to lower total operating costs—beyond what they could achieve by themselves if they were operating independently. Thus, the objectives in the four perspectives of the enterprise Balanced Scorecard should answer the following questions.

Financial: How Can We Increase the Shareholder Value of the Business Units in Our Strategic Business Unit (SBU) Portfolio?
Corporate financial synergy revolves around issues such as where to invest, where to harvest, how to balance risk, and how to create an investor brand. The corporate headquarters in holding companies and highly diversified corporations (such as Berkshire Hathaway, FMC Corporation, and Textron) creates value mainly by its superior ability to allocate capital among its operating units. The corporate value to these diversified enterprises comes from operating an internal capital market that is more effective and efficient than if each autonomous company were an independent and publicly owned company.

Other corporations, in addition to striving for financial synergies from superior resource allocation and governance processes, play an active role in creating synergies among the three other Balanced Scorecard perspectives.

Customer: How Can We Share the Customer Interface to Increase Total Customer Value?
A satisfied customer is a precious asset. The goodwill generated by a positive customer relationship translates into the potential for repeat purchases and an extension of the relationship to other company products and services, particularly those packaged under the same brand. Companies with homogeneous retail outlets—such as retail banks, stores, and franchisers like Hilton Hotels and Wendy's—seek to promote standardization throughout their dispersed units to deliver a common, consistent

Figure 1-2 Building the Enterprise Scorecard

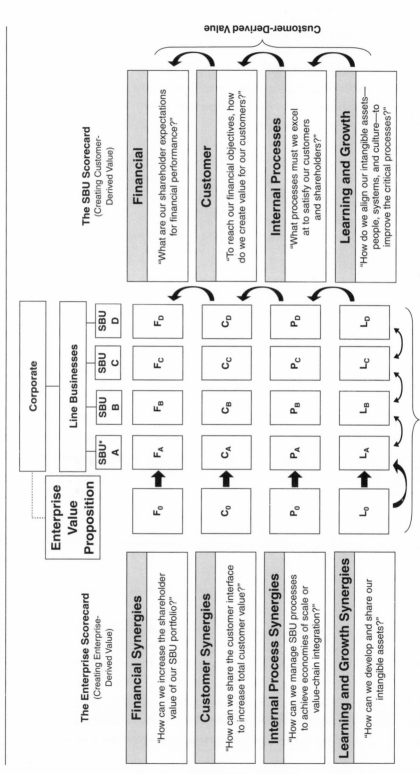

The Enterprise Scorecard
(Creating Enterprise-Derived Value)

Financial Synergies

"How can we increase the shareholder value of our SBU portfolio?"

Customer Synergies

"How can we share the customer interface to increase total customer value?"

Internal Process Synergies

"How can we manage SBU processes to achieve economies of scale or value-chain integration?"

Learning and Growth Synergies

"How can we develop and share our intangible assets?"

The SBU Scorecard
(Creating Customer-Derived Value)

Financial

"What are our shareholder expectations for financial performance?"

Customer

"To reach our financial objectives, how do we create value for our customers?"

Internal Processes

"What processes must we excel at to satisfy our customers and shareholders?"

Learning and Growth

"How do we align our intangible assets—people, systems, and culture—to improve the critical processes?"

Customer-Derived Value

Enterprise-Derived Value

Corporate

Line Businesses

Enterprise Value Proposition

*SBU = strategic business unit

customer experience at every location, one that reinforces and enhances the corporate brand.

In more diversified corporations, a single business unit may initiate a customer relationship and develop it modestly, but ultimately the unit may be limited by the breadth of its products or services. Other business units in the corporation can enhance the relationship by offering complementary products and services to the same customer. A producer of medical instruments, for example, may have satisfied and loyal customers for its range of products. But it can generate an additional—and perhaps more profitable and certainly more stable—source of revenue through post-sales service and maintenance performed by the company's field services business unit. By expanding the marketing message and redesigning the selling process, corporations can bring the products of several business units to the customer, thus increasing revenue per customer through cross-selling.

For example, the former strategy of Northwestern Mutual, a financial services company, was based on providing superior life insurance through a single sales force of insurance specialists. The company's new strategy expanded on this base by adding a full range of investment products and advisory services to address the needs of its customers for financial protection, capital accumulation, estate preservation, and asset distribution. Northwestern Mutual created a network of specialists to assist the insurance sales force with the advice and support required to serve customers and cross-sell this broader set of services. The corporate role was to create value by broadening the set of services available to customers, who were now exposed to the knowledge of the account team as well as the capabilities of multiple products that were now linked to create a more complete solution. The corporation created teamwork across business units that previously had operated autonomously.

Internal: How Can We Manage SBU Processes to Achieve Economies of Scale or Value-Chain Integration?

Large organizations have opportunities to create economies of scale to enhance their competitive advantage and shareholder value. The purchasing and distribution processes of Wal-Mart (private sector) and Defense Logistics Services (public sector) operate at a scale that rivals the GNPs of small countries. Every multiunit corporation can create scale economies by examining common processes required by its multiple business units.

For example, one corporate department in a retailer such as The Limited contracts for and manages real estate used by all retail outlets.

Another corporate-level department negotiates supplier relationships for all the business units. Automobile manufacturers, such as Daimler-Chrysler, coordinate the design and development of new products on a global basis. In our earlier books, we described how the marine engineering division of Brown & Root created value by integrating the offerings of its previously independent engineering, design, fabrication, installation, and logistics business units so that it could supply a complete, turnkey solution to customers.

Learning and Growth: How Can We Develop and Share Our Intangible Assets?

Perhaps the greatest opportunity for a beneficial headquarters role is to develop and share critical intangible assets: people, technology, culture, and leadership. Professional service organizations such as SAS Institute (software), Accenture (consulting), and Schering (pharmaceuticals) consciously manage the movement of ideas throughout their enterprises. Citicorp and Goodyear were pioneers in creating a global culture by rotating a cadre of executives in their worldwide offices to support their strategies for global expansion. Organizations like British Petroleum (BP) have centralized IT organizations that share the sophisticated, specialized knowledge of IT professionals with diverse organizational units. Intangible assets have become a new force in business strategy. They present an opportunity, and a mandate, for headquarters offices to manage them in a way that creates synergy and sustained competitive advantage.

Figure 1-3 summarizes various sources of enterprise-level synergies, organized by the four perspectives of an enterprise Balanced Scorecard. We describe and illustrate this structure in more detail in Chapters 3 and 4, where we describe successful private, public, and nonprofit enterprise applications.

THE ALIGNMENT SEQUENCE

Figure 1-4 shows a typical sequence used to create enterprise-derived value. The process starts when the corporate headquarters articulates an enterprise value proposition that will create synergies among operating units, support units, and external partners. The enterprise Strategy Map and Balanced Scorecard articulate and clarify corporate priorities and clearly communicate them to all business and support units.

Figure 1-5   Sources of Enterprise Synergy

The Enterprise Scorecard

Sources of Enterprise-Derived Value (Strategic Themes)

Financial Synergies

"How can we increase the shareholder value of our SBU portfolio?"

- *Internal capital management:* Create synergy through effective management of internal capital and labor markets.
- *Corporate brand:* Integrate a diverse set of businesses around a single brand, promoting common values or themes.

Customer Synergies

"How can we share the customer interface to increase total customer value?"

- *Cross-selling:* Create value by cross-selling a broad range of products and services from several business units.
- *Common value proposition:* Create a consistent buying experience, conforming to corporate standards at multiple outlets.

Internal Process Synergies

"How can we manage SBU processes to achieve economies of scale or value-chain integration?"

- *Shared services:* Create economies of scale by sharing the systems, facilities, and personnel in critical support processes.
- *Value-chain integration:* Create value by integrating contiguous processes in the industry value chain.

Learning and Growth Synergies

"How can we develop and share our intangible assets?"

- *Intangible assets:* Share competency in the development of human, information, and organization capital.

Figure 1-4 Building Alignment into the Planning Process

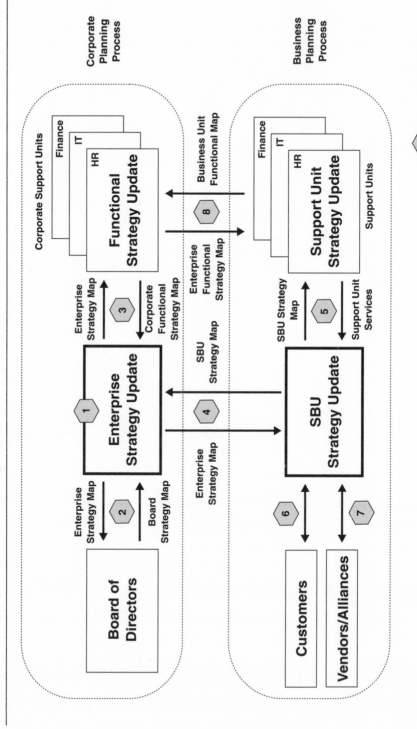

Aligning Enterprise Headquarters with Operating Units

After the corporate headquarters develops its strategy and value proposition, each business and support unit develops its long-range plan and Balanced Scorecard to be consistent with the enterprise scorecard. The process helps business units balance their challenging tasks. They, of course, must be formidable competitors in their local markets. They often choose their targeted customers and the value proposition to be offered to customers and then develop their people, systems, and culture to enhance internal operating processes, customer management processes, and innovation processes that deliver value to customers and their corporate parent. Business units must also contribute to corporate-level synergies, incorporating corporate themes, servicing corporate customers, and integrating and coordinating with other business units for additional sources of value creation. Business unit Strategy Maps and Balanced Scorecards must reflect both local excellence and corporate contribution. We discuss such alignment in Chapters 3 and 4.

Aligning Internal Support and Service Units

Next, shared-service units, such as human resources, information technology, finance, and planning, develop their long-range plans and Balanced Scorecards to support the strategies of the business units and enterprise priorities. For example, the enterprise value proposition may require that the human resource department create synergy by developing new programs to recruit, train, retain, and share key personnel throughout all organizational units. If enterprise strategy dictates an emphasis on risk reduction from terrorism, for example, then the information technology department can lead a disaster planning and prevention program that applies to all units. To be effective, internal service units must understand the enterprise strategy and must align their activities with that strategy.

Traditionally, however, companies have treated their service units as *discretionary expense centers*. Each year, during the budgeting process, they decide how much they can spend on each service unit, and then, during the subsequent year, they monitor service units' actual expenses against budgeted amounts. Treating these units as discretionary expense centers does little to align them to serve their customers: the internal business units and the corporate headquarters. Creating Strategy Maps and Balanced Scorecards for service units enables companies to create incremental enterprise value through alignment of the units' customer, process, and learning and growth objectives with the business unit objectives. The process transforms service and support groups from expense centers to strategic partners. Chapter 5 describes the process of creating Strategy Maps and Balanced Scorecards that link service unit strategies with corporate and business unit strategies.

Corporations have followed various paths to align business and shared-service units. Some have started by defining strategy at the headquarters level and then cascading this strategy to all operating and service units. This logical and orderly process has occurred within some highly structured, hierarchical enterprises, such as the U.S. Army and Petrobras, the Brazilian national oil, gas, and energy company. Alternatively, many if not most corporations have started their Balanced Scorecard programs in a single business unit or even a service group. These corporations did not want the BSC program to be viewed as one led and mandated by headquarters. They deliberately started the program bottom-up, postponing the definition of the enterprise value proposition and enterprise-wide coordination until all the operating units were on board with the new management system. We discuss these various implementation paths in Chapter 6.

Aligning External Organizations

Beyond the alignment of internal business and service units, an enterprise can exploit additional alignment opportunities by formulating plans and scorecards that define relationships with its board of directors and external partners, such as customers, suppliers, and joint ventures. The CEO and CFO can use the Balanced Scorecard to enhance corporate governance and to improve communication with shareholders. Companies align their boards of directors with the strategy by making the enterprise and business unit Strategy Maps and Balanced Scorecards the board's central information resource. Some companies go further, working with their boards to construct Strategy Maps and scorecards for the boards themselves. The map and scorecard describe the board's objectives for investors, shareholders, regulators, and the community, define the critical board processes that must be performed well to deliver on constituents' expectations, and identify the skills, information, and culture required of the board and its deliberations.

Once the board has become comfortable with the description and measurement of strategy in the enterprise Balanced Scorecard, the CEO and CFO can use the enterprise BSC to structure communication and disclosure with shareholders. Several companies are communicating their Strategy Maps in annual reports to shareholders and are using BSC measures as the framework for discussions and conference calls with analysts. Effective governance, disclosure, and communication reduce the risk faced by investors when they entrust their capital to company managers, and thereby lower the company's cost of capital. We discuss these applications in Chapter 7.

Building a scorecard with an external partner—a key customer, supplier, or joint venture partner—provides another opportunity to create value through alignment. The process enables the senior managers of the two entities to work together to reach a consensus about the objectives for the relationship. The process also builds understanding and trust across organizational boundaries, leading to lowered transaction costs and reduced misalignment between the two parties. And the scorecard itself provides the explicit contract by which interorganizational performance will be measured. Without a Balanced Scorecard, external contracting focuses on financial measures, such as price and cost. The scorecard provides a more general contractual mechanism that allows the venture to explicitly incorporate measures of relationship, service, timeliness, innovation, quality, and flexibility, as well as cost and price, as we discuss in Chapter 8.

MANAGING ALIGNMENT AS A PROCESS

Each of the activities we have identified is an opportunity to create synergy and value. Most organizations attempt to create synergy, but in a fragmented, uncoordinated way. They do not view alignment as a management process. When no one is responsible for overall organization alignment, the opportunity to create value through synergy can be missed.

To create synergy, we require more than a concept and a strategy. The enterprise value proposition defines the strategy for value creation through alignment, but it doesn't describe how to achieve it. The alignment strategy must be complemented with an *alignment process*. The alignment process, much like budgeting, should be part of the annual governance cycle. Whenever plans are changed at the enterprise or business unit level, executives likely need to *realign* the organization with the new direction.

The alignment process, of necessity, should be cyclic and have a top-down bias. The targeted corporate synergies should be defined at the top and realized in the business units. Just as the CFO coordinates the budgeting process, a senior executive should coordinate the alignment process—a responsibility for the Office of Strategy Management (OSM).[6] The annual planning process provides an architecture around which the alignment process can be executed. Following are the eight alignment checkpoints (see Figure 1-4) for corporate, business units, and support units of a typical multibusiness organization to hit during the annual planning process.

1. *Enterprise value proposition*: The corporate office defines strategic guidelines to shape strategies at lower levels of the organization.
2. *Board and shareholder alignment*: The corporation's board of directors reviews, approves, and monitors the corporate strategy.
3. *Corporate office to corporate support unit*: The corporate strategy is translated into those corporate policies that will be administered by corporate support units.
4. *Corporate office to business units*: The corporate priorities are cascaded into business unit strategies.
5. *Business units to support units*: The strategic priorities of the business units are incorporated in the strategies of the functional support units.
6. *Business units to customers*: The priorities of the customer value proposition are communicated to targeted customers and reflected in specific customer feedback and measures.
7. *Business support units to suppliers and other external partners*: The shared priorities for suppliers, outsourcers, and alliance partners are reflected in business unit strategies.
8. *Corporate support*: The strategies of the local business support units reflect the *priorities* of the corporate support unit.

Using these eight checkpoints as a point of reference, an organization can measure and manage the degree of alignment, and hence the synergy, being achieved across the enterprise. Organizations that master this process can create competitive advantages that are difficult to dislodge. In Chapter 9, we discuss this ongoing process of sustaining alignment. It requires the modification of existing management processes so that they stay focused on identifying and capturing corporate-level synergies.

Although it is not strictly part of organizational alignment—the primary focus of this book—the enterprise must also align its employees and management processes with the strategy. Having aligned and integrated strategies at all organizational units yields little if employees are not aware of the strategy and are not motivated to help their organizational unit implement it. Enterprises must have active policies to communicate, educate, motivate, and align employees with the strategy. They must also align their ongoing management processes—for resource allocation, target setting, initiative management, reporting, and reviews—with the strategy. In Chapter 10, we discuss these additional alignment processes.

CASE STUDY: SPORT-MAN INC.

We illustrate many of the alignment issues with a disguised case study, Sport-Man Inc. (SMI). The company founded in 1925 to manufacture and market men's work boots. Its early success was attributed to a classic waterproof, lace-up boot that became the standard for workers in construction, farming, and other professions that require strenuous outdoor labor. SMI built a successful national sales base from its headquarters in Massachusetts by establishing channels with large department and specialty shoe stores.

During World War II, SMI received a large contract from the U.S. Army that put its combat boots on the feet of more than two million soldiers. Its success carried into the postwar boom economy. Building on the Sport-Man brand, the company added a line of hiking boots and became more aware of opportunities for growth in the leisure market. In the 1960s, it added a line of men's casual shoes sold through company-owned retail stores. The 1970s saw a diversification into men's clothing, a new line of business (LOB) that focused on outdoor clothing for work or play. The clothes soon became synonymous with the "hunter look." Capitalizing on the growth of suburban malls, SMI soon had more than one hundred retail stores, mostly in the Northeast. During the 1980s, it took the product nationwide, with outlets in more than four hundred malls.

Growth slowed in the mid-1990s. Sport-Man was a great brand, but its market for men's outdoor shoes and clothing had become saturated. A comprehensive strategy review revealed that the Sport-Man brand could be extended to other apparel lines. Furthermore, its retail footprint in major malls throughout the United States provided an excellent channel for opening new stores for the new product lines. The new retail stores could be located in space contiguous to existing Sport-Man stores to make for convenient cross-selling opportunities with existing customers. Finally, SMI's competency, developed over the forty-year postwar period, in sourcing products from factories in Europe and Asia would allow rapid growth in its new apparel lines, as well as permit significant cost economies.

Thus, the company embarked on its first major diversification program in thirty years by broadening its offerings under the Sport-Man brand. The specifics of the strategy were as follows:

- Add two new lines of business to complement the two current lines of men's shoes and men's outdoor clothing:
  - A new LOB of men's casual clothing
  - A new LOB focused on sporting goods: clothing, athletic shoes, and equipment
- Achieve distribution synergies by sharing real estate in the four hundred malls that SMI already occupies.
- Share customer lists and credit cards with the new businesses.
- Share the company's competency in product purchasing.
- Share key management skills with the new LOBs.

Financially, SMI had dual objectives: maintain market share in its core outdoor shoes and clothing product lines and grow the new LOBs to a similar share over the next five years. SMI would harvest cash from its mature businesses to invest in the growth of the new businesses.

SMI's executives recognized that this strategy required extraordinary alignment and teamwork throughout the business lines. They wanted customers to view each brand as a stand-alone business, but they wanted the business units to cooperate by redistributing cash among them and sharing customer lists, credit cards, real estate, vendors, technology, key employees, and knowledge. With the exception of real estate, current businesses had been allowed to manage themselves independently, so the teamwork required by the new strategy would be a significant change.

SMI management turned to the Balanced Scorecard to help create the necessary organization alignment in the following ways:

- Clearly define corporate's strategy for each of the business units and, in particular, how they would work together to create synergy.
- Align the business units with the corporate strategy.
- Align the support units with the business units.
- Create a governance process to ensure that alignment is perpetually maintained.

Figure 1-5 shows the first step in this process: the creation of the enterprise scorecard, which describes how synergy will be created. Financial synergy at SMI will be achieved by using the surplus cash flow from the mature businesses to invest in the growth of the new businesses. The corporate measure, *sales growth per store,* emphasizes that existing stores must participate in normal industry growth while the new stores experience targeted revenue growth. The corporate scorecard also measures the amount of cash flow generated and invested.

Synergies	Enterprise Value Proposition	Enterprise Scorecard
Financial Synergies "How can we increase the shareholder value of our SBU portfolio?"	**Internally Funded Growth** - Aggressively invest in growth businesses. - Harvest cash from mature businesses.	- Sales growth (per store) - Strategic investment level - Free cash flow
Customer Synergies "How can we share the customer interface to increase total customer value?"	**Migrate Customers** - Migrate mature customer base to new growth businesses. **Build Brands** - Build niche brands around dominant categories.	- % revenue from common customers - Total sales per customer (annual growth) - Market share in dominant category (e.g., running shoes)
Internal Processes Synergies "How can we manage SBU processes to achieve economies of scale or value-chain integration?"	**Destination Stores** - Build mall clusters to encourage cross-brand traffic. **Sourcing Economies of Scale** - Build long-term partnerships to ensure access to high-quality and reliable product.	- Sales per square foot - Multistore traffic - Returns - Order fulfillment
Learning and Growth Synergies "How can we develop and share our intangible assets?"	**Build the Infrastructure** - Share strategic jobs and skills. - Create organization alignment. - Share key systems and knowledge.	- Human capital readiness - Key staff rotation - Alignment index - Common systems (vs. plan) - Best-practice sharing

The customer synergy comes from sharing SMI's current customer base with the new businesses. The corporate customer measure, *percentage of revenue from common customers,* monitors this objective directly, and *annual growth in sales per customer* emphasizes the importance of cross-selling across product lines.

SMI expected three sources of internal process synergies: (1) using a dominant product category to attract the customer into the store (measured by the category *market share*); (2) sharing real estate in malls by building clusters of SMI stores and brands (measured by *sales per square foot* and *multistore traffic*); (3) purchasing economies of scale (measured by *returns* and *order fulfillment*).

Finally, learning and growth synergies would be achieved by rotating experienced professionals to key jobs in the new companies (*key staff rotation*), by sharing computer systems (*common systems versus plan*) and knowledge (*best-practice sharing*), and, finally, by creating full organization alignment (*alignment index*).

This enterprise scorecard captures the essential elements of the overall strategy (alignment checkpoint 1). It provides SMI with the top-down guidance from corporate to the business and service units that needs to be reflected in their strategic planning.

Figure 1-6 shows how the business units translate the corporate scorecard into their own business unit scorecards (alignment checkpoint 4). The primary distinction is between the mature businesses and the growth businesses.

From a financial perspective, the mature businesses are expected to generate positive cash flow by maintaining their revenues (*same-store sales*) and improving productivity (*inventory turns* and *expense growth*). The corporate objective from the customer perspective requires the sharing of customers across business units. All businesses measure the same objectives: *shared customer revenues* and *sales per customer.* The mature businesses will focus on *customer loyalty,* whereas the new businesses will emphasize *customer satisfaction,* a precondition for customer loyalty.

In the internal process perspective, all business units monitor their *brand recognition* in the marketplace. They also monitor *sales* and *market share* in targeted categories. The growth businesses focus more on the acquisition of new customers, measuring *new credit card accounts.* All business units monitor the same measures regarding sourcing: *returns* (surrogate for poor quality) and *order fulfillment.*

Objectives and measures for the learning and growth perspective are the same for all business units, reflecting the sharing of people (*strategic*

Sport-Man Inc. (Corporate)

Lines of Business ④

Support Units ③

	Enterprise Value Proposition ①	Enterprise Scorecard	Growth Business — Sporting Goods	Growth Business — Men's Casual	Mature Business — Men's Outdoor	Mature Business — Men's Shoes	Support Units
Financial	Internally funded growth	• Sales growth per store • Investment level • Free cash flow	• Sales growth		• Same store sales • Cash flow • Inventory turns • Expense / sales growth		**Corporate Finance**
Customer	Migrate mature customers	• % revenue, common customers • Sales per customer	• Shared customer revenues • Sales per customer • Customer satisfaction		• Shared customer revenues • Sales per customer • Customer loyalty		**Corporate Marketing** ⑤
Internal	Build niche brands ― ― ― ― Destination stores Sourcing economies	• Market share ― ― ― ― • Sales psf • Multistore traffic • Returns (poor quality) • Fulfillment (vs. plan)	• Brand recognition • Sales growth (category) • New accounts opened ― ― ― ― • Sales psf • Multistore traffic • Returns (poor quality) • Fulfillment (vs. plan)		• Brand recognition • Sales by category • Market share ― ― ― ― • Sales psf • Multistore traffic • Returns (poor quality) • Fulfillment (vs. plan)		**Real Estate** **Purchasing**
Learning and Growth	Strategic jobs and skills ― ― ― ― Organizational alignment Common systems	• Human capital readiness • Key staff rotation ― ― ― ― • Alignment index ― ― ― ― • Common systems vs. plan • Best-practice sharing	• Strategic job readiness ― ― ― ― • Alignment index ― ― ― ― • Strategic system readiness • Best-practice sharing		• Strategic job readiness ― ― ― ― • Alignment index ― ― ― ― • Strategic system readiness • Best-practice sharing		**Human Resources** **Information Technology**

⑧ = Alignment checkpoint

job readiness), technology (*strategic system readiness*), and knowledge (*best-practice sharing*). The *alignment index* measures the extent to which the goals of corporate are formally aligned with those of the business units. For example, 87 percent of the measures on the corporate scorecard appear directly on the business unit scorecards. Two measures are unique to corporate: (1) *investment level,* a measure of how much is being invested in the growth businesses, and (2) *key staff rotation,* which measures the extent to which corporate is facilitating the movement of key staff. The *strategic job readiness* measure in the business units reflects the success from such employee mobility. Approximately 80 percent of the measures on the business unit scorecards are held in common. This reflects not only the similarities of the business units but also the significant amount of sharing occurring across the business units.

The corporate service units help the business units execute the corporate priorities (alignment checkpoint 3). For example, the key staff rotation objective would require a program run by the corporate human resource department to select, cultivate, and place the employees.

Figure 1-7 describes the Balanced Scorecard of the purchasing division (alignment checkpoint 8), which selects and manages the vendors that manufacture the shoes, clothing, and equipment that SMI sells. The products are designed to SMI specifications. Good vendors offer the following features: excellent quality, innovative styles, reliable delivery, fast development of new products, and perfect order fulfillment. Selecting and managing a high-quality stable of vendors are keys to the entire operational part of SMI's strategy. It is particularly important that the ever-changing needs of the business units be understood and translated into contracts with reliable vendors.

The purchasing department serves as the intermediary in creating alignment between the needs of the business units and the vendors. A relationship manager from purchasing is assigned to each of the business units. Her role is to be a strategic partner, managing the product sourcing needs of the business unit. Each year, as part of the annual planning and budgeting process, purchasing negotiates a service agreement with each business unit (alignment checkpoint 5). The service agreement discussion starts by examining the long-range plan, Strategy Map, and BSC of the business unit.

From this plan, the relationship manager and the business unit head establish performance measures and targets for eight parameters of purchased goods (e.g., quality, delivery, and price), as shown in Figure 1-7, and this constitutes the service agreement for the subsequent year. Each quarter,

Figure 1.7 Support-Unit Alignment at Sport-Man Inc.

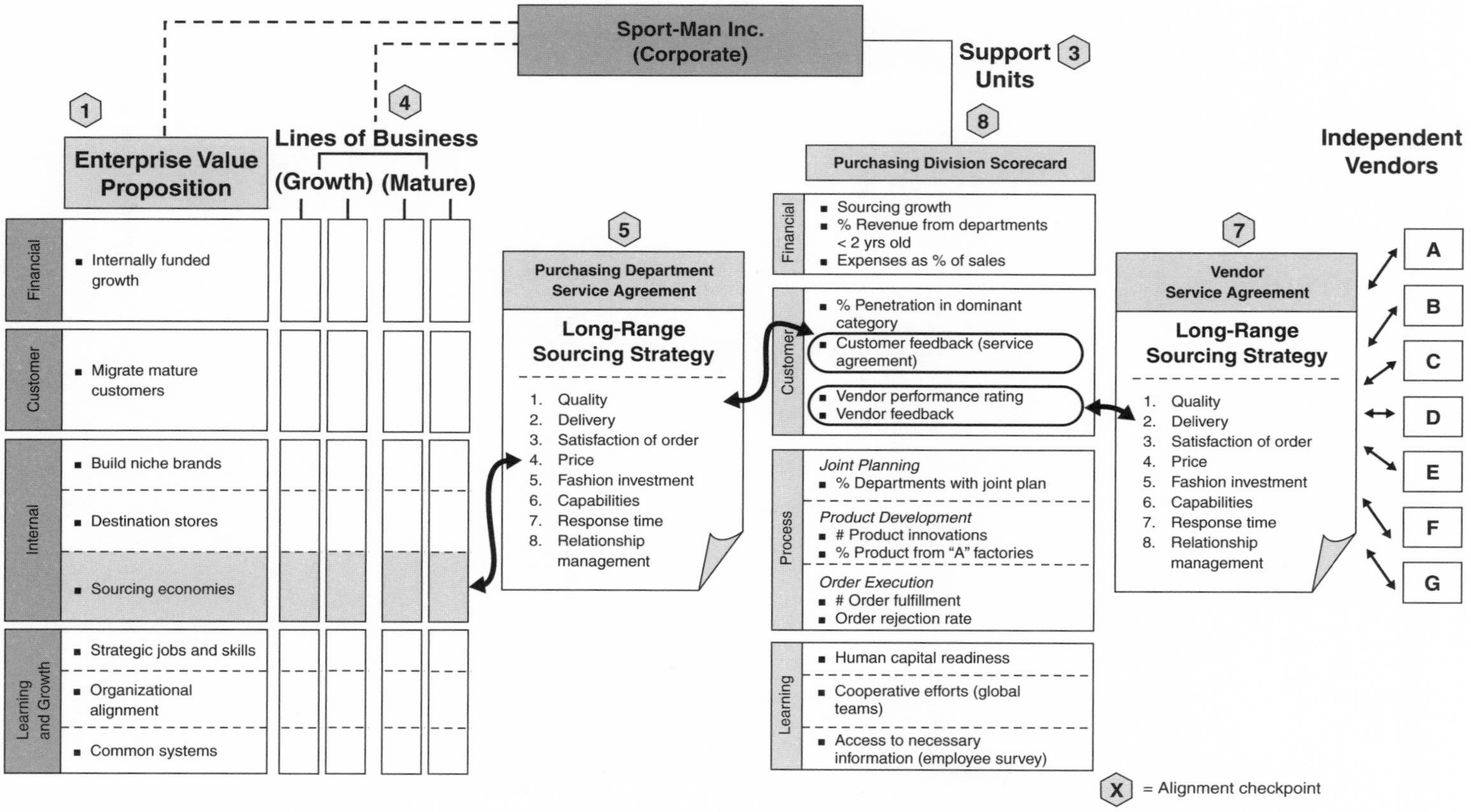

the business unit provides written customer feedback describing its assessment of the performance of the purchasing department against the eight parameters in the service agreement. This feedback provides the customer score on the purchasing division's scorecard and is used as the agenda for a quarterly meeting between the relationship manager and the business unit head to discuss performance. The purchasing division uses an identical approach to link its numerous vendors to itself and to SMI's business units through scorecards and service agreements (alignment checkpoint 7).

To ensure that organization alignment is managed as a continual process, SMI management has made the cascading and integration approach a permanent part of its management calendar. As shown in Figure 1-8, the annual strategic planning process begins in March with an update of SMI's three-year forecast and strategic issues. In June, the corporate executive team meets to translate this strategic thinking into an updated corporate value proposition, Strategy Map, and BSC. In July, the business units update their strategies and cascade the corporate scorecard into updated business unit Strategy Maps and BSCs. Soon after, the cascading process is continued with service units for their strategy updates. In September, the Board of Directors reviews the corporate, business unit, and service unit strategies, with accompanying Balanced Scorecards. Simultaneously, SMI updates service agreements and scorecards with its external partners, the key manufacturing vendors.

The budgeting process begins in September and continues through year end. During this time, the finance officer and the strategy management officer review, select, and fund strategic initiatives. The service units finalize service agreements with the business units. Final approval and presentation of the budget to the board take place in December.

Finally, each individual in the organization develops a personal scorecard. The objectives and targets on those scorecards for the following year are agreed to in December. These scorecards are linked to the business unit or service unit scorecard to which the person belongs, thus ensuring complete top-to-bottom alignment.

Figure 1-9 summarizes the strategic alignment of Sport-Man, Inc., using the alignment map to describe the eight alignment checkpoints. SMI has particularly strong alignment on seven of the eight checkpoints. Only the customer interface (checkpoint 6) lacks a clear, defined alignment mechanism. This is not unusual in retail segments having large numbers of active or potential customers, where statistical measures of customer satisfaction or focus groups are used to monitor the customer interface. Business-to-business sectors with a relatively small number of

Figure 1-8 The Alignment and Governance Process at Sport-Man Inc.

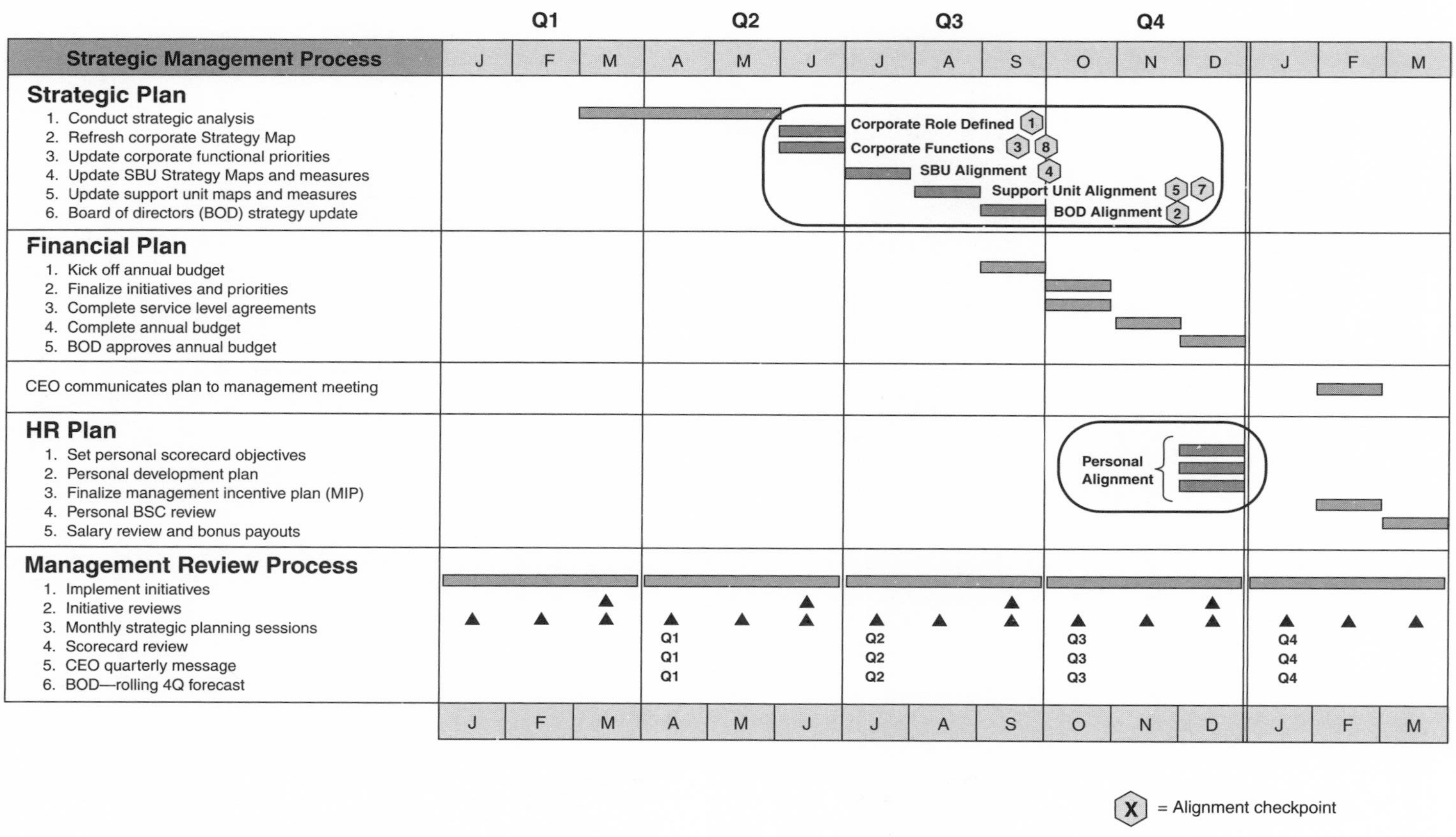

Figure 1-9 Organization Alignment Map at Sport-Man Inc.

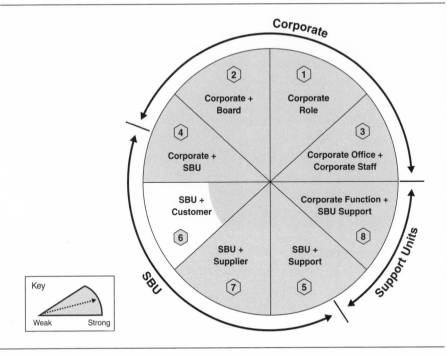

customers—such as chemicals, electronics, and engineering services—tend to use more formal mechanisms, such as service-level agreements, to create customer alignment.

SMI has clearly defined its corporate role and uses scorecards and service agreements to align the corporate strategy with business and service unit strategies. It uses corporate, business unit, and service unit scorecards to communicate and gain approval of the strategy with its board of directors. During the subsequent year, the board monitors the success of the strategy through quarterly scorecard updates. SMI aligns personal performance plans with the strategies of their business or support units. SMI has created a tight web of alignment that focuses the energies of the entire organization and its strategic partners on achieving an ambitious, integrated strategy.

SUMMARY

Corporations must continually search for ways to make the whole more valuable than the sum of its parts. Alignment is critical if enterprises are to achieve synergies throughout their business and support units. A new measurement and management system, based on Strategy Maps and Balanced Scorecards, helps corporations define and capture the benefits of organizational alignment.

Before proceeding to the process for creating a corporate-level Strategy Map and Balanced Scorecard to describe the enterprise value proposition, we embed our approach in an historical perspective. Chapter 2 describes how organizations have struggled for more than a century to find the ideal structures to manage their strategies. We believe that the search for the perfect structure will remain frustrating unless companies also use a third lever—their measurement and management systems—to align structure with strategy.

NOTES

1. Information on the Balanced Scorecard Hall of Fame can be found at http://www.bscol.com/bscol/hof.
2. These are the five principles documented in R. S. Kaplan and D. P. Norton, *The Strategy-Focused Organization: How Balanced Scorecard Companies Thrive in the New Competitive Environment* (Boston: Harvard Business School Press, 2000).
3. D. Rigby, *Management Tools* (Boston: Bain & Company, 2001).
4. R. S. Kaplan and D. P. Norton, *Strategy Maps: Converting Intangible Assets into Tangible Outcomes* (Boston: Harvard Business School Press, 2004).
5. The following are among the important references on corporate strategy:

   A. D. Chandler Jr., *Strategy and Structure: Chapters in the History of the Industrial Enterprise* (Cambridge, MA: MIT Press, 1962); *Scale and Scope: The Dynamics of Industrial Capitalism* (Cambridge, MA: Harvard University Press, 1990); and "The Functions of the HQ Unit in the Multibusiness Firm," *Strategic Management Journal* (1991): 31–50.

   M. E. Porter, "From Competitive Advantage to Corporate Strategy," *Harvard Business Review* (April–May 1987): 43–59.

   B. Wernerfelt, "A Resource-based View of the Firm," *Strategic Management Journal* (1984): 171–180.

   M. Goold, A. Campbell, and M. Alexander, *Corporate-Level Strategy: Creating Value in the Multibusiness Company* (New York: John Wiley & Sons, 1994); A. Campbell, M. Goold, and M. Alexander, "Corporate Strategy: The Quest for Parenting Advantage," *Harvard Business Review* (March–April 1995): 120–132.

   D. J. Collis and C. A. Montgomery, "Competing on Resources: Strategy in the 1990s," *Harvard Business Review* (July–August 1995): 118–128; "Creating Corporate Advantage," *Harvard Business Review* (May–June 1998): 70–83; and *Corporate Strategy: Resources and the Scope of the Firm* (Chicago: Irwin, 1997).

   C. Markides, "Corporate Strategy: The Role of the Centre," in *Handbook of Strategy and Management,* 1st edition, eds. A. Pettigrew, H. Thomas, and R. Whittington (London: Sage Publications, 2001).

J. Barney, "Firm Resources and Sustained Competitive Advantage," *Journal of Management* (1991): 99–120.

J. Bower, "Building the Velcro Organization," *Ivey Business Journal* (November–December 2003): 1–10.

K. M. Eisenhardt and S. L. Brown, "Patching: Restitching Business Portfolios in Dynamic Markets," *Harvard Business Review* (May–June 1999): 72–82.

6. R. S. Kaplan and D. P. Norton, "The Office of Strategy Management," *Harvard Business Review* (October 2005): 72–80.

CHAPTER TWO

CORPORATE STRATEGY AND STRUCTURE
HISTORICAL PERSPECTIVE

THE PROTOTYPICAL ORGANIZATION, at the dawn of the Industrial Revolution, was Adam Smith's pin factory, a small, focused enterprise producing a narrow range of products for its local customers. The organization structure of Smith's pin factory was simple: an owner-entrepreneur with perhaps a supervisor and several hired workers. The owner-manager ordered materials, hired and paid the employees, supervised production, and performed marketing, sales, billing, and cash collections.

The Second Industrial Revolution, starting in the middle of the nineteenth century, saw the growth of much more complex capital-intensive industries, such as primary and fabricated metals, chemicals, petroleum, machinery, and transportation equipment. The dominant corporations in these industries enjoyed enormous economies of scale because of their significant capital investments in production and distribution facilities. To cope with their larger investment base and extended range of customers, the companies needed a more elaborate organization than Smith's pin factory to coordinate and gain the scale economies from their purchasing, manufacturing, marketing, distribution, and product development activities. They also needed, of course, more managers to staff these departments and to coordinate products and processes. Figure 2-1 illustrates the *centralized functional organization* that evolved to manage the typical late-nineteenth-century industrial enterprise.[1]

In the centralized functional organization, the two largest functional departments—production and sales—performed the primary value-adding activities. A third department, finance, performed two important

Figure 2-1 The Multiunit, Multifunctional Enterprise

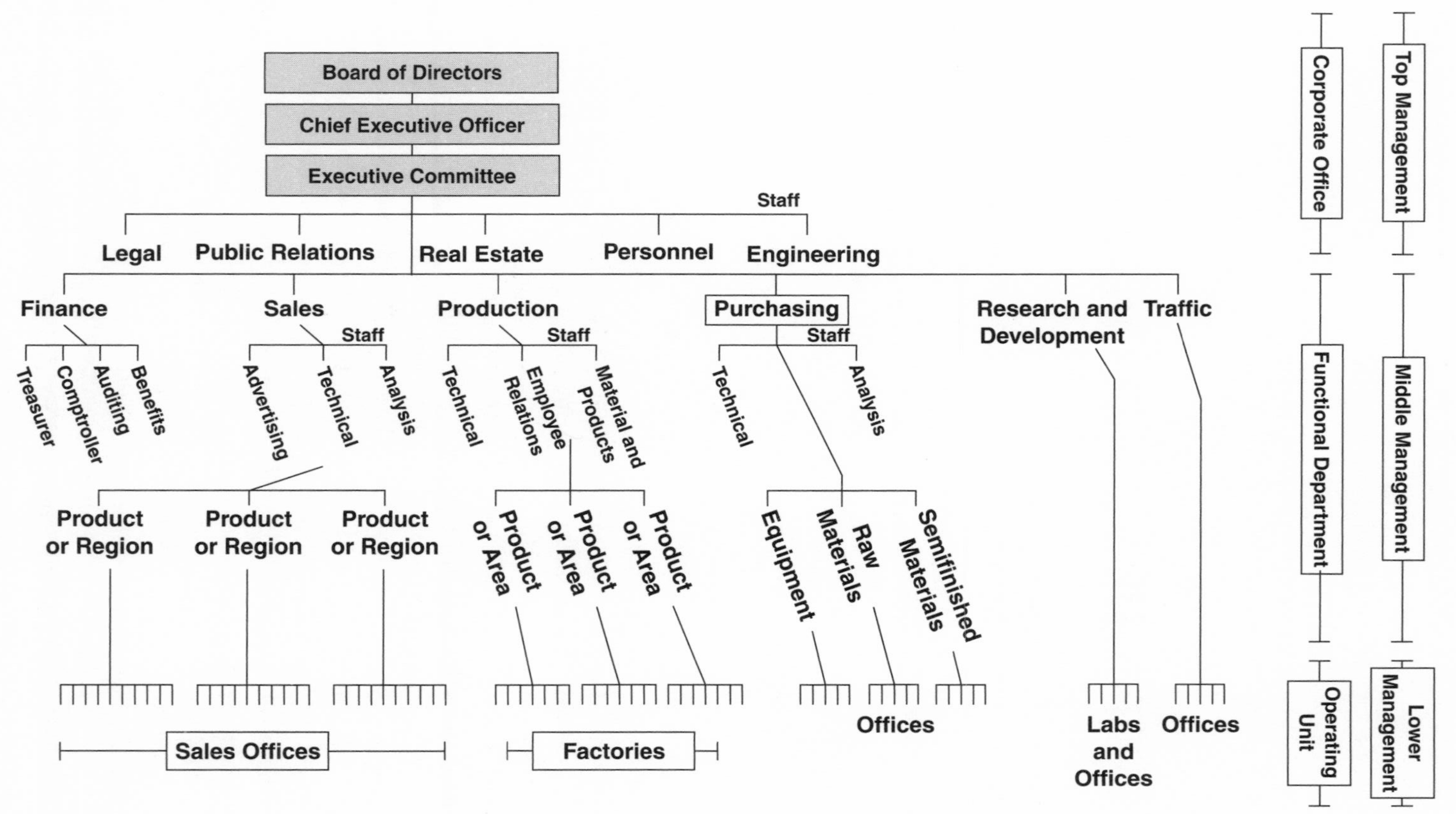

functions: (1) coordinating the flow of funds to and from the various operating departments and (2) providing information to senior executives so that they could monitor the operating units' performance and allocate resources among them. The enterprise also needed departments to perform specialized activities such as purchasing, research and product development, logistics, engineering, legal, real estate, human resources, and public relations. The heads of the major functional departments, along with the president and chairman of the board, constituted the corporation's senior decision-making team. Regular meetings of the senior executive team coordinated the activities across the corporation's functional departments.

The centralized functional structure in late-nineteenth-century corporations offered considerable advantages for the enterprise. Individuals in each functional department had considerable experience and expertise in their fields. They collaborated with department colleagues to perform their assigned tasks—in production, purchasing, product development, legal, and marketing—effectively and efficiently. And the large clusters of people doing similar tasks provided excellent opportunities for coaching, mentoring, and promotion from within.

Successful industrial companies continued to grow in the early twentieth century. Some acquired competitors through horizontal combinations. Several, such as Ford Motor, undertook vertical integration to better coordinate the flow of materials into and out of factories. Most companies expanded geographically so that they could leverage their physical and organizational economies of scale in their domestic markets to reach customers in more distant markets. And many exploited their existing production and distribution infrastructure, as well as their extensive organizational and managerial capabilities, to diversify into new product lines and market segments.

So by the early twentieth century, the simple, focused, local manufacturing company familiar to Adam Smith a hundred years earlier had morphed into a giant, multiproduct, multifunctional, multiregional corporation. The management challenge was to continue to offer attractive, innovative, low-priced products to a broad customer base without collapsing from the complexity of operations that were now internalized within a single corporation.

As centralized functionally organized companies expanded and diversified, they encountered new problems. Coordination and handoffs between departments were often inefficient, costly, and time-consuming. The lack of shared information among marketing specialists and salespeople (who dealt with customers), engineers (who designed new products and services), and operating people (who built the products and provided the services) often led to expensively designed products and services that were costly to manufacture and deliver and didn't meet customers' expectations and needs. Functional organizations typically were also slow to respond to changes in customer preferences and new opportunities or threats in the marketplace.

Alfred Chandler summarized the problems faced by these centralized, functional organizations:

> *The lack of time, of information, and of psychological commitment to an overall entrepreneurial viewpoint were not necessarily serious handicaps if the company's basic activities remained stable, that is, if its sources of raw materials and supplies, its manufacturing technology, its markets, and the nature of its products and product lines stayed relatively unchanged. But when further expansion into new functions, into new geographical areas, or into new product lines greatly increased all types of administrative decisions, then the executives in the central office became overworked and their administrative performance less efficient. These increasing pressures, in turn, created the need for the building or adoption of the multidivisional structure with its general office and autonomous operating divisions.[2]*

Companies such as DuPont, General Motors, General Electric, and Matsushita introduced a new organization form in the 1920s and 1930s. The *multidivisional company* was organized around divisions focused on specific product lines and geographic regions. Each division brought together employees with skills from all the business functions to work together to develop, build, and deliver a specific product line sold to customers in defined market segments (see Figure 2-2). A general manager headed each division, assisted by a staff that included the heads of functional activities for the division. So each product or geographic division became a replica of the original enterprise, with its own centralized functional department organization, except that the general manager was now a middle manager reporting to the senior executives in the corporate headquarters.

Executives in the corporate office no longer ran the business. Their role was to evaluate the performance of the operating divisions and do the strategic planning and resource allocation of funds, facilities, and personnel to the divisions. The corporate office also included staff who had specialized skills to support the corporate executives and who

Figure 2-2 DuPont Corporation: An Example of Multidivisional (M-form) Structure

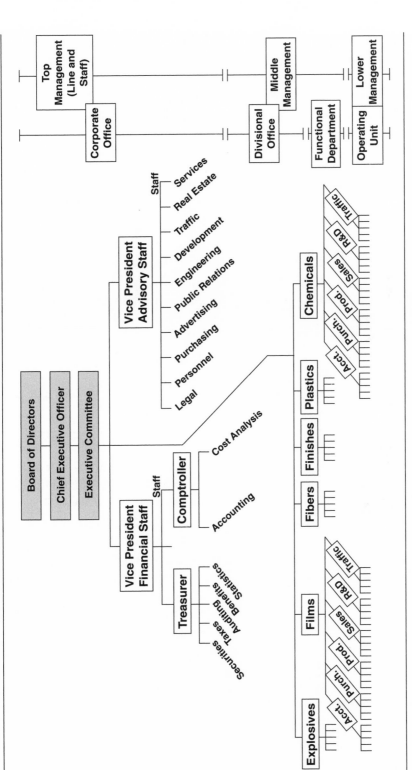

Source: Alfred D. Chandler, *Scale and Scope: The Dynamics of Industrial Capitalism* (Cambridge, MA: Harvard University Press, 1990).

advised and coordinated the work done by their counterparts in the operating companies.

The introduction of the multidivisional organization, although enabling the product and geographic divisions to be more responsive to local opportunities and threats, had its own management challenges. The smaller product divisions lost many of the efficiencies—the scale economies and learning curve effects—associated with focused, functional organizations whose resources could be shared throughout multiple product lines, market segments, and geographies. Customers became confused and often complained when multiple salespersons, from what they previously thought was a single corporate entity, called on them, each one promoting a narrow product line. Also, companies risked losing deep functional expertise when they dispersed specialists throughout the organization into the small heterogeneous groups in each operating division, rather than cluster them where they could educate and solve problems with each other in homogeneous groups.

The 1960s saw the birth of the *conglomerate*, a new organization form. Rather than achieve growth through expansion from core businesses, technologies, and capabilities or through acquisition in related businesses and industries, several companies grew by acquiring and merging unrelated businesses. Companies such as ITT, Litton Industries, Textron, and Gulf + Western became a collection of autonomous operating companies with no apparent synergies among them.

One apparent motivation for conglomerate growth was to reduce the risk of business cycles by investing in a diversified portfolio of businesses. This rationale, of course, was more about reducing the risk to the senior executive team, because shareholders could diversify by owning shares in a broad portfolio of companies and thereby avoid the high costs of mergers and acquisitions and the deadweight loss of a corporate office. A more plausible, economically grounded rationale was that the senior executives in these conglomerates were exceptional managers and could use their superior knowledge and skill to create more value from the collection of companies they owned than would occur if the companies operated independently without the benefit of the corporate office.

A similar organization form arose in many developing nations. Business groups, such as the Tata Group in India, the Koç Group in Turkey, Siam Cement in Thailand, and the Samsung and Hyundai chaebols in South Korea, are massive collections of unrelated businesses that operate mostly within their country of origin. These groups evolved within each country because their local governments followed an explicit policy of import substitution by erecting trade and capital barriers that limited foreign competition. The business groups, typically headed by a skilled entrepreneurial family, prospered locally by substituting for institutional gaps in their countries' infrastructures, such as poorly functioning capital and labor markets, limited consumer information and recourse about product quality, and uncertain and frequently corrupt judicial and political environments.[3]

But most of the countries in which business groups developed and thrived are now joining the global economy. With their countries now open to global markets, the previously protected business groups are now subject to vigorous competition from abroad. The headquarters of these country-specific business groups must now evaluate the benefits of having hundreds of unrelated businesses operate within a single corporate structure. They must address how the executive team at the business group headquarters adds, rather than subtracts from, the value being created by its local operating companies.

Beyond the development of conglomerates and emerging market business groups, the current information- and knowledge-based global economy has created new opportunities for a corporate headquarters to create synergy. Some corporations have delivered consistently excellent performance by operating effective management systems among their business units, with all managers following similar business strategies. For example, a company like Cisco has exceptional skills for integrating technology companies procured in acquisitions. Others are effective at managing innovative product development throughout a collection of companies by following product leadership strategies. At the other extreme, some headquarters are adept at managing mature, commodity-type companies to foster continual cost reductions, process improvements, supply-chain management, and cooperative labor relations.

Several companies have become enormously successful by leveraging a well-known *brand* across diverse businesses. Disney movies create animal characters, such as Mickey Mouse and the Lion King, which Disney then leverages into theme parks, television programs, and consumer retail outlets. Richard Branson founded Virgin Airlines and subsequently leveraged the Virgin brand—associated with fun, high quality, excellent service, and a particular lifestyle—into businesses as diverse as trains, resorts, finance, soft drinks, music, mobile phones, cars, wines, publishing, and bridal wear.

Other corporations, such as financial services and telecommunications companies, have exploited their *customer relationships* to offer one-stop shopping for a wide array of services within their industry. Corporations such as Microsoft and eBay have become dominant in their sectors by leveraging an industry-standard *platform* into a broad array of services. Pharmaceutical and biotechnology corporations leverage their basic and applied *research* about specific disease categories into new drugs and treatments that enable them to dominate their sectors.

In all these examples, individual businesses are worth far more within the corporate structure than if they were operated as independent units. The key organizational question for any sizable enterprise, therefore, is how the corporate headquarters adds value to its collection of functional, product, channel, and geographical business units. For the corporate office to add value, the benefits from its monitoring, coordination, and resource allocation must exceed the cost of its operations. The corporate headquarters destroys value when it introduces delays in decision making, is not responsive to emerging local opportunities and threats, and makes errors in resource allocation and direction because of its lack of contact with local market conditions, competitors, and technologies.

If the corporate headquarters does not add value, then the market for corporate control will operate to restructure the company. The leveraged buyout (LBO) and management buyout (MBO) movement of the 1980s was a reaction that unleashed the value contained in collections of business units. Enabled by innovation in capital markets, this movement eliminated or dramatically reduced the role of corporate offices, particularly in diversified corporations, that were perceived to be destroying rather than creating shareholder value.

ALIGNING STRUCTURE WITH STRATEGY

Much of the academic as well as managerial literature on strategy focuses on business-level strategy: how a business unit positions itself and leverages its resources for competitive advantage.[4] If all companies were akin to Adam Smith's pin factory, this treatment would be sufficient. But because most companies are now a complex mixture of centralized functional and decentralized business units, corporate headquarters have tried various ways of coordinating activities and creating synergies.

Many companies have attempted to solve the coordination problem by adopting a *matrix organization*.[5] Figure 2-3 shows a typical matrix organization in which a manager reports both to a senior corporate functional executive and to a product or line-of-business manager. Figure 2-4 shows

Figure 2-3 The Matrix Organization

Business Function \ Business	Business Unit 1	Business Unit 2	...	Business Unit n
R&D	R&D Manager, BU_1	R&D Manager, BU_2	...	R&D Manager, BU_n
Purchasing	Purchasing Manager, BU_1	Purchasing Manager, BU_2	...	Purchasing Manager, BU_n
Manufacturing	Manufacturing Manager, BU_1	Manufacturing Manager, BU_2	...	Manufacturing Manager, BU_n
Marketing	Marketing Manager, BU_1	Marketing Manager, BU_2	...	Marketing Manager, BU_n
Sales	Sales Manager, BU_1	Sales Manager, BU_2	...	Sales Manager, BU_n

a matrix organization that attempts to align local operating companies with global product groups and local country managers.

ABB, a global electrical products company, made the product line–geographical matrix approach popular in the 1990s, when it organized its hundreds of local business units around the world. In the new structure, each local business unit reported to both a country executive and a worldwide line-of-business executive. The matrix organization apparently

Figure 2-4 The Matrix Organization Across Global Product Groups and Countries

	Country 1	Country 2	...	Country n
Product Line 1	BU_{11}	BU_{12}	...	BU_{1n}
Product Line 2	BU_{21}	BU_{12}	...	BU_{2n}
Product Line 3	BU_{31}	BU_{32}	...	BU_{3n}
> > >	> > >	> > >	v v v	> > >

allowed the corporation to achieve the benefits of centralized coordination, functional expertise, and economies of scale for product groups while maintaining local divisional autonomy and entrepreneurship for marketing and sales activities.

In practice, despite their appeal, matrix organizations have proven difficult to manage because of the inherent tension between the interests of the senior executives responsible for managing either a row or a column of the matrix. A manager stuck at a matrix intersection struggles to coordinate between the preferences of his "row" and "column" managers, leading to new sources of difficulty, conflict, and delay. The ultimate source of accountability and authority in a matrix organization remains ambiguous. Newer, so-called post-industrial forms of organization have been proposed. Examples include virtual and networked organizations that operate across traditional boundaries, and Velcro organizations, which can be snapped apart and reassembled in new structures in response to changing opportunities.[6]

With all the innovation in new structures, a purely organizational solution to balancing the tension between specialization and integration remains elusive. This should not be surprising. In McKinsey's famous 7-S Model for designing aligned organizations, strategy and structure are only two of the seven S's.[7] A third S—systems—must also be mobilized to create organizational alignment. McKinsey defined *systems* as follows: "the formal processes and procedures used to manage the organization, including the management control systems, performance measurement and reward systems, planning, budgeting, and resource allocation systems, information systems, and distribution systems."

McKinsey conducted its research for the 7-S Model in 1980, before the development of Strategy Maps, the Balanced Scorecard, and the five principles—mobilize, translate, align, motivate, and govern—for creating a strategy-focused organization.[8] We can now see how the Balanced Scorecard innovation enables companies to design their operating systems to align structure with strategy and also to contribute to the four other S's: staffing, skills, style, and shared values.[9] The insight from our work with hundreds of organizations is that organizations should not search for the perfect structure for their strategy. Instead, they should choose a structure that is reasonable and seems to work without major conflicts, and then design a customized, cascaded *system* of linked Strategy Maps and Balanced Scorecards to tune the *structure*—the corporation and its collection of centralized functions and decentralized product groups and geographical units—to the *strategy*.

BALANCED SCORECARD: A SYSTEM FOR ALIGNING CORPORATE STRATEGY AND STRUCTURE

Chandler's work and extensions by Michael Porter affirm that strategy precedes structure and systems. We must start, therefore, with a brief discussion of corporate strategy before illustrating how Strategy Maps and the Balanced Scorecards align organization structure with corporate-level strategy. Goold, Campbell, and Alexander argue that corporate strategy—the rationale for operating multiple businesses within the same corporate entity—must derive from the company's "parenting advantage."[10] The corporation must demonstrate what we call the enterprise value proposition: how corporate headquarters creates more value from the businesses it owns and operates than its rivals would if they owned the same set of businesses, or if the businesses operated completely independently.[11] The four Balanced Scorecard perspectives provide a natural way to categorize the various types of enterprise value propositions that can contribute to corporate synergies:

Financial Synergies
- Effectively acquiring and integrating other companies.
- Maintaining excellent monitoring and governance processes across diverse enterprises.
- Leveraging a common brand (Disney, Virgin) across multiple business units.
- Achieving scale or specialized skills in negotiations with external entities such as governments, unions, capital providers, and suppliers.

Customer Synergies
- Consistently delivering a common value proposition across a geographically dispersed network of retail or wholesale outlets.
- Leveraging common customers by combining products or services from multiple units to provide distinct advantages: low cost, convenience, or customized solutions.

Business Process Synergies
- Exploiting *core competencies* that leverage excellence in product or process technologies across multiple business units.[12] Consider competencies in microelectronics fabrication, optoelectronics, software development, new product development, and just-in-time production and distribution systems that lead to competitive advantage in multiple industry segments. Core competencies can also include

knowledge in how to operate effectively in particular regions of the world.

- Achieving economies of scale through shared manufacturing, research, distribution, or marketing resources.

Learning and Growth Synergies

- Enhancing *human capital* through excellent HR recruiting, training, and leadership development practices across multiple business units.
- Leveraging a *common technology*, such as an industry-leading platform or channel for customers to access a wide set of company services, that is shared across multiple product and service divisions.
- Sharing best-practice *capabilities* through knowledge management that transfers process quality excellence across multiple business units.

Collis and Montgomery summarize such effective corporate strategies:[13]

> An outstanding corporate strategy is not a random collection of individual building blocks but a carefully constructed system of interdependent parts . . . [I]n a great corporate strategy, all of the elements [resources, businesses, and organization] are aligned with one another. That alignment is driven by the nature of the firm's resources—its special assets, skills and capabilities.[14]

Strategy Maps and the Balanced Scorecard turn out to be ideal mechanisms to describe enterprise value propositions and subsequently to align enterprise resources for superior value creation. The headquarters executive team uses its corporate Strategy Map and Balanced Scorecard to articulate the theory of the enterprise: how the enterprise generates additional value by having business units operate within its hierarchical structure rather than have each unit operate as an independent entity, with its own governance structure and source of financing.

NOTES

1. This brief summary of a complex history is drawn from Chapter 2, "Scale, Scope, and Organizational Capabilities," in A. D. Chandler Jr., *Scale and Scope: The Dynamics of Industrial Capitalism* (Cambridge, MA: Harvard University Press, 1990), 14–49.
2. A. D. Chandler Jr., *Strategy and Structure: Chapters in the History of the Industrial Enterprise* (Cambridge, MA: MIT Press, 1962), 297.

3. T. Khanna and K. Palepu, "Why Focused Strategies May Be Wrong for Emerging Markets," *Harvard Business Review* (July–August 1997): 41–51.

4. We explored the role of Strategy Maps and Balanced Scorecards in describing and implementing business unit strategy in the book *Strategy Maps: Converting Intangible Assets into Tangible Outcomes* (Boston: Harvard Business School Press, 2004).

5. S. Davis and P. Lawrence, "Problems of Matrix Organizations," *Harvard Business Review* (May–June 1978); H. Kolodny, "Managing in a Matrix," *Business Horizons* (March–April 1981).

6. L. Hirschhorn and T. Gilmore, "The New Boundaries of the 'Boundaryless' Company," *Harvard Business Review* (May–June 1992); M. Raynor and J. Bower, "Lead from the Center: How to Manage Divisions Dynamically," *Harvard Business Review* (May 2001); J. Bower, "Building the Velcro Organization: Creating Value Through Integration and Maintaining Organization-Wide Efficiency," *Ivey Business Journal* (November–December 2003): 1–10.

7. R. H. Waterman, T. J. Peters, and J. R. Phillips, "Structure Is Not Organization," *Business Horizons* (1980).

8. R. S. Kaplan and D. P. Norton, *The Strategy-Focused Organization* (Boston: Harvard Business School Press, 2000).

9. R. S. Kaplan, "The Balanced Scorecard: Enhancing the McKinsey 7-S Model," *Balanced Scorecard Report* (March 2005).

10. D. Collis and C. Montgomery, *Corporate Strategy: Resources and the Scope of the Firm* (Chicago: Irwin, 1997), refer to essentially the same concept as the "corporate advantage." We will use the more vivid image of the corporate as parent to its various offspring.

11. M. Goold, A. Campbell, and M. Alexander, *Corporate-Level Strategy: Creating Value in the Multibusiness Company* (New York: John Wiley & Sons, 1994); A. Campbell, M. Goold, and M. Alexander, "Corporate Strategy: The Quest for Parenting Advantage," *Harvard Business Review* (March–April 1995): 120–132.

12. *Core competencies* has been defined by Markides as the "pool of experience, knowledge and systems within the corporation that can be deployed to reduce the cost or time to create or extend a strategic asset"; strategic assets are the "imperfectly imitable, imperfectly substitutable, and imperfectly tradable assets that promote cost advantage or differentiation." See C. Markides, "Corporate Strategy: The Role of the Centre," in *Handbook of Strategy and Management,* 1st edition, eds. A. Pettigrew, H. Thomas, and R. Whittington (London: Sage Publications, 2001).

13. D. J. Collis and C. A. Montgomery, "Competing on Resources: Strategy in the 1990s," *Harvard Business Review* (July–August 1995): 118–128; and "Creating Corporate Advantage," *Harvard Business Review* (May–June 1998): 70–83.

14. Collis and Montgomery, "Creating Corporate Advantage," 72.

CHAPTER THREE

ALIGNING FINANCIAL AND CUSTOMER STRATEGIES

ENTERPRISES CAN CREATE organizational synergies in many ways. Some enterprises leverage financial synergies through effective merger and acquisition policies and skilled management of internal capital markets. Others leverage a common brand or customer relationship across multiple business units and retail outlets. Still others gain scale economies by having multiple business units share common processes and shared services, or they generate economies of scope through effective integration of units across an industry value chain. And finally, enterprises create synergies when they develop and share human, information, and organization capital across multiple units. Corporate headquarters must be explicit about the synergies it expects to create and then must implement a management system to communicate and capture them.

In this chapter, we describe examples of corporations that create value by leveraging financial and customer synergies. In Chapter 4, we continue the analysis by presenting opportunities for leveraging critical internal processes and for integrating learning and growth capabilities across the enterprise. In both chapters, we show how private-sector companies, public-sector agencies, and nonprofit organizations have created enterprise-derived value through specific attention to sources of synergy.

FINANCIAL SYNERGIES: THE HOLDING COMPANY MODEL

All enterprises have the opportunity to generate synergies by using centralized resource allocation and financial management, but we get the purest example by focusing on holding companies, which consist of business units or companies that operate largely as independent entities. These companies create synergies only through their financial competencies and practices. Typically, a holding company's operating units are located in different regions, operate in different industries, sell to different customers, use different technologies, and craft their own strategies.

Such a situation also occurs in the public sector, where governmental departments often consist of a collection of independent agencies whose operations overlap little and do not have to be tightly coordinated. Consider the U.S. Department of Transportation, which consists of thirteen mostly autonomous agencies, including the Federal Aviation Administration, Federal Highway Administration, Federal Transit Association, Federal Motor Carrier Safety Administration, Federal Railway Administration, Federal Maritime Administration, and the National Highway Transportation Safety Administration. Each of these agencies has its own constituency (e.g., airlines, railroads, public transit, trucking, ships, and automobiles), mission, and strategy.

Chapter 2 describes how 1960s-era corporations—such as Litton Industries, ITT, Textron, and Gulf + Western—followed a strategy of aggressive acquisitions, putting together under one organizational structure a collection of companies that had few shared capabilities, technologies, or customers. The espoused rationale for this conglomerate movement was twofold: first, the corporation gained access to new industries that promised more growth and less competition than its existing businesses, and second, the acquisition strategy reduced the corporation's risk by holding a portfolio of companies whose business cycles were not correlated.

Neither rationale eventually stood up to economic scrutiny and practical experience. Although some businesses do have higher growth opportunities than others, the current stockholders of those higher-growth companies normally understand these opportunities reasonably well, and the growth is already reflected in the current share price. Therefore, the acquiring company pays a considerable premium to purchase the growth company. Many studies have shown that in a merger or acquisition, sellers generally capture all the gains, and purchasers suffer a winners' curse, overpaying for growth and subsequently earning below-market returns from their acquisitions.

On the alleged risk-reduction benefits, most investors already own a sufficient number of companies to achieve their own diversification from firm-specific risk. They don't need to have company managers pay a premium price to perform this diversification for them. And, in any case, most conglomerates failed even in their home-grown risk-reduction strategy. During the economic slowdown of the 1970s, virtually all the companies they owned suffered together, leading to major difficulties in servicing the debt taken on during the aggressive acquisition phase of the 1960s.

The conglomerates realized disappointing earnings growth and risk reduction during the 1970s, and this disappointment was followed, in the late 1970s and through the 1980s, by a wave of takeovers, divestitures, and management replacement. Nevertheless, the lure of growth and the reduced risk to executives of diversified companies continue (to say nothing of the high fees earned by the investment banks that organize companies' merger and acquisition activities), and many such corporations still exist. The huge challenge faced by the executive teams in their corporate headquarters is how to overcome historical experience. They must demonstrate that they can select and manage a collection of unrelated businesses to create value superior to what the businesses could earn separately.

The leading examples of companies in this category, such as Berkshire Hathaway and Kohlberg Kravis Roberts (KKR), are pure investment or private equity corporations. Each company in an investment or holding company portfolio is managed and financed independently. Each has its own board of directors, which usually includes representatives of the parent corporation. There are no cross holdings, and cash flow from one company cannot be used in another company.

The gains from this type of corporation arise from two sources of financial synergy. First is the investment acuity of the principal owners, such as Warren Buffett at Berkshire Hathaway and the KKR senior partners. These owners create corporate value by their ability to identify undervalued or turnaround company situations. They also follow an excellent due diligence process to support their initial opportunity identification. In effect, this capability requires having superior information or performing superior analysis so that the corporation can "buy low and sell high" consistently.

The second source of financial value creation comes from operating an effective governance system that monitors and guides the long-term performance of the portfolio companies and their senior executives. Holding companies frequently assist in the acquisition and assignments of key personnel as well as introduce professional management approaches.

For example, FMC Corporation, one of the earliest adopters of the Balanced Scorecard, operated more than two dozen companies in the machinery, chemicals, minerals, and defense industries. Senior corporate executives had extensive experience within the operating companies. They also had private information about the opportunities, threats, capabilities, and weaknesses of their operating companies and their markets. The headquarters executives used their extensive experience and private information to make better decisions about resource allocation than the public capital markets would have made. For example, one of FMC's companies produced airport equipment for baggage handling, passenger transportation to and from aircraft, and jetways and loading ramps. During one of the typical down cycles of the airline industry, investment was depressed throughout the industry. FMC's company made a strategic investment to acquire its largest competitor at a price highly discounted from what FMC executives perceived was its long-term value. This decision was more than validated during the next upswing in airport expansion and investment.

So the enterprise value proposition for a highly diversified corporation includes a superior ability to allocate capital and manage risks in its diverse businesses. The financial objectives on its corporate scorecard should include common high-level metrics such as economic value added and return on net capital employed. The financial metrics provide a common benchmark for measuring the financial contribution of each company in the corporate portfolio. Of course, even in a highly diversified corporation, the headquarters executives are active portfolio managers and can highlight different financial metrics among the varied portfolio to facilitate resource allocation. They may choose to emphasize sales and market share growth for a company early in its product life cycle, while emphasizing the generation of free cash flow for a company in its more mature phase.

The case studies here of Aktiva and New Profit Inc. show how enterprises seeking such financial synergies can deploy the Balanced Scorecard to play a central role in their governance system for a portfolio of unrelated business units.

CASE STUDY: AKTIVA

Aktiva, a private investment holding company, was founded in Slovenia in 1989 and currently is headquartered in Amsterdam, with offices in Geneva, Ljubljana, London, Milan, and Tel Aviv. Company assets in first quarter 2004 were €600 million, and the assets in the thirty companies in fourteen countries that Aktiva controls directly or with strategic partners exceed €12 billion.

Aktiva uses an active governance approach that transfers leading-edge management theory, practice, and discipline to its portfolio companies. Aktiva's initial strategy used value-based management and measures of economic value added to provide financial discipline and focus for its operating companies. By 2000, it saw the opportunity to more actively assist its portfolio companies by requiring each company to develop a Balanced Scorecard to describe and implement its strategy. Aktiva started by developing a Balanced Scorecard for itself that described how it would maximize its value through active management and governance of its portfolio companies (see Figure 3-1). It then assisted each of its portfolio companies to develop and implement its own Balanced Scorecard.

Aktiva established what it called an "active governance group" in its corporate structure. The managers in this group move to the geographic locations of member companies. There, they provide day-to-day help, coaching the company's executive teams in their development of the Strategy Maps and Balanced Scorecards that describe and help the company managers implement their strategies. Each assigned member of the active governance group participates in the incentive scheme of the portfolio company, gaining a strong incentive to help the company succeed. Incentive schemes for upper and middle managers in each portfolio company are linked to personal scorecards and to the company scorecard.

Aktiva executives meet quarterly (and often monthly) with the executive team of each portfolio company to review its performance on its Balanced Scorecard and to suggest ways to solve problems and improve performance. These meetings, attended by corporate active governance group members, also provide an opportunity for knowledge and experience generated in one portfolio company to be rapidly transferred to all the others.

Aktiva's active governance process, using value-based management and the Balanced Scorecard, has been highly successful. The return on net assets of Aktiva's largest investments rose from a negative 2 percent in 1998 to positive 12 percent in 2003. Pinus TKI, a Slovenian-based agricultural chemicals company in its portfolio, doubled its sales from 1996 to 2003 and transformed a negative €1.5 million economic value added in 1996 to a positive €1.5 million in 2003.

Aktiva, as an investment company and not as an operating company, periodically sells a company when it can get a price that fully reflects the company's underlying value that Aktiva has helped to generate. Interestingly, companies that Aktiva has sold, even when no longer under Aktiva's active governance mandate, continue to use their Balanced Scorecards—a tribute to the belief, within each portfolio company, of the value of this management and governance tool. Aktiva CEO Darko Horvat testified to the value of the Balanced Scorecard for his private investment company:

Figure 3-1 Aktiva Corporate Active Governance Strategy Map

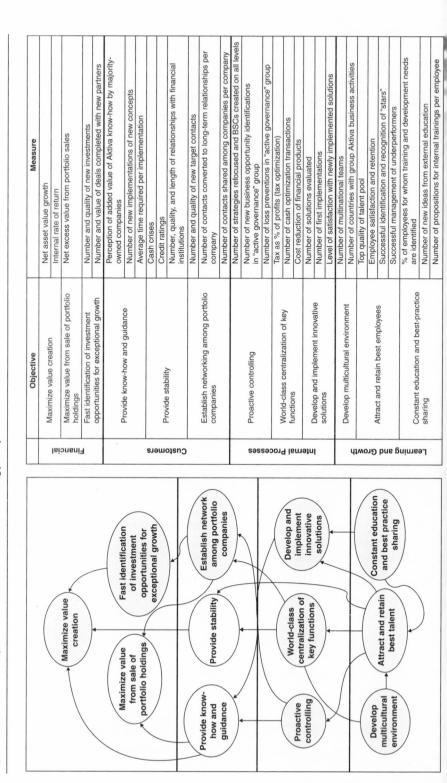

	Objective	Measure
Financial	Maximize value creation	Net asset value growth
		Internal rate of return
	Maximize value from sale of portfolio holdings	Net excess value from portfolio sales
Customers	Fast identification of investment opportunities for exceptional growth	Number and quality of new investments
		Number and value of deals completed with new partners
	Provide know-how and guidance	Perception of added value of Aktiva know-how by majority-owned companies
		Number of new implementations of new concepts
		Average time required per implementation
	Provide stability	Cash crises
		Credit ratings
		Number, quality, and length of relationships with financial institutions
	Establish networking among portfolio companies	Number and quality of new target contacts
		Number of contacts converted to long-term relationships per company
		Number of contacts shared among companies per company
Internal Processes	Proactive controlling	Number of strategies refocused and BSCs created on all levels
		Number of new business opportunity identifications in "active governance" group
		Number of loss preventions in "active governance" group
	World-class centralization of key functions	Tax as % of profits (tax optimization)
		Number of cash optimization transactions
		Cost reduction of financial products
	Develop and implement innovative solutions	Number of solutions evaluated
		Number of first implementations
		Level of satisfaction with newly implemented solutions
Learning and Growth	Develop multicultural environment	Number of multinational teams
		Number of countries with group Aktiva business activities
	Attract and retain best employees	Top quality of talent pool
		Employee satisfaction and retention
		Successful identification and recognition of "stars"
		Successful management of underperformers
	Constant education and best-practice sharing	% of employees for whom training and development needs are identified
		Number of new ideas from external education
		Number of propositions for internal trainings per employee

Before we implemented the BSC, Aktiva was growing exceptionally fast, but there was always a danger of focusing too much on only financial KPIs (key performance indicators). We were aware that such financial results are not sustainable for several years. By implementing the BSC, our focus moved from EVA to the other three perspectives, which, in the end, are those that contribute most to the future as well as to the financial success of the company. For us, the BSC is irreplaceable and is the backbone of how we conduct our business in a strategy-focused way. We look on it as an essential part, deeply integrated into the way of our success.[1]

CASE STUDY: NEW PROFIT INC.

A nonprofit version of the investment company model has also enjoyed great benefits from use of the Balanced Scorecard. New Profit Inc. (NPI), a venture philanthropy organization, attracts large donations from individuals, foundations, and corporations interested in contributing to entrepreneurial nonprofit organizations that can demonstrate proven track records and have the potential to go to scale.[2] NPI provides multiyear funding to its portfolio organizations that enables them to build capacity for growth. Much like private-sector venture capital firms, NPI holds its portfolio organizations accountable to achieve mutually agreed-upon targets on measurable performance criteria. NPI sustains its funding to these organizations as long as they continue to reach their goals.

Unlike private-sector investment, private equity, or venture capital firms, NPI cannot use financial measures to assess the performance of its investments in nonprofit organizations. The success of its portfolio organizations is measured by their social impact, not their ability to raise funds or balance their budgets. NPI's founding partners turned to the Balanced Scorecard as the best tool for establishing a performance contract with, and subsequently evaluating the performance of, each of its portfolio organizations.

NPI started by developing a corporate-level Balanced Scorecard for itself (see Figure 3-2). NPI developed its scorecard with its own board and with potential and existing investors so that it could be held accountable for its own performance, much as it would demand that portfolio organizations be accountable for theirs. The NPI corporate-level scorecard served as a template for the scorecards subsequently developed in the portfolio organizations. This allowed all portfolio organization scorecards to have a similar structure, facilitating communication with NPI board members and investors while still allowing the portfolio organizations to

Figure 3-2 New Profit 2005 Balanced Scorecard

New Profit mission: to demonstrate a new approach to philanthropy that provides the strategic and financial resources to enable visionary social entrepreneurs and their organizations to create transformative, sustainable impact.

Aspect	Objectives	Measures

Social Impact	A. Create a world-class philanthropic fund to select and scale social entrepreneurs.	(1) Portfolio organizations are achieving superior performance against their mission.
		  (a) Reach and growth: aggregate annual growth in lives impacted across the portfolio
		  (b) Growth: aggregate annual growth of revenue across the portfolio
		  (c) Quality: % of portfolio organizations meeting quality metric (within 5%)
		  (d) Sustainability: average change in "graduation checklist" score across the portfolio
		(2) Addition of high-potential organizations to portfolio
		  (a) X new investments in organizations meeting due diligence criteria

	B. Leverage results, experience, and network to build a strong environment for high-growth social entrepreneurs.	(3) Recognition of New Profit as a leader that can influence the actions of key players in the field to improve the environment for high-growth social entrepreneurs.
		  (a) Success in convening key leaders on social entrepreneurship and creating action-oriented initiatives
		  (b) Creation of a detailed strategy to make progress on key sector-wide initiatives and metrics to measure success. In addition to specific milestones for individual initiatives, measures of success here might include:
		    i. Inclusion of New Profit by others in important events/discussions
		    ii. Increase in the number and/or scale of other philanthropic organizations adopting a "New Profit"–like model of philanthropy
		    iii. Long-term increase in number of social entrepreneurs who have achieved "scale"

Constituent	C. New Profit investors are highly satisfied.	(4) Survey result on investor satisfaction.
	D. Social entrepreneurs in portfolio recognize value of working with New Profit.	(5) Survey result on overall satisfaction.
	E. Monitor Group North American partners are highly satisfied with TMG's commitment of resources to New Profit.	(6) Survey result of satisfaction of Monitor North American partners with New Profit relationship.

Financial	F. Grow amount of revenue raised.	(7) Total $ in new commitments from campaign.
		    ■ Increase % of funding coming from high-contributing investors
		    ■ Increase total $ raised by board of directors

	G. Create a more systematic, predictable process that doesn't rely solely on the founder.	(8) Close one new joint venture. (9) Increase in $ raised from investors per senior partner investment of time. (10) # of qualified prospects in the pipeline (personal referrals from existing investor or contact with last 3 months where specific investment amount was proposed) going into next year.
	H. Leverage direct $ investment in portfolio organizations with additional resources and funding.	(11) "Leverage ratio" (total value of resources brought by New Profit to portfolio/direct $ investment from New Profit).
Internal Operations	I. Strengthen internal financial controls around key operating decisions.	(12) New investments not made without at least 100% funding coverage. (13) Meet expense targets in budget. (14) Timely collection of investor commitments.
Organizational Capacity	J. Reinvigorate effective, consistent, high-quality portfolio management process.	(15) 100% of portfolio organizations have full "campaign plan" in place with quarterly evaluations of progress and results. (a) New portfolio organizations have clear investment thesis and campaign plan at time of investment
	K. Create a highly motivated, efficient, and productive organization	(16) 100% of staff members with formal goals. (17) Increased retention of New Profit staff.
	L. Increase effectiveness of NPI-Monitor relationship.	(18) Concrete proposal for "next generation" NPI-Monitor relationship agreed to by all key decision makers

customize the objectives in the various scorecard perspectives to fit their individual missions and constituents.

Once NPI built its corporate scorecard, its personnel worked with the portfolio organizations, helping them design and implement Balanced Scorecards tailored to their specific goals. NPI now monitors the performance of its portfolio organizations by how well they deliver on their individual Balanced Scorecard measures and targets. In semiannual reporting, NPI partners share with "investors" (i.e., contributors) a summary of each organization's Balanced Scorecard so that the investors see the social impact and performance of each portfolio organization.

NPI's enterprise value proposition includes an excellent due diligence process that identifies promising investing opportunities for social impact and growth. NPI also maintains an active monitoring and governance process that holds the social entrepreneurs accountable for delivering measurable results, and it provides management consulting to coach and advise the entrepreneurs on how to build more effective and efficient organizations. Because there is no capital market for funding the growth of nonprofit organizations, NPI creates substantial social value by enabling high-performing social enterprises to access long-term financing for growth and capacity building.

Each portfolio organization, in thought partnership with New Profit, creates its own scorecard, based on its mission, constituents, and value proposition. NPI provides only the broad template—showing perspectives for social impact, clients, financial, people, and resources—and each portfolio organization fills in its own scorecard.

FINANCIAL SYNERGIES:
CORPORATE BRANDS AND THEMES

Corporate headquarters can also create value by proactively leveraging resources, capabilities, or information throughout the individual entities. For example, highly diversified corporations, such as General Electric, Emerson, and the FMC Corporation, consist of a group of mostly autonomous sectors or companies in different industries. The enterprise value proposition for such highly diversified corporations comes primarily from headquarters executives' ability to operate internal capital markets better than external market mechanisms do (as with holding companies), and, in addition, the sharing of common themes or information across the units in a way that would not occur were each operating company to be an independent, market-facing entity.

Such diversified corporations follow a bottom-up approach, with the corporate parent approving the company-level scorecards as each is created and then monitoring each operating company according to its specified strategy for value creation. The corporate parent may impose a structure—such as which financial metrics must appear in each scorecard—and general themes for the various perspectives: "become our customers' most valued supplier," "achieve six sigma levels of quality in all operations," "be the industry leader in environmental and safety performance," "recruit the best talent," and "leverage technology for process improvement." The operating companies interpret these general guidelines in their own contexts and build their individual scorecards to capture their local strategies in a way that is consistent with corporate guidelines.

Many other corporations, although not exactly conglomerates, also fall into this category. All the operating units may be in the same broad industry category, such as financial services or discrete part manufacturing, but they still operate with different strategies and in different industry segments. For example, suppose a corporation consists of life sciences companies; some companies are innovative product leaders, others produce commodity products and compete on low cost and excellent quality and delivery, and still others offer an integrated set of products and services to their targeted customers. These corporations too must identify their enterprise value proposition: how their loosely connected set of companies can produce additional value by operating within the same corporate structure.

Most successful diversified corporations have distinct competencies that they leverage throughout their operating companies. For example, Emerson's companies operate in mature industries, involving engineered products, where success involves highly efficient manufacturing processes using electrical and mechanical technologies. FMC's companies operate in mature, capital-intensive industries, with slowly evolving technological processes. Many of General Electric's eclectic collection of businesses—including locomotives, aircraft engines, financial services, health care, energy, water treatment, and broadcasting—have long development and contracting cycles. Such homogeneity provides the opportunity for the corporate parent to add value throughout the operating units.

Some highly diversified corporations find it beneficial to develop a branding strategy to promote cohesion in the eyes of investors and customers. The values represented by the brand transcend the strategies of operating companies. General Electric has, over its history, branded its corporate businesses with a series of overarching themes: "We Bring Good Things to Life," "Progress Is Our Most Important Product," and "Live Better Electrically." Today, to signify a renewed emphasis on innovation, GE has introduced a new theme, "Imagination at Work." Each GE operating company now communicates how imagination brings new products, services, and solutions to customers.

For more than a century, Emerson Electric was known as an organization of companies that offered low-cost engineered products to customers. With its new (shortened) name, Emerson has repositioned its brand, as did GE, to stress innovation and technology. It communicates that each of its operating companies, all of whose names now begin with the company name, Emerson, will deliver on the corporate brand promise:

> *At Emerson, we bring together technology and engineering to create solutions for the benefit of our customers. We deliver the forward-thinking answers our customers require to succeed in a world in action. We are driven without compromise to bring our customers quality solutions deserving of the Emerson name.*
>
> *For businesses around the world, the Emerson brand represents global technology, industry leadership and customer focus. For the investor, the Emerson name symbolizes our proven management model, successful growth strategy, and strong financial performance. For employees, the Emerson experience means opportunities to grow, prosper, and make a difference.[3]*

The Balanced Scorecards of highly diversified corporations may also have customer and internal process objectives. The customer perspective in the corporate Balanced Scorecard can include desired customer outcomes, such as brand image and customer acquisition, satisfaction, retention, market share, and profitability. The objectives typically do not include objectives or measures describing a customer value proposition because each operating company will have its own customized value proposition for its targeted customers.

For the internal perspective, diversified companies often articulate corporate-level themes for critical processes such as six sigma quality, e-business capability, and excellent environmental, safety, and employment practices. For example, many corporations have embraced quality, such as six sigma programs, as a corporate theme. Headquarters encourages its operating companies to compete for national and international quality awards to demonstrate leadership in quality processes. Companies operate internal quality award programs to foster competition among their operating companies.

To avoid the consequences to the entire corporation from a local failure or incident, the corporate parent may also want each operating company to excel at regulatory and social processes. A product liability problem, a company bribery incident, a dismal environmental reputation, or frequent employee safety and health concerns in any single operating company can produce highly unfavorable publicity that affects the financial resources and viability of the entire corporation. On a more positive note, exceptional performance on employment, environmental, health, safety, and community objectives may attract customers, investors, and employees for all the corporation's companies.

Excellence in regulatory and social processes can help the corporate brand to the benefit of all its operating companies. For example, business groups such as Tata and Siam Cement require that their operating companies live up to contracts in order to earn a reputation as a good company to do business with, even though strict contract enforcement may not be required given the lower incidence of independent and bribery-free judiciaries in the developing nations in which these business groups operate.[4] Amanco, based in Central and South America, has developed a Strategy Map and Balanced Scorecard based on three bottom-line performance measures—economic, environmental, and social—to position itself as a leading progressive corporation in all regions in which it operates.[5] Diversified corporations that expect to leverage gains from excellent performance in operating, regulatory, and social processes can reflect objectives on these corporate-level themes in the internal perspective of their corporate Strategy Map and Balanced Scorecards.

We illustrate the development of a diversified company Strategy Map and Balanced Scorecard with Ingersoll-Rand, a corporation that generated increased shareholder value by clarifying its corporate brand and focusing its line businesses on common themes.

CASE STUDY: INGERSOLL-RAND

Founded more than 130 years ago as a specialist in construction and mining equipment, Ingersoll-Rand (IR) is now a diversified manufacturing corporation with annual sales of more than $10 billion. Its corporate portfolio consists of numerous successful brands, such as Thermo King (refrigeration), Bobcat (construction), Club Car (golf carts and utility vehicles), and Schlage (security and safety).

IR historically was a product-centered business, with each brand having its own customers and sales channels. IR's operating companies delivered strong results, and growth in corporate earnings per share exceeded 20 percent for six consecutive years, from 1995 to 2001.

Herb Henkel became president and CEO of IR in 1999. He wanted to continue the IR businesses' product-driven excellence that had delivered past success, but he now wanted to unleash cross-business integration that would provide a new source of revenue and growth. Cross-business integration would let IR better leverage its sales channels, products, and customer base as well as the knowledge and experience of its people. Henkel recognized, however, that such cross-business integration was countercultural at IR. A major transformation of IR, from top to bottom, would be required.

The change started with the creation of a new corporate architecture based on the corporate strategy (see Figure 3-3). Henkel organized all the previously independent product businesses into four global growth sectors: Climate Control, Industrial Solutions, Infrastructure, and Security and Safety. The sectors would create more market focus, share sales channels, and provide opportunities to cross-sell products. Companies within the sectors would strive to create new customer value by providing solutions to customer problems instead of simply selling products. Teamwork within these sectors would be the primary source of synergy.

The corporate center would create enterprise-derived value by implementing cross-business integration and by increasing the value of IR's brand with investors. The corporate center now had five key missions:

1. Build the new corporate identity for the benefit of customers, employees, and investors.
2. Create leverage and synergy with IR's resources.
3. Enhance the performance of the sectors.
4. Provide strategic leadership.
5. Satisfy legal requirements.

Henkel collected IR's shared-service organizations into a new unit, Global Business Services (GBS), which represented the third element of the new architecture. In the past, shared services had often micromanaged business issues. GBS was now responsible for creating standard processes and for proliferating best practices to facilitate and enhance

IR is a global, diversified industrial enterprise with market-leading brands serving customers in the growth markets of climate control, industrial solutions, infrastructure, and security and safety.

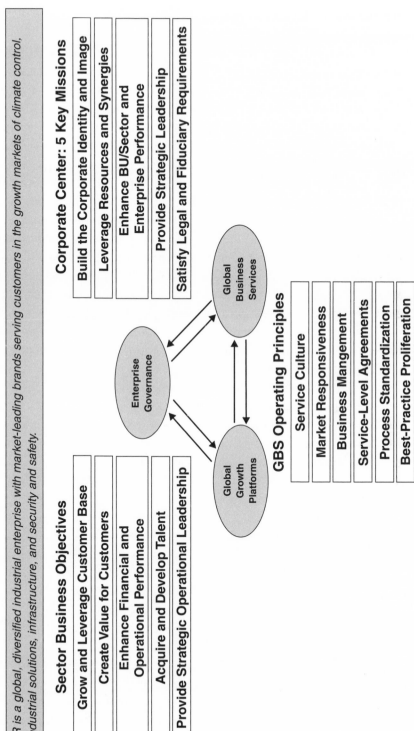

Corporate Center: 5 Key Missions

- Build the Corporate Identity and Image
- Leverage Resources and Synergies
- Enhance BU/Sector and Enterprise Performance
- Provide Strategic Leadership
- Satisfy Legal and Fiduciary Requirements

Sector Business Objectives

- Grow and Leverage Customer Base
- Create Value for Customers
- Enhance Financial and Operational Performance
- Acquire and Develop Talent
- Provide Strategic Operational Leadership

Enterprise Governance

Global Business Services

Global Growth Platforms

GBS Operating Principles

- Service Culture
- Market Responsiveness
- Business Mangement
- Service-Level Agreements
- Process Standardization
- Best-Practice Proliferation

cross-business synergies. Service-level agreements between GBS and the sectors provided the mechanism for achieving such synergies.

The creation of the corporate architecture was an important and essential first step in the IR strategy execution. It unfroze the IR executives, showing the need for change in spite of six consecutive years of exceptional performance. It created a new way of managing and established clear accountability; both objectives were designed to move executives outside the comfort zone of their past. Having created the management infrastructure, IR then developed its enterprise Strategy Map to translate the high-level corporate strategy into operational terms. The enterprise Strategy Map used corporate themes as guidelines for sector planning.

The Strategy Map template described a common philosophy—the philosophy of the new Ingersoll-Rand—that would provide the foundation for the strategy of each business unit. As shown in Figure 3-4, the financial objectives were straightforward: increase revenue, reduce costs, and use assets efficiently. The customer perspective captured the essence of the new strategy from the perspective of customers and markets. Providing solutions would shift the business focus from a narrow product strategy to one based on personal relationships that exploited the knowledge of IR personnel.

The process dimension of the scorecard was organized around the three fundamental process themes—operational excellence, customer intimacy, and product innovation—that each sector would subsequently adopt and adapt to its situation. For example, "drive operational excellence" required each sector to develop strategies that would continuously improve health, safety and environment, manufacturing, and technology. "Drive demand through customer intimacy" required each sector to develop customized marketing programs with key customers. "Drive dramatic growth through innovation" required each sector to develop innovative, differentiating applications and solutions. The specifics of the approaches developed by sectors and business lines would differ dramatically, based on the unique features of their situation. Yet all sectors and businesses would now use a common framework to view the marketplace.

The people perspective of the strategy identified the most important dimension of the corporate change agenda: dual citizenship. Historically, all personnel worked for a single line of business. Although this strategy provided clear benefits, it meant that tangible and intangible assets were locked up, incapable of being used elsewhere in the corporation where additional payoffs could be realized. Dual citizenship sent a message to all employees in the organization to think beyond the limits of their individual business

Figure 4-1. Ingersoll-Rand Enterprise Strategy Map

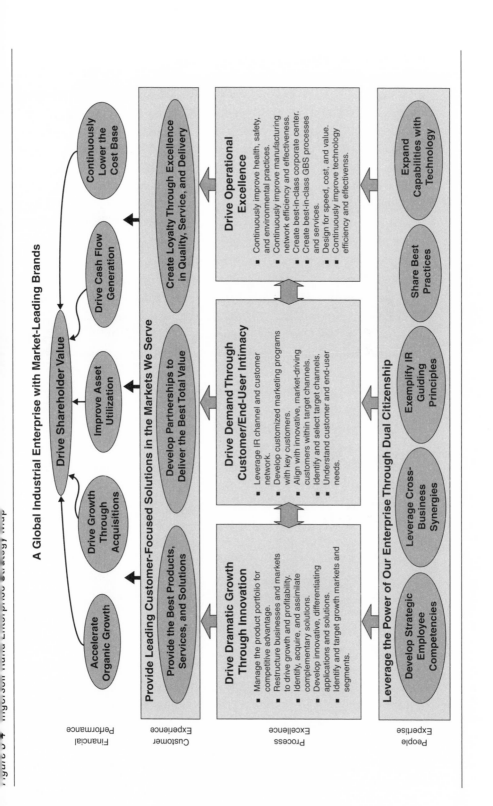

A Global Industrial Enterprise with Market-Leading Brands

Drive Shareholder Value

Accelerate Organic Growth

Drive Growth Through Acquisitions

Improve Asset Utilization

Drive Cash Flow Generation

Continuously Lower the Cost Base

Provide Leading Customer-Focused Solutions in the Markets We Serve

Provide the Best Products, Services, and Solutions

Develop Partnerships to Deliver the Best Total Value

Create Loyalty Through Excellence in Quality, Service, and Delivery

Drive Dramatic Growth Through Innovation
- Manage the product portfolio for competitive advantage.
- Restructure businesses and markets to drive growth and profitability.
- Identify, acquire, and assimilate complementary solutions.
- Develop innovative, differentiating applications and solutions.
- Identify and target growth markets and segments.

Drive Demand Through Customer/End-User Intimacy
- Leverage IR channel and customer network.
- Develop customized marketing programs with key customers.
- Align with innovative, market-driving customers within target channels.
- Identify and select target channels.
- Understand customer and end-user needs.

Drive Operational Excellence
- Continuously improve health, safety, and environmental practices.
- Continuously improve manufacturing network efficiency and effectiveness.
- Create best-in-class corporate center.
- Create best-in-class GBS processes and services.
- Design for speed, cost, and value.
- Continuously improve technology efficiency and effectiveness.

Leverage the Power of Our Enterprise Through Dual Citizenship

Develop Strategic Employee Competencies

Leverage Cross-Business Synergies

Exemplify IR Guiding Principles

Share Best Practices

Expand Capabilities with Technology

Financial Performance

Customer Experience

Process Excellence

People Expertise

units and find ways to create cross-business value for other IR businesses. Ultimately, this theme would result in divisions sharing factories, and employees selling the products of other divisions to their customers. IR set a target to create several hundred million dollars' worth of such cross-business value, all of which would be new, an increment to business as usual.

The corporate scorecard was cascaded to each of the sectors and business units, which, in turn, developed their own Strategy Maps consistent with the corporate template. The corporate strategy was supported by a set of "One Company" initiatives, shown in the rightmost column of Figure 3-5. These initiatives provided the actions necessary to execute the corporate dimensions of the new strategy.

As the final dimension of IR's transformation and alignment strategy, Henkel created a new Enterprise Leadership Team (ELT) consisting of key executives from the sectors, from Global Business Services, and from the corporate center. Each executive was responsible for the operation of his own business or support unit, but collectively they accepted the mission to be stewards of the performance of Ingersoll-Rand, the corporation.

ELT responsibilities included the following:

- We are leading (corporate financial success) together.
- We help define dual citizenship and remove barriers to its success.
- We lead the strategic initiatives together.
- We lead IR's communication team.
- We own talent and diversity.
- We are mentors creating mentors.

The creation of the Executive Leadership Team, the new corporate architecture, the corporate Strategy Map, the corporate Balanced Scorecard, and One Company initiatives provided an operational framework to make Ingersoll-Rand more valuable than the sum of its parts.

Since 2001, the company's reported diluted earnings per share have tripled; its cash flow generation has greatly expanded, with virtually a tenfold increase in cumulative cash generated compared with the decade earlier period between 1991 to 1994; and its operating margins have improved from 6.3 percent in 2001 (excluding restructuring charges) to 11.9 percent in 2004.

At the same time, the company has doubled its base of recurring revenues through a focus on services and aftermarket business (which is a critical piece of the company's growth strategy) and has dramatically

Corporate Synergies		Enterprise Value Proposition	Enterprise Scorecard	Corporate Initiatives
Financial	◐	■ Drive shareholder value.	■ Total shareholder return ■ Total revenue growth ■ Organic revenue growth ■ Operating income growth ■ Cash flow	■ Finance as a growth engine ■ Acquisition and integration ■ Corporate tax
Customer	◐	■ Provide leading customer-focused solutions.	■ Customer survey ■ Target account performance ■ % Perfect orders	■ Retail solutions
Internal Process	◐	■ Drive dramatic growth through innovation.	■ Revenue from new solutions ■ Product/SBU portfolio performance	■ IR distribution
		■ Drive demand through customer/end-user intimacy.	■ Revenue from cross-selling	■ Supplier solutions
		■ Drive operational excellence.	■ % Revenues supported by standard technology platform ■ IR quality index ■ Lost workdays ■ Hazardous waste	■ Enterprise-wide technology
Learning and Growth	◐	■ Leverage the power of our exterprise through dual citizenship.	■ Employee survey ■ Leadership development plan ■ Performance management plan participation	■ Strategic management system ■ IR University/Leadership Institute ■ Communications

Key: Corporate Role

◯ Common/linked processes and measures

◐ Common themes

improved its balance sheet, reflected by a debt-to-capital of 24.2 percent at the end of 2004 compared with 46.3 percent at the end of 2001.

SYNERGIES FROM SHARED CUSTOMERS

Many decentralized corporations have business units that sell to the same customers. For example, Datex Ohmeda (DO), a subsidiary of Instrumentarium Corporation (now part of GE Healthcare), was historically organized by product units. These units developed innovative products for acute-care health systems, including anesthesia machines, ventilators, and drug-delivery systems. The different product lines, many added through acquisition, were sold by different sales forces, each focusing on the technical merits of its individual hardware system.

DO executives saw an opportunity to leverage its multiple business units by shifting from a product-driven strategy to a customer relationship approach that emphasized total solutions for its health-care delivery customers. By integrating the sales force to create customer account teams, DO increased the scope of its products and services to customers, leading to greatly increased revenue per account.

In general, corporations whose operating companies sell to common customers have the opportunity to leverage their multiple products and services to create unique customer solutions, resulting in customer satisfaction and loyalty that less diversified and more focused corporations cannot match.

The BSC customer perspective of such corporations features the outcomes and value proposition related to providing customers with more complete solutions. For example, a customer outcome objective might be to increase the share of the customer's wallet, measured by the percentage of the customer's spending in its category that is being captured by the corporation as a whole. Other objectives are to increase the number of different products and services used by targeted customers, the lifetime profitability of acquired customers, and the quality of complete solutions offered to customers. Objectives for internal customer management processes include acquiring high-potential-value customers that could benefit from receiving integrated solutions, cross-selling existing customers to acquire additional products and services, and retaining and growing the business of these targeted customers.

Some public-sector organizations have also adopted a corporate strategy to share customers across business units. The municipalities of Charlotte, North Carolina, and Brisbane, Australia, recognized that their operating departments had common customers, in their cases, the citizens and businesses in the city. Charlotte and Brisbane each developed a city-level Balanced Scorecard to articulate a strategy to make it the number one city in the region in which to live, work, and recreate. The operating units in the city—such as police, fire, sanitation, utility, planning, housing, parks, and recreation—then built their scorecards to deliver the citywide value proposition that would differentiate Charlotte and Brisbane and make them better than communities that operated with less focus and attention to their common customer, the citizen. Each department had to integrate its offerings with those of other city departments to provide a uniquely great experience for local residents and businesses.

The following case study of Media General describes a corporate Strategy Map and Balanced Scorecard designed to realize the benefits of sharing customers across multiple business units.

CASE STUDY: MEDIA GENERAL

Media General is a southeastern U.S. media company with revenues in 2003 of $837 million and nearly eight thousand employees. As of 2003, it owned twenty-five daily newspapers with a combined circulation of more than one million; more than one hundred weekly newspapers; twenty-six network-affiliated television stations reaching more than 30 percent of TV households in the Southeast (8 percent in the United States); and more than fifty Web sites related to its newspapers and TV stations.

Media General was founded more than 150 years ago and until the 1990s had a history of somewhat unsystematic growth, purchasing diverse publishing and media properties around the United States. Competitive pressures and the explosive growth of cable TV and the Internet, however, had depressed the value of Media General's stock. When J. Stewart Bryan III became chairman and CEO in 1990, the company embarked on a massive transformation, shedding old businesses and acquiring others to refocus on its historic roots in the Southeast. It divested all properties outside the region and, in 1995, owned only three newspapers, three television stations, and interest in a cable company and a newsprint company. During the next five years Media General purchased twenty-two newspapers and twenty-three TV stations, all in the Southeast, and sold its cable and newsprint interests.

The company could now exploit its regional concentration to embark on a new strategy based on convergence. Bryan wanted to create synergy by exploiting the individual and collective strengths of Media General's three divisions: newspapers, TV, and interactive media. His goal was to coordinate different media in a given market to provide quality information in the way that each does best—but delivered from a comprehensive and unified perspective.

Media General would bring together the unique strengths of print, broadcast, and interactive media to give customers in its core regional markets continual access to a seamless set of content platforms. It would leverage its three properties in each region to make them the preferred local sources of news and content for local residents. The concentration of the three related properties would also enable Media General to offer advertisers a high-quality audience to which they could direct integrated multimedia advertising packages.

The new convergence strategy would not be a natural action for the Media General properties. Historically, newspapers and broadcast media have competed for the same audience and advertisers' dollars, and the operators of interactive media regarded TV stations and newspapers as "old economy" relics. Bryan saw that his convergence strategy for creating new revenue sources required the use of the Balanced Scorecard to develop strong teamwork, communication, and cooperation across business lines.

Media General started by crafting its mission statement: "to be the leading provider of high-quality news, entertainment, and information in the Southeast by continually building on our position of strength in strategically located markets." The corporation continued by developing a corporate Strategy Map (see Figure 3-6) that described the convergence strategy. Here, we identify and analyze several objectives in each perspective, starting with the foundation—learning and growth—to highlight how Media General's corporate Strategy Map incorporated the convergence strategy.

Learning and Growth

The overall goal of the learning and growth objectives was to have a convergence focus that would guide every employee's everyday activities. The "focus on career and skills development" objective featured sales personnel receiving training on multimedia and multimarket sales development so that they could effectively sell new multimedia packages to advertisers. The objective "promote culture of change and employee empowerment" involved education to help employees understand the benefits of working as parts of a single regional Media General team rather than thinking, within a silo, as employees of a newspaper, a TV station, or a Web page.

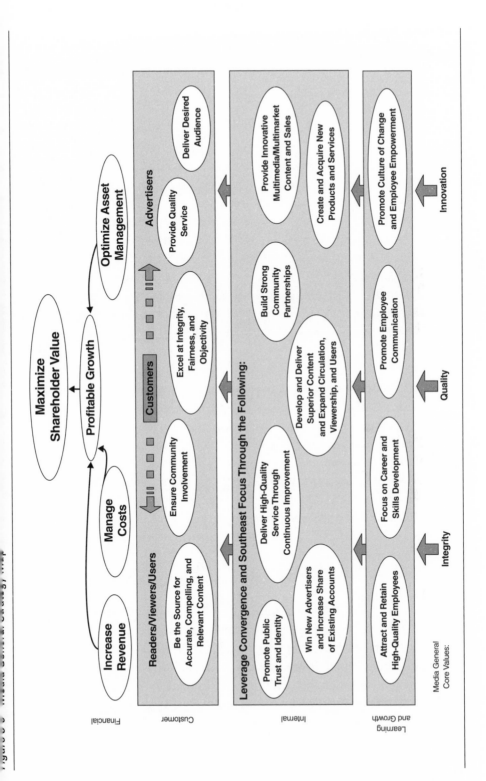

Figure Media General Strategy Map

Internal

The objective "develop and deliver superior content" signaled how the newsrooms from all three divisions should work together to jointly develop stories. The goal was to have more stories to share, along with higher-quality products and content delivered in a more timely fashion. The objective "provide innovative multimedia/multimarket content and sales" was a direct convergence objective. Metrics for this objective included the number of targeted (advertiser) convergence accounts successfully sold through cooperative efforts from the three divisions, new nontraditional advertisers gained, and new programs sold.

The company expected that both of these internal process objectives would influence a third, "build strong community partnerships." The synergies gained when properties in the three divisions worked together, rather than competed, were expected to increase local awareness of Media General's brand.

Customer

The customer objective "provide quality service" was based on a newly developed online advertiser survey. The survey's aim was to learn whether Media General's new value proposition of integrated multimedia content was indeed giving local advertisers additional vehicles to get their message out to the public and generating more consumer traffic to their places of business. The objective "ensure community involvement" tracked customers' perception of Media General as a strong community citizen. This objective directly measured the scope benefit of Media's convergence strategy, a larger community presence due to its having multiple properties in the same region.

Financial

Ultimately the success of the corporation's convergence strategy would be measured by its delivery of improved financial results. The "increase revenue" objective had one measure that identified the convergence revenue that was incremental to revenue earned from the existing, traditional base of properties in the three divisions. It directly measured the increased revenue resulting from the purchase of the new multimedia/multimarket packages by existing advertisers as well as revenues from new advertisers acquired through convergence offerings.

A second measure for this objective tracked growth in traditional advertising revenue; it motivated the three divisions to continue to focus on their core businesses while also contributing to the new convergence business. The objective "manage costs" represented scale economies that the executives expected to gain by consolidating news production among the three divisions, by reengineering processes, and by sharing best practices throughout the three divisions.

Cascading

Once Media General had developed the enterprise Strategy Map and Balanced Scorecard, each of the properties in the three divisions then developed its individual scorecard. These scorecards reflected the balance between the convergence priorities on the corporate scorecard and each division's local business situation.

A unique feature of the Media General implementation was a subsequent step to create a Strategy Map and scorecard for each region. Initially, a local, cross-business team consolidated the maps and scorecards from the three divisions in the region. The team then created a regional "convergence" Strategy Map and scorecard to reflect synergy opportunities, and it shared the scorecard with the three properties, asking them to update their local scorecards to reflect convergence objectives in their region (see Figure 3-7).

Results

In 2002, a particularly difficult year in the publishing industry, earnings per share from continuing operations almost tripled on revenue growth of 4 percent. Multimedia advertising packages contributed to a 42.5 percent revenue gain in the interactive media division. Revenue growth increased only slightly in 2003, but income from continuing operations increased more than 10 percent. The publishing division was second in the nation in its peer group of newspapers in total revenue growth, and the interactive media division increased revenues by 60 percent.

SYNERGIES FROM A COMMON CUSTOMER VALUE PROPOSITION

Many corporations generate value by offering and consistently delivering a common customer value proposition throughout their decentralized

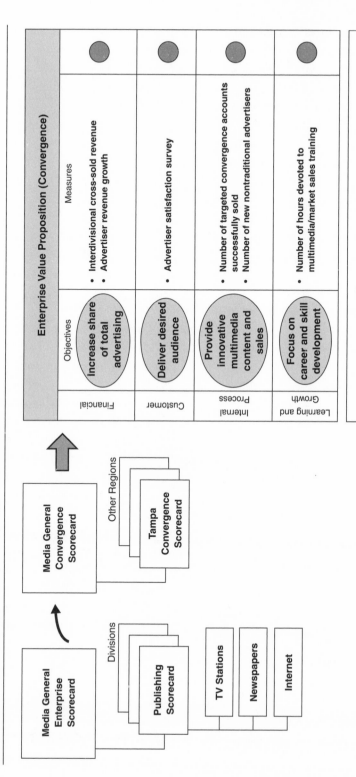

Figure 3-7 Cascading the Convergence Strategy at Media General

units. Customers can be assured that they will get the same products, services, value, and buying experience at any corporate unit they transact with.

Examples of homogeneous units operating under a corporate structure are branded fast food and restaurant outlets, hotels, gasoline stations, apparel stores, convenience stores, and retail branch banks. A company that operates such retail units brands its strategy with every customer contact at every unit. The enterprise value proposition is to create satisfied, loyal customers by offering a consistent experience, conforming to the corporate quality standards, at each outlet for every customer contact.

The financial perspective of the corporate scorecard identifies the financial metrics used by the company to evaluate the success of its strategy. These are often industry specific, such as same-store sales growth (for retail stores) and revenue per available room (for hotels). Customer objectives relate to creating satisfied, loyal customers from every buying experience. Internal process objectives communicate the importance of having each unit conform to the corporate standard for delivering the customer value proposition, including standards for speed, quality, and friendly service. Learning and growth objectives emphasize retention and development of employees, because the customer's experience with the company is usually delivered by frontline employees.

Companies in this category have the simplest cascading process. Executives at corporate headquarters decide on the strategy and the value proposition to be offered at each unit. The executives translate the strategy into a Balanced Scorecard of key metrics, which is communicated and applied at every retail outlet.

To illustrate this alignment role for the Balanced Scorecard, we present two case studies: from the private sector, Hilton; and from the nonprofit sector, Citizen Schools.

CASE STUDY: HILTON HOTELS

In 2005 Hilton Hotels Family of Brands included over 2,300 owned, managed, and franchised properties, totaling over 360,000 rooms. Hilton initially introduced the Balanced Scorecard Program at its owned and managed hotel properties in 1997, after a period of stagnant performance. At the corporate level, senior executives developed five strategic value drivers (perspectives), and from these value drivers, developed KPIs for the individual SBUs, its hotels (see Figure 3-8). This allowed

Figure 3-8 Case Study: Hilton Hotels

Value Drivers	Enterprise Value Proposition	Enterprise Scorecard
Financial: Operational Effectiveness, Revenue Maximization	Provide a common understanding of the measures of success.	■ GOP $ (Gross Operating Profit) ■ GOP % ■ Rev/PAR: Revenue per available room ■ Rev/PAR Index: Compared with competitive set

Customer Loyalty	Create satisfied, loyal customers from each customer contact point.	■ Guest loyalty index (measuring)
		  ■ Satisfaction
		  ■ Likelihood to return
		  ■ Likelihood to recommend

Operations	Consistently deliver the customer value proposition.	■ Brand consistency index
		  ■ Brand standards
		  ■ Physical condition
		  ■ Overall service
		  ■ Cleanliness

Learning and Growth	Retain and develop team members.	■ Team member loyalty ■ Training index ■ Diversity

the hotels to align with the corporate strategic direction while having their own unique KPI measures based on prior year actuals, plus an improvement factor.

The common scorecard format for each property enabled a clear and consistent message to be delivered throughout the chain. The promise of a brand requires that customers experience the same level of quality and services at each Hilton property, and individual hotel scores would now be benchmarked internally against all Hilton properties. With corporate strategic direction now linked to hotel measures, managers at each Hilton property could then communicate these measures to every team member. Hotel teams built awareness and understanding of the measures into team members' orientation and training programs, and continually updated the scores on the nine KPI measures so that team members could track current performance and trends. Finally the hotel's BSC performance was linked to executive pay through bonus plans. And, to make sure the BSC aligned every team member throughout the hotel, *all* team members at hotels getting all green zones for all nine KPIs shared a portion of an annual $1 million "Go for the Green" award.

From 1997 to 2000, Hilton realized profit margins three percentage points higher than other full-service hotels. This financial performance was achieved through improvements in the revenue per available room (RevPAR) index, customer satisfaction, post-stay loyalty (delivering the highest scores in the company's history).

By 2004, following the spin-off of gaming hotels and the merger of Promus Hotels (Doubletree, Embassy Suites, Homewood, Hampton Inn) Hilton's Balanced Scorecard was embedded in a comprehensive perfor-mance management program that included planning, budget-goal setting, measurement (BSC), continuous improvement process, operational sup-port, and reward and recognition (see Figure 3-9).

Hilton's new Performance Management System is Web based, which allows for drill-down capabilities so managers can determine the root causes and detail information behind the numbers to assist in their con-tinuous improvement effort. And Hilton was now using its extensive cross-sectional database to develop statistical linkage among its processes, objectives, and leading/lagging indicators. The indicators helped to iden-tify the relationship between variables, and opportunities for finding root causes of problems, and subsequently measured whether implemented so-lutions were having the desired effects. Finally, the system allows the scorecard to cascade through the organizational hierarchy from the enter-prise, regional, and hotel rollup scorecards, to the department and ulti-mately to the individual level, optimizing alignment and accountability throughout the organization.

CASE STUDY: CITIZEN SCHOOLS

Citizen Schools, one of the portfolio companies of New Profit Inc. (NPI was discussed earlier in this chapter), is a nonprofit example of this common value proposition model. Citizen Schools operates after-school and summer programs for children aged nine through fourteen in Boston and across the United States. Through apprenticeships with local ex-perts, children learn real-world skills, build self-confidence, and connect with their communities.

Citizen Schools' Balanced Scorecard (see Figure 3-10) follows the five-perspective framework of New Profit Inc. The scorecard includes

Figure 3-9 Hilton Corporation Balanced Scorecard

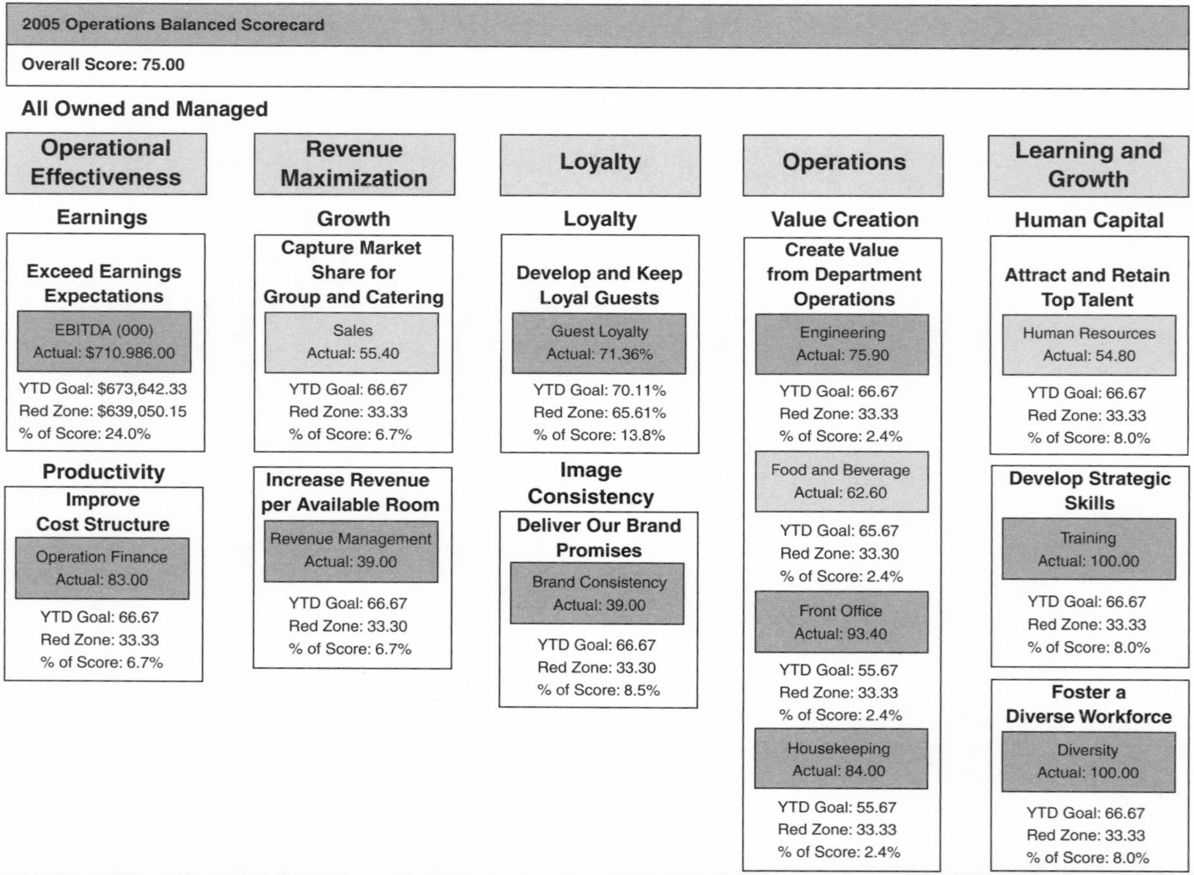

2005 Operations Balanced Scorecard

Overall Score: 75.00

All Owned and Managed

Operational Effectiveness	Revenue Maximization	Loyalty	Operations	Learning and Growth

Earnings

Exceed Earnings Expectations

EBITDA (000)
Actual: $710.986.00

YTD Goal: $673,642.33
Red Zone: $639,050.15
% of Score: 24.0%

Productivity

Improve Cost Structure

Operation Finance
Actual: 83.00

YTD Goal: 66.67
Red Zone: 33.33
% of Score: 6.7%

Growth

Capture Market Share for Group and Catering

Sales
Actual: 55.40

YTD Goal: 66.67
Red Zone: 33.33
% of Score: 6.7%

Increase Revenue per Available Room

Revenue Management
Actual: 39.00

YTD Goal: 66.67
Red Zone: 33.30
% of Score: 6.7%

Loyalty

Develop and Keep Loyal Guests

Guest Loyalty
Actual: 71.36%

YTD Goal: 70.11%
Red Zone: 65.61%
% of Score: 13.8%

Image Consistency

Deliver Our Brand Promises

Brand Consistency
Actual: 39.00

YTD Goal: 66.67
Red Zone: 33.30
% of Score: 8.5%

Value Creation

Create Value from Department Operations

Engineering
Actual: 75.90

YTD Goal: 66.67
Red Zone: 33.33
% of Score: 2.4%

Food and Beverage
Actual: 62.60

YTD Goal: 65.67
Red Zone: 33.30
% of Score: 2.4%

Front Office
Actual: 93.40

YTD Goal: 55.67
Red Zone: 33.33
% of Score: 2.4%

Housekeeping
Actual: 84.00

YTD Goal: 55.67
Red Zone: 33.33
% of Score: 2.4%

Human Capital

Attract and Retain Top Talent

Human Resources
Actual: 54.80

YTD Goal: 66.67
Red Zone: 33.33
% of Score: 8.0%

Develop Strategic Skills

Training
Actual: 100.00

YTD Goal: 66.67
Red Zone: 33.33
% of Score: 8.0%

Foster a Diverse Workforce

Diversity
Actual: 100.00

YTD Goal: 66.67
Red Zone: 33.33
% of Score: 8.0%

measures of students' academic and social development and provides guidance and feedback for the training and development of staff.

Central to Citizen Schools' strategy is to replicate its model at multiple sites around its Boston home base and to affiliates and franchises that operate throughout the United States. By 2004, Citizen Schools units were operating in six other cities in Massachusetts and in San Jose and Redwood City, California; Houston, Texas; Tucson, Arizona; and New Brunswick, New Jersey. As the organization expands, it uses its Balanced Scorecard template to communicate the common strategy to all sites.

In general, personnel at the new sites are not familiar with the Balanced Scorecard and its terminology. But they all understand the perspectives of social impact and the customer. Citizen Schools uses key BSC measures to communicate performance expectations and to track results at each site. Now that it has more than a dozen sites operating with the same scorecard measures, Citizen Schools benchmarks performance data from all the units and identifies opportunities for best-practice sharing. Having a common measurement and management system is a key ingredient for Citizen Schools in rapidly scaling its operations to a national level while still delivering a consistent experience and value proposition at each newly opened site.

SUMMARY

Even the most diversified enterprise can create value when it operates an internal capital market that is more effective than having each business unit in its portfolio seek its own financing independently from external capital providers. Such enterprises can describe and monitor their objectives for value creation through high-level financial metrics.

Diversified enterprises also create value when they articulate corporate-level themes that brand each operating company with an image and that leverage capabilities related to such objectives as good governance, product quality, customer-focused solutions, community responsibility, or environmental excellence. Customer-based value can be created when diverse business units combine their products and services to offer customers convenient, integrated solutions. Customer-based value also arises when homogeneous, geographically dispersed units give customers a consistent, high-quality buying experience of products or services. In such enterprises, the corporate headquarters articulates the branded, common experience and uses Balanced Scorecards to motivate and monitor the delivery of service throughout its dispersed units.

Figure 3-10 Citizen Schools Balanced Scorecard (*FY* 2001)

Aspect	Objectives	Measures and Goals
Social Impact	A. Deliver a superior quality program that educates children and strengthens community by building skills (writing, data analysis, and oral presentation), access, leadership, and community interactions.	1. Student impact rating of 4.0 or higher on a 5-point scale (composite of up to 10 key questions from various stakeholders). 2. 75% (or more) of students at campuses focusing on writing (currently 9 of 11) will increase by one rubric level their writing skills during the academic year. 75% (or more) of all students will improve their oral presentation skills (data from both rubrics and staff assessments). *Stretch Goal:* Greater than 80%
Financial	B. Receive $7.5 million in cash or commitments toward four-year, $25 million campaign.	3. Reach the $7.5 million goal by end of year. *Stretch Goal:* Greater than $8.5 MM of above measurement. *Stretch Goal 2:* Nonfoundation funding increases (minimum of >10% versus growth targets) faster than expenses between 2000–2001
	C. Stay within 2001 budget.	4. Post 5%+ surplus and stay within budget of $4.8 million.
Customer	D. *Students:* Expand student demand and enrollment.	5. Increase student enrollment from 1,248 in FY2000 to 1,530 (±5%). *Stretch Goal:* demand grows significantly as evidenced by 2/3 of campuses with a waitlist of 10% or more enrollment for fall 2001 program
	E. *Citizen teachers:* Provide outstanding volunteer experience and thereby increase pool of volunteers.	6. 85% or more of CTs surveys indicate they would (a) return and teach a future apprenticeship, (b) refer a friend to teach an apprenticeship, and (c) rate the experience as 4.0 or greater on its positive impact on the volunteer.
	F. *Training partners:* Deliver high-quality, high-impact training to first-year CSU partners.	7. 4.0 (or better) rating of quality and impact of training by executive directors and participating staff from 2+ partners.

Operations	G. Develop more precise evaluation instruments for measuring program impact.	8. Complete the following: hire external evaluator for three-year evaluation, revise constituent surveys, and develop strong measurement tools in all key outcome areas.
	H. Set stage for national leverage of CS model.	9. Publishing: Document and internally publish Version 1.0 CS Best Practices.
		10. Policy: Four meetings with local officials, four with state/national officials, and favorable coverage in five media outlets.
	I. Deepen school partnerships.	11. Eight of twelve campus directors, and eight of twelve school principals (or primary school liasons) rate the following components of the partnership as 4.0 or greater: (a) academic alignment, (b) enrollment demand, and (c) community engagement.
	J. Consistently implement action plan.	12. Successfully accomplish 75% or more action plan goals within one quarter of goal. *Stretch goal:* 85% or more of action plan
Learning and Growth	K. Maintain high full-time staff retention and increase staff diversity.	13. Retention of full-time staff at 75% or higher for staff employed as of January 2001. *Stretch goal:* 85% retention
		14. Develop recruitment strategy to increase hiring and retention of people of color.
	L. Technology serves as a reliable communication and operational tool.	15. By the end of the second quarter, each workstation has the following functioning software: database, e-mail, Internet, MS Office. Each full-time staff member has access to e-mail and voice mail.
	M. Further develop full-time staff training program.	16. All full-time staff employed throughout 2001 will participate in the following trainings: CS strategic plan, CS Balanced Scorecard, database, office technology, and two other organization-wide topics as determined by leadership. *Stretch goal:* Trainings receive a participant satisfaction rating of 4 or greater from CS staff.
	N. Improve communication by developing and implementing high-quality human resource procedures and protocols.	17. All staff will have by year-end: (a) job description, (b) performance reviews, and (c) ongoing benefits training, and CS will develop a new employee checklist and exit interview process.

NOTES

1. Private correspondence to Balanced Scorecard Collaborative.
2. R. S. Kaplan and D. P. Norton, *The Strategy-Focused Organization* (Boston: Harvard Business School Press, 2000).
3. http://www.gotoemerson.com/about_emerson/index.html
4. T. Khanna and K. Palepu, "Why Focused Strategies May Be Wrong for Emerging Markets," *Harvard Business Review* (July–August 1997).
5. R. S. Kaplan and D. P. Norton, *Strategy Maps: Converting Intangible Assets into Tangible Outcomes* (Boston: Harvard Business School Press, 2004), 192–195.

CHAPTER FOUR

ALIGNING INTERNAL PROCESS AND LEARNING AND GROWTH STRATEGIES:
INTEGRATED STRATEGIC THEMES

CHAPTER 3 COVERS the synergies from enterprise value propositions that align financial and customer capabilities across a collection of business units. In this chapter, we explore the opportunities organizations can exploit by aligning their internal business processes and their intangible assets to achieve enterprise-level synergies. We discuss four types of enterprise value propositions: shared processes and services, vertical integration, intangible assets, and corporate-level strategic themes.

SYNERGIES FROM SHARED PROCESSES AND SERVICES

Among the most common ways to create enterprise-derived value is by sharing common processes and services among multiple business units. The value from sharing processes and services arises in two ways. First, enterprises gain economies of scale by centralizing processes. Second, they capture the benefits of creating a centralized resource having specialized knowledge and expertise in how to operate a key process or service.

Attaining economies of scale in business processes has long been the goal and competitive advantage of large organizations. From the earliest days of the modern business era, size has created opportunity. More than a century ago, Standard Oil created a dominant advantage through the economies of its large refineries and distribution system. Today, megabanks such as Citigroup and Bank of America create scale economies by merging the back offices of the banks and other financial institutions they acquire. The Limited, a retailer of fashion clothing for men, women, and children, consolidates the purchasing of its several divisions to create dramatic savings and benefits. It creates similar benefits by centralizing the real estate management of its retail chains. In both cases, if the processes were not centralized, the divisions would be competing with themselves in the open market for fabric and space and would lack the scale to get the best deals from overseas manufacturers or real estate developers.

The management of information technology is another function that creates opportunities for scale economies. The economics of purchasing and operating large processing centers in organizations like Citicorp (in financial services), Allstate (in insurance), and British Petroleum (BP) (in energy)—companies that spend more than a billion dollars per year on IT—create natural opportunities to reduce costs, achieve critical scale in expertise, and improve productivity. Sharing the sophisticated capabilities required for effective IT also allows organizations to improve data center security, adopt flexible standards for operating platforms, and remain current with the never-ending wave of new technologies.

Gaining economies of knowledge in business processes offers similar potential for large organizations. Although the physical management of processes may remain decentralized, the sharing of common philosophies, programs, and competencies can create significant benefits. For example, the *quality movement* encompasses such programs as total quality management (TQM), the Baldrige National Quality Program, the European Foundation for Quality Management (EFQM), and, most recently, six sigma. *Activity-based management* stimulates process improvement and management insight, starting from the organization's cost model. *Customer management*—embodied in customer value management, customer relationship management, and customer life-cycle management—is designed to focus managers and employees on operational improvements to yield better performance for customers.

These approaches to process management have helped many organizations achieve dramatic improvements in the quality, cost, and cycle times of their manufacturing and service-delivery processes. Many of the same organizations that adopt the BSC to implement their strategies inevitably need to integrate their BSC system within a management approach that often includes one or more of these management disciplines. But some organizations are confused about the relative roles of these programs and do not know how to integrate them, especially if one is already in place.

With the leadership of a corporate program, the BSC can be effectively combined with one or more of these approaches to achieve advantages beyond what any one of them could deliver on its own. The BSC imbues each with organization-wide legitimacy, giving the program a strategic context and anchoring it to the overall management system in a holistic way. The BSC's cause-and-effect links help highlight those process improvements and initiatives that each program identifies as having the greatest impact on the organization's strategic success.

CASE STUDY: BANK OF TOKYO-MITSUBISHI (HQA)

The Bank of Tokyo-Mitsubishi (BTM) is one of the world's largest banks. HQA, the bank's New York–based headquarters for the Americas, manages the wholesale offerings of BTM throughout North and South America. In 2001, HQA introduced a Balanced Scorecard management program to help clarify and communicate its strategy at multiple levels, to increase accountability, to improve collaboration, and to reduce risk. We described HQA's Strategy Map in a previous book.[1] The map, reproduced here in Figure 4-1, shows the three major themes of HQA's strategy: grow revenues, manage risk, and enhance productivity. The risk-management theme provides an outstanding example of a corporate role in the management of a common business process to create enterprise-derived value.

In the Americas region, BTM focused on the wholesale banking business, with twelve branches, eleven subsidiaries, two loan production offices, and four representative offices. Overlying this grassroots organization were four independently managed business units (global corporate banking, investment banking, treasury, and corporate center), each reporting directly to its counterpart in Tokyo. The complex organization produced many challenges to effective communication and, in particular, to effective risk management. Constant tensions existed, for example, between business promotion and credit approval. Centralized direction versus local autonomy, and expatriate versus local personnel, introduced other challenges to clear accountability.

The Strategy Map framework required BTM to articulate the strategy for all organization levels from the top down. This made it easier to identify the risks associated with implementing the strategy. COSO-based risk and control self-assessment (CSA), a methodology based on the framework developed by the Committee of Sponsoring Organizations (COSO) of the Treadway Commission, was introduced on a bankwide basis to proactively manage risks derived from strategy execution. This process, shown on the Strategy Map as "proactive risk management and compliance," was adopted as a common bankwide objective. As shown in Figure 4-2, CSA was conducted at the lowest level of the organization. The self-assess-

Figure 4-1 Bank of Tokyo-Mitsubishi

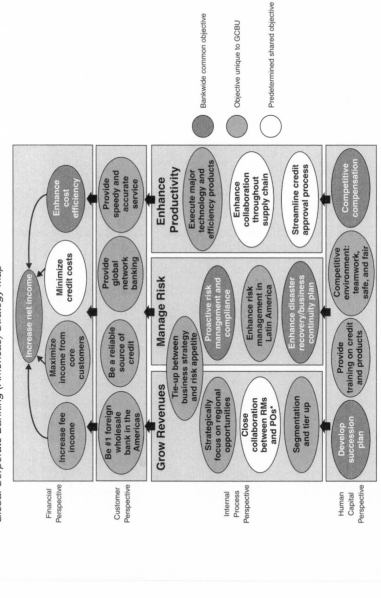

Global Corporate Banking (Americas) Strategy Map

*RM - Relationship Managers, PO - Product Managers

Source: R. S. Kaplan and D. P. Norton, *Strategy Maps: Converting Intangible Assets into Tangible Outcomes* (Boston: Harvard Business School Press, 2004), Figure 1-4.

Figure 4-2   Cascading and Managing the Risk Management Process at
BTM/HQA

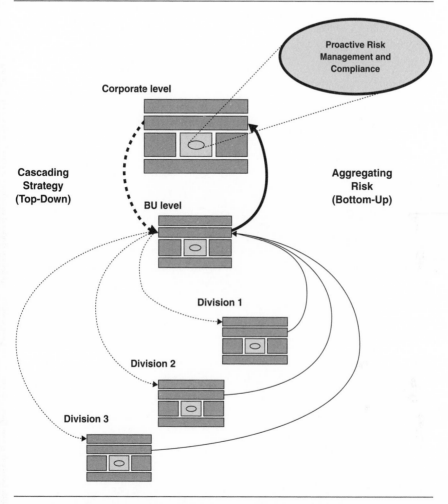

Source: BSCol Conference, December 11–13, 2002, Cambridge, MA, Bank of Tokyo.

ment was based on the premise that a business is more aware of its own risks than are external parties who might perform risk audits. The CSA results were aggregated from the bottom up into two enterprise-level Balanced Scorecard measures:

- *Share of issues identified by business lines (target = 50 percent).*
  This measure highlighted, out of all the issues identified by other parties (including internal and external auditors and regulators), the percentage of the risk issues identified by the COSO self-

assessment. This measure had the immediate effect of making the business lines proactively identify risks they had previously ignored or not reacted to.

- *Share of issues closed during the period (target = 100 percent).* The review of this measure on a monthly basis forced quicker resolution of risk issues.

By cascading the Strategy Map and Balanced Scorecard from the corporate office to the business units, HQA defined an element in its enterprise value proposition: develop a common methodology for the risk-management process, linked to measures on the Balanced Scorecard, to significantly reduce business risk and secure shareholder value.

SYNERGIES FROM VALUE-CHAIN INTEGRATION

Virtually every organization is part of a broader competitive (or cooperative) environment in which customers combine the products or services of one business with those of another service provider to achieve some higher-level value proposition. For example, when buyers purchase new automobiles, usually they must also secure financing. The automobile manufacturer can elect simply to sell cars and let customers secure their own loans, or it can set up a new line of business to provide the financing. Customers must also have the automobile serviced and repaired. Again, the manufacturer can elect to let customers find their own service shops, or it can set up a new line of business that provides factory-trained mechanics to service its cars.

Both of these businesses—financing and service—create an opportunity for the manufacturer to expand the customer relationship, to increase its share of customers' automobile-related spending, and to increase the likelihood that customers will purchase their next new vehicles from the manufacturer. The manufacturer can offer an attractive customer value proposition, one-stop shopping, by adding these new businesses.

Many industries present similar opportunities for enterprises to expand their scope into related areas in the customer value chain. For example, IBM, originally a product organization focused on computer hardware and software, expanded into the front end of the customer value chain by creating a consulting services division. This entity designs solutions for customers—solutions that, in turn, include the company's products. IBM added another line of business on the back end of the customer value chain: an outsourcing business that takes responsibility for operating and maintaining customers' computer-based systems.

Brown & Root Engineering Services created a new customer value proposition by combining the services of six stand-alone profit centers (engineering, procurement, construction, installation, operations support, and supply) into one integrated service. It offered customers one-stop shopping as well as a new level of operating efficiency that created dramatic cost reductions for customers.

An active headquarters role is essential to the success of such value-chain integration. Each profit center in the examples we've cited would have been happy to stay focused on its current market, customers, and services. But the new strategies called for separate profit centers to integrate their activities. For example, the automobile manufacturer had to modify its selling process to encourage cross-selling the financing and service businesses at the time of purchase. IBM had to create an account-management process that provided a balanced presentation of its full range of services. And the Brown & Root businesses had to learn how to go to market as teams instead of separate companies. In each case, top-down corporate priorities required the SBUs to expand their scope of activities to accommodate the corporate strategy.

Figure 4-3 shows a generic corporate value proposition for a value-chain integration strategy, along with a typical scorecard. The financial objectives focus on the desired outcomes of the cross-business dimension of the strategy. Each SBU might be given the target to create new revenue by cross-selling other units' services or selling integrated services. Similarly, it would be asked to create cost reductions resulting from cross-business activity. For example, the automobile manufacturer might look to the service company working with the dealer sales representative to help trigger a new purchase.

The cost of customer retention is a fraction of the cost of new customer acquisition. The customer perspective of the corporate scorecard describes the benefits, such as one-stop shopping and cost reductions, that the new integrated strategy creates for the customer. These benefits could be measured by the expanded breadth of the relationship, the length of the relationship, the share of customer spending, the number of services used, and reduced cost from shared or integrated services.

The internal perspective focuses on the new business processes that are needed to support the cross-business strategy. These might include order processing, which crosses business lines, integrated account management, cross-selling, marketing, and development of new services.

The learning and growth perspective focuses on the new behaviors and competencies that the cross-business strategy necessitates. Typical issues here are the need to increase cross-business awareness, product-line knowledge, teamwork, and shared incentives.

Figure 4-3 Strategic Architecture: Value-Chain Integration

Synergies	Enterprise Value Proposition	Typical Scorecard Measures
Financial	To define the cross-business goals for revenue growth and productivity to be achieved by integrating the value chain	■ % Revenue from integrated services ■ Life-cycle cost reduction
Customer	To define the new customer value proposition made possible by the integration of SBU services	■ Length of relationship ■ Value-chain services used (#, %) ■ Share of wallet
Internal Process	To define the new processes required to seamlessly integrate SBU activities	■ Order management—productivity ■ Customer management—effectiveness ■ Key process cycle time
Learning and Growth	To define the knowledge, systems, and culture required to integrate the value chain	■ Cross-business knowledge ■ Teamwork ■ Shared incentives

The enterprise value proposition and scorecard shown in Figure 4-3 defines the specific cross-business objectives that the value-chain integration strategy requires. These corporate objectives are then cascaded to the SBUs, which then internalize the corporate objectives in their own strategies.

CASE STUDY: MARRIOTT VACATION CLUB (MVCI)

The Marriott name is synonymous with quality hotels and resorts. In addition to its flagship Marriott properties, the parent corporation includes such brands as Renaissance, Courtyard, Fairfield Inn, and Ritz-Carlton. Its frequent traveler program, Marriott Rewards, is the largest in the industry.

In 1984, Marriott entered the time-share business with the acquisition of American Resorts Group. A time-share is the purchase of an interval of time, typically one week, of product use. The approach appeals to individuals and families seeking the pleasures of a second home without the hassles. What was a fledgling industry in 1984 has expanded with unabated double-digit growth over the past twenty years. Today, Marriott Vacation Clubs consists of four brands: MVC International (MVCI), Horizons, Grand Residence Club, and The Ritz Carlton Club. Each brand addresses a different market segment. In 2003, revenues were approximately $1.2 billion and three to five new resorts were being added each year to help sustain the company's double-digit growth.

The dramatic success of MVCI was not without its challenges. The core economic model consisted of four very different businesses, each occupying an adjacent link in the industry value chain, as shown in Figure 4-4. The land development, architecture, and construction group selected locations, acquired permits and property, and designed and built resorts. The sales and marketing group sold the resort shares to end customers. The mortgage bank group supported the sales process by providing customer financing. The resort management group operated the completed resort and had the ultimate responsibility for customer service.

Although the interdependency of these four groups was obvious, their cultures and competencies could not have been more disparate. Over time, the work of these four groups evolved into silos; each group performed its own activities, with limited interaction among others. For example, if the development team ran into problems or delays, it kept these problems to itself. In the meantime, the sales and marketing team, assuming that the product would be available, began its marketing campaign, rounding up

Figure 4-4   The Industry Value Chain for Marriott Vacation Club International (MVCI)

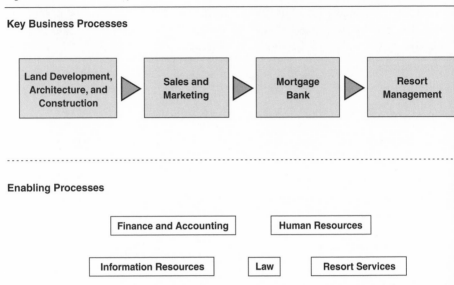

Key Business Processes

| Land Development, Architecture, and Construction | ▷ | Sales and Marketing | ▷ | Mortgage Bank | ▷ | Resort Management |

Enabling Processes

Finance and Accounting   Human Resources

Information Resources   Law   Resort Services

customers and selling the properties. The operations group, assuming that the product was soon to be available, began hiring and assembling a team of specialists from all over the world. Because the value chain was sequential, small problems escalated as they moved downstream. Clearly, MVCI was missing a major opportunity to create synergy and value by integrating its value chain.

Roy Barnes, a twenty-year veteran of the hospitality business, was assigned by MVCI to address this problem. His title, senior VP of strategy management and customer strategy, described his agenda: to help evolve MVCI from an entrepreneurial to a strategically managed mind-set. Barnes's specific objective was to restructure the company, jettisoning its four siloed departments and creating a set of integrated business processes tied to the enterprise strategy. He chose the Balanced Scorecard as his framework to support this evolution.

Figure 4-5 shows MVCI's enterprise-level Strategy Map, which describes its strategy in an integrated and holistic manner. The map reflects the shift in mind-set of viewing the business as a whole instead of as a set of stand-alone, siloed functions. The corporate map defined the goal for integrated team behavior at the lower levels of the organization.

Figure 4-6 shows how the enterprise Strategy Map and Balanced Scorecard, once completed, were then cascaded through the four levels of the organization: from the MVCI enterprise level to the lines of business, from the LOBs to the four value-chain departments (referred to as "key business processes"), from the departments to the regions, and ultimately, from the regions to each specific resort property. Each level would align its own strategy with the higher-level one that had been cascaded to it.

Although the Strategy Maps and Balanced Scorecards gave Barnes the tools he needed, he still needed an extended implementation process to bring about the desired change in behavior. His change management approach consisted of five steps:

1. *Sell the BSC concept.* Meet with business leaders from all organization levels to personally sell the new strategy and the Balanced Scorecard framework for managing it.
2. *Link the BSC to all other governance.* Integrate the BSC into the annual cycle of strategy development, planning, budgeting, goal setting, performance reviews, and adjustment.
3. *Communicate the BSC strategy.* Identify the target audiences. Determine appropriate messages and channels for delivery. Communicate each message seven times in seven different ways.
4. *Link the BSC to compensation.* Tie personal incentives to the Balanced Scorecard.
5. *Maintain focus on the BSC.* Use the BSC to monitor performance and manage the corporate agenda, thereby ensuring that the business strategy gets consistent executive visibility.

It took more than a year for MVCI to internalize the new way of managing, but the benefits from the effort were substantial. Now, each group understands the key success drivers of the group in front of it to help monitor the status of activities on which it is dependent. As a result, when the development team runs into trouble, the other groups are aware of it and act accordingly. In just one example of better coordination along the value chain, MVCI documented savings in the millions of dollars. The corporate strategy of value-chain integration was creating major synergies.

SYNERGIES FROM LEVERAGING INTANGIBLE ASSETS

Any enterprise, no matter how diversified, can create enterprise-derived value by proactively managing its leadership and human capital development. In the knowledge-based global economy, intangible assets like

Figure 4-5 MVCI's Enterprise Strategy Map

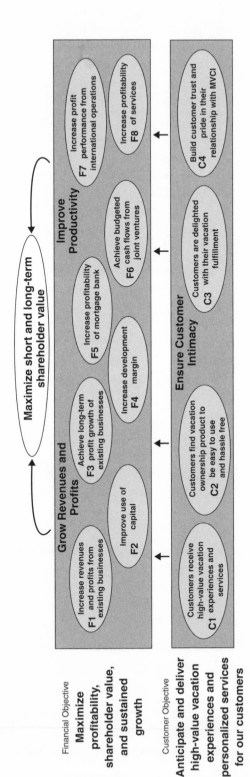

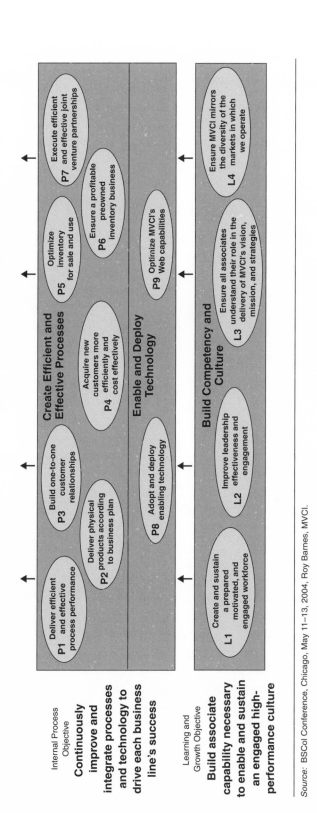

Internal Process Objective
Continuously improve and integrate processes and technology to drive each business line's success

Create Efficient and Effective Processes

P1 Deliver efficient and effective process performance

P2 Deliver physical products according to business plan

P3 Build one-to-one customer relationships

P4 Acquire new customers more efficiently and cost effectively

P5 Optimize inventory for sale and use

P6 Ensure a profitable preowned inventory business

P7 Execute efficient and effective joint venture partnerships

Enable and Deploy Technology

P8 Adopt and deploy enabling technology

P9 Optimize MVCI's Web capabilities

Learning and Growth Objective
Build associate capability necessary to enable and sustain an engaged high-performance culture

Build Competency and Culture

L1 Create and sustain a prepared motivated, and engaged workforce

L2 Improve leadership effectiveness and engagement

L3 Ensure all associates understand their role in the delivery of MVCI's vision, mission, and strategies

L4 Ensure MVCI mirrors the diversity of the markets in which we operate

Source: BSCol Conference, Chicago, May 11–13, 2004, Roy Barnes, MVCI.

Figure 4-6 Cascading the Enterprise Scorecard at MVCI

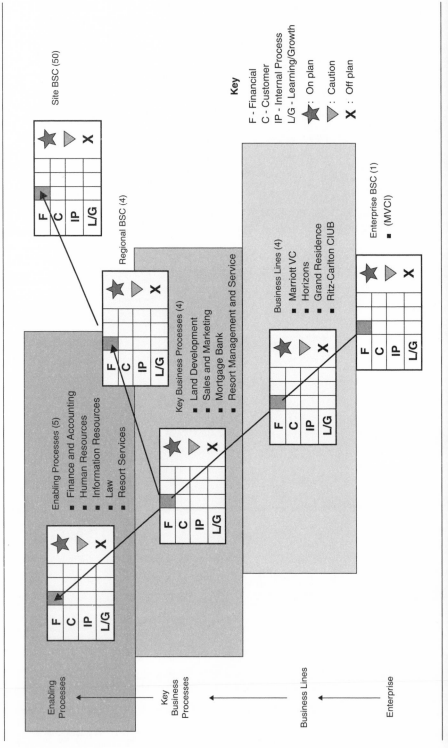

human capital account for nearly 80 percent of an organization's value. Converting intangible assets to tangible results represents a new way of thinking for most organizations. Those who master this process, generally emanating from the HR organization, can create substantial competitive advantage.

Because every organization has workers and leaders who require development, and a climate that requires shaping, the enterprise value proposition can be to offer an effective process for developing these human capital assets. Such a process will transcend the specifics of various SBUs; the specific competencies, for example, will be different, but the process for developing them and aligning them will be the same. The corporate headquarters can mobilize three processes for developing human and organization capital across its portfolio of SBUs: (1) leadership and organization development, (2) human capital development, and (3) knowledge sharing.

Leadership and Organization Development

Modern human resource organizations are expected to guide the development of leaders and to help shape the organization's culture. Although it is difficult to quantify, good leadership and a supportive culture are essential enablers of the successful execution of strategy. The primary objective in developing these assets is to ensure their alignment with the enterprise strategy. Leaders must understand the strategy toward which they are mobilizing their organization, and they must create the values that support this strategy. The enterprise value proposition here is to ensure the alignment of leadership and culture with the strategy.

As an example of a company that was initially failing to exploit an enterprise value proposition for leadership and human capital development, consider the audit conducted by the corporate HR organization at one of the strategic business units of Global Chemical, Inc. (see Figure 4-7). The point of reference for this evaluation was the organization's change agenda, a set of seven behaviors that the SBU's new strategy required.[2] The center panel in the figure shows the set of cultural values that the SBU was promoting in its staff-development programs. Although the SBU's strategy required a shift from product-dominated approaches to a consultative, customer solutions strategy, no mention of customer focus was found in its "aspirational values."

Similarly, the SBU's strategy called for the development of regional centers of excellence. Although this specialization created significant

Figure 4-7 Aligning Leadership and Culture with the Strategy at Global Chemical, Inc.

New Behaviors Required by the Strategy	GCI's Organization Change Agenda	GCI's Aspirational Values	Alignment Index	GCI's Leadership Model	Alignment Index
1. Customer Focused	Be viewed by the customer as a knowledgeable partner who understands their business	?	○	?	○
2. Innovative	Sustain a culture that is open to new ideas, to experiment and take controlled risk	We value empowerment to promote fast decision making	●	Our leaders identify the need and opportunity for change—they overcome old ways of thinking	●
3. Deliver Results	Build a culture that has bottom-line awareness, cost-effectiveness, and efficiency	We drive for results with a focus on business outcomes	●	Our leaders delegate to the best level of competence—they provide the necessary resources	●
4. Understands Strategy	Strengthen the worldwide corporate identity	We communicate strategy and goals clearly	◑	Our leaders translate the company strategy into a vision for specific parts of the organization	◑
5. Accountable	Empower people and give accountability	We expect clear assignment of accountability and personal targets	●	Our leaders set clear goals and priorities for action	●
6. Open Communications	Ensure the transfer of knowledge across functions and regions	We appreciate an open exchange of views	◑	Our leaders listen to ideas, alternatives, and concerns	◑
7. Teamwork	Manage business processes across locations and cultures	?	○	?	○
			70%		70%

Key: ● Good alignment   ◑ Partial alignment   ○ Not aligned benefits, it called for high levels of teamwork around the globe. The aspirational values defined by the HR organization of the SBU were silent on the teamwork issue. The measure of the alignment of the organization's aspired culture with its strategic change agenda was only 70 percent.

The rightmost panel in Figure 4-7 shows the leadership model being used by the SBU to develop its cadre of leaders. Again, the model developed by the HR organization in the SBU was silent on the subjects of customer focus and teamwork. The gap in the leadership and organization development programs revealed by the audit resulted in several major revisions to the SBU program. The corporate initiative thus improved the SBU's ability to gain strategic benefits from these important intangible assets.

Human Capital Development

Corporations can create enterprise-derived value by improving the development of human capital throughout their business units. Even highly diversified companies operating in many different industries can create value by operating an efficient labor market among their operating companies.

Consider the example of business groups such as India's Tata Group. The educational systems in developing nations generally do an inadequate job of preparing most students with the fundamental skills required for successful employment. Large conglomerates in these countries can afford to invest in their own education and training programs for entry-level employees and then capture the benefits as their employees pursue lifetime careers with the company. In countries having more developed and more mobile labor markets, the individual receiving the company training would capture most of the benefits through higher wages and the threat of joining a competitor if salary increases were not forthcoming. The corporate Balanced Scorecard of a holding company that actively managed its internal labor market would include objectives relating to rotation of key staff throughout its companies and promotion of executives from one company to another.

Large diversified companies, such as General Electric, also offer exceptional career development opportunities for employees in their various businesses. Steve Kerr, former chief learning officer at General Electric, described how the product lines and geographic diversity of GE allow it to provide unique opportunities for young, promising managers at "popcorn stands" around the world—small businesses whose success or failure would not affect any of the first three digits of GE's annual operating income.[3] GE uses the information it gathers about managers' performance at these small businesses to assess which managers it should promote, invest in further, and give greater responsibility to in a different GE company that operates in a different part of the world. At the culmination of twenty or so years of such experiences, GE has produced a cadre of proven leaders capable of major responsibility at its large product and geographic divisions.

Corporate learning and growth objectives relate to recruiting the best talent into the operating companies, operating an outstanding corporate university for internal training and education, providing varied career development opportunities for emerging leaders in the corporation, and sharing best-practice knowledge about similar processes throughout the operating companies.

The greatest payoff comes from an increased focus on strategic competencies. Many organizations are creating the specialized role of chief learning officer (CLO) to accomplish this objective. Strategic competencies are the skills and knowledge the workforce must have to support the strategy. Investing in employee learning and development constitutes the true starting point for any long-term, sustainable change. For knowledge-based organizations, the ability to improve business processes that support a customer value proposition depends on employees' ability and willingness to change their behavior and apply their knowledge to the strategy. Therefore, organizations that want to ensure the success of their strategies need to understand the required human competencies. They need to assess the current level of strategic competencies and develop programs that will fill any gaps in the organization's competency profile.

Although competency development programs are not a new idea, tying such programs to the strategy—something that is made possible through the use of the Balanced Scorecard—is new. In recent years, organizations have begun to define *strategic job families,* or competency "clusters" associated with specific strategic processes. By identifying the relevant strategic job families, organizations can ensure that they develop the right competencies—those that will accelerate strategic results. The importance of understanding and managing strategic job families has been underscored by John Bronson, senior vice president of human resources at San Francisco–based Williams-Sonoma, who estimated that people in only five out of all the company's many job families determine 80 percent of his company's strategic performance.[4] (At the average midsize to large corporation, only about 10 percent of all job families are strategic.)

Several approaches can be used to close the gap in strategic competencies: recruiting, training, career planning, and outsourcing. The right mix of these approaches will be determined by the strategy's timetable as well as by the flexibility afforded by the available talent pool.

Kinnarps, a Swedish furniture manufacturer, used its Balanced Scorecard to align the competency development for every employee to strategy execution. The company's internal training group, Kinnarps Academy, maps every employee's competency and compares the employee's competency profile with the actual competencies required for the position as specified by the strategy. The academy then develops customized competency development programs for employees to acquire the skills needed to meet the company's strategic objectives. The head of Kinnarps Academy says that the BSC has helped the academy be more proactive and goal-oriented in its competency development.[5] Kinnarps uses an IT program to track competency development investments; the program maps skills to strategy and shows how much is financially lost or gained by an employee's competency level. The importance of closing the competency gap can thus be understood in terms of its financial impact.

Knowledge Sharing

All enterprises can benefit from knowledge sharing throughout the organization. Even highly diverse business units, having different targeted customers and diverse value propositions, still conduct many similar or identical processes, such as payroll, monthly financial reporting, recruiting, annual employee performance reviews, purchasing, vendor selection and payment, shipping, receiving, and scheduling.

By sharing information about common processes, the enterprise has more opportunity to identify a best practice that can be implemented quickly across all business units. This best-practice knowledge capture and sharing will occur sooner and at lower cost than if independent companies had to contract among themselves for periodic benchmarking studies. For knowledge sharing , the larger and more diverse the corporation, the greater the chance that a process innovation will occur that can be leveraged into benefits throughout the corporate business units.

In many cases, responsibility for knowledge capture and transfer has been assigned to a new organization position, the chief knowledge officer (CKO). Although the field of best-practice management is mature, ways to link specific best practices to strategic outcomes is less well understood. Traditional approaches to leveraging best practices are typically independent of strategy. We are now seeing many organizations use their BSC reporting capabilities to identify high-performing teams, departments, or units based on their ability to deliver strategic results. This makes it possible to document the reasons for high performance and to disseminate this information broadly throughout the organization, thus educating and training others about how they can improve their performance.

Crown Castle International's (CCI) knowledge management system, CCI-Link, is a comprehensive database and library of the company's best practices. This knowledge management tool centralizes and shares performance information and best-practice knowledge throughout this global and highly decentralized company.

CCI uses the BSC to benchmark each of its forty district offices on strategic performance measures. Benchmarking helps executives discover which strategic processes and practices are performed best within the firm and helps them train people in other areas of the organization on these processes and practices so that they can meet the highest performance levels. A focus on internal best practices allows Crown Castle to incorporate the lessons learned and helps integrate the strategy, scorecard, process improvement, and training activities throughout the organization.

Crown Castle's knowledge management practice has contributed immensely to alignment and operational efficiencies, especially amid a period of job cuts. CCI-Link's core architecture is common across diverse geographies. Countries have common, traditional functions listed, such as finance, assets, and human capital, but the content is largely local. A detailed analysis helps differentiate between geographic areas so that managers can understand the true basis for performance differences.

In a Nutshell

Building the human capital and organization capital of the enterprise is everyone's job; the HR organization is expected to take the leadership role. Our experience indicates that if these processes are linked to strategy, the value of the enterprise's human capital increases dramatically. We have described elsewhere how creating alignment and measuring strategic readiness enable HR executives to manage these processes.[6] Strategy Maps provide another tool for aligning human capital with the strategy.

Clearly, the science of managing human capital is emerging. New management processes are needed to apply this science. Although a promising 43 percent of HR organizations appoint a representative to help business units manage their HR relationship, according to a survey by Balanced Scorecard Collaborative and the Society for Human Resource

Management, only 19 percent actually integrate their strategic plans with those of the enterprise.[7] Developing these new processes will increase the value of an organization's intangible assets.

CASE STUDY: IBM LEARNING

The quality of its people, its leadership, and its culture has long been a differentiator of IBM and fundamental to its success. Through the decades of the 1960s, 1970s, and 1980s, IBM's people created the most successful company in business history. They combined leadership in the evolution of new technologies with a powerful marketing and sales process to generate strong customer loyalty. IBM invested heavily in the development of its people's competencies and leadership—the foundations of its success.

This success came to an abrupt end in the 1990s. Although IBM's laboratories continued to develop the technologies of the future, the enterprise organization could not change its traditional business model. IBM's strong culture, which had been one of its major assets, turned into a liability. It became a barrier to change in an industry where change was a constant. IBM lost more than $16 billion in the early part of the decade. Many people felt that the company should be broken into pieces and sold.

Lou Gerstner, who had been hired as CEO from outside the company, came to the opposite conclusion. He believed that customers wanted a company that could integrate the diverse spectrum of information technologies and that IBM was best positioned to be that integrator. History has shown the brilliance of that insight. By the year 2000, IBM had returned to its position of industry leader. Under the leadership of Sam Palmisano, the new IBM continues to evolve. The role of leadership, culture, and staff learning remains central to the IBM strategy.

In May 2001, Ted Hoff joined IBM as vice president of learning to help develop these intangible assets. As IBM's chief learning officer, Hoff was responsible for learning initiatives across the company, developing management training, functional guidance for employees, technical and sales training, and technology-enabled learning. He became a member of IBM's senior leadership group and the global HR leadership team.

Hoff found, upon his arrival, that IBM was still investing heavily in learning; more than $1 billion per year was being spent. In spite of this significant investment, however, line managers did not know how much they were spending nor what they were getting in return. Learning was an "HR issue." No strategic planning process existed to integrate learning with the business. Learning was not positioned to be a key driver of business and organization success. Hoff's corporate mandate was to change this.

Figure 4-8 summarizes the approach IBM used to align its $1 billion learning investment with the company's strategy. As shown in the box on the left, IBM has a well-defined strategy formulation process and a leadership-driven approach to execution. The box on the right summarizes the investments in learning that support the strategy. Historically, however, there had been no effective way to ensure that these investments were, in fact, aligned. The Strategy Map of the business unit, shown in the center box, proved to be the missing link. The business strategy was translated into a Strategy Map, a step that enabled the learning organization to focus its investments on strategic priorities.

A five-step Strategic Learning Planning approach was developed and used in each major business unit. Before starting the process, however, a strong partnership relationship had to be built with line management. Hoff assigned a "Learning Leader" from his organization to each unit. This person's role was to serve as the integrator by (1) understanding the BU's strategy and (2) developing an appropriate learning strategy.

Step 1—Understand and validate business priorities. The Learning Leader was responsible for research and analysis of the BU strategy. Strategy documents, marketplace information, budgets, business plans, and the Internet, as well as direct interaction with the BU, were typical sources. The Learning Leader partnered with other support teams such as HR, Finance, and Strategy to execute its mission.

Step 2—Translate business priorities into a Strategy Map. Based on the research and interactions, the Learning Leader created a draft Strategy Map of the BU. The draft identified specific issues, objectives, and strategic themes. Through a series of executive interviews, the Leader then validated the Strategy Map. These interviews helped to identify the critical business areas on which the learning programs should be focused. A validated Strategy Map resulted.

Step 3—Identify business measures. A Balanced Scorecard of measures and targets was then derived from the Strategy Map. The Learning Leader used this process to educate the client on the link between intangible assets and tangible business results.

Step 4—Identify and prioritize learning solutions. The culmination of this planning process was the development of a set of learning solutions to support the strategy. Figure 4-9 illustrates the alignment of potential

Figure 4-8 Aligning Strategic Learning with Business Units at IBM

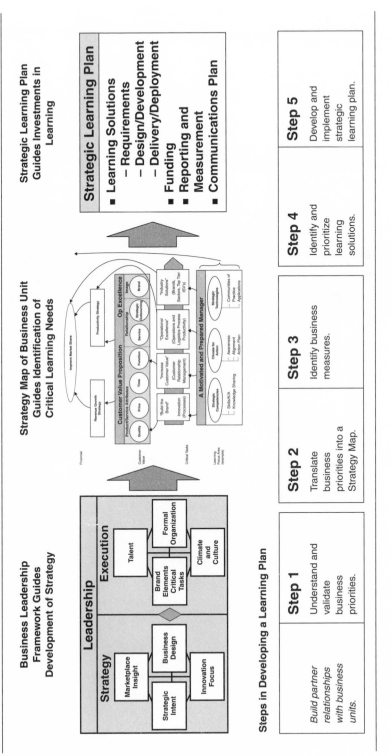

Figure 4-9 Aligning Performance Solutions with Business Partners at IBM

Strategic Theme	Critical Task	Business Measure	Business Measure Target	Potential Learning Solution	Estimated Cost	Priority
	Target specific applications and customer growth opportunities.	New Product Placements	20% YTY Growth	■ Blend training program, new products (e-learning), and 3-day opportunity workshop. ■ Include customer module in sales school.	■ $100K (e-learning) module; $50K workshop design and development; $500 per person delivery and deployment cost ■ $50K, no additional delivery cost	2 4
"Build the Brand"	Work with field offices to drive sales.	Revenue	Increase by 16%	■ 15 road shows in U.S., Central Europe, and SE Asia	■ $50K	1
	Strengthen relationship with business partners.	Business Partner Satisfaction Metric	85% Satisfied/Very Satisfied by year end	■ Train territory sales reps on channel sales operations with Web lectures and new handbook ■ Incent BPs for multi-customer placements	■ $80K for development plus $3 per handbook cost of printing and distribution ■ Nonlearning solution	3 n/a

Note: Management targets and cost estimates for illustration only.

solutions to enable critical business imperatives. BU sponsors were identified for each program. Solutions that fell outside the learning domain (e.g., climate, incentives) were identified for subsequent discussion with HR and line management. The cost of developing and deploying each potential solution was identified. The potential investments were then ranked based on their anticipated impact on scorecard measures. This list provided the final input for construction of the BU's support plan.

Step 5—Develop and implement strategic learning plan. The business analysis and planning performed in Steps 1 through 4 were then consolidated into the final Strategic Learning Plan for the BU. Funding was gained to implement the solutions. A communication plan to support the deployment of the plan was developed and a process of measuring, reporting, and reviewing progress against the plan was developed.

Through the use of Strategy Maps and the Balanced Scorecard, learning investments at IBM now have "line of sight" alignment with business goals. The approach has made a material difference on the integration of different parts of the IBM organization. As described by Ted Hoff, "We are now at the table with the business."[8] The learning organization participates in strategic planning, budgeting, and investment/return discussions. They have access to senior executives as needed. Learning organization staffs are now accountable for results. Most importantly, IBM is converting this most intangible of assets (learning programs) into tangible business results.

INTEGRATION USING CORPORATE STRATEGIC THEMES

Large multiproduct, multiregion organizations strive to achieve competitive advantage through economies of scale and scope among their decentralized units. These companies have a difficult task because the business units must be responsive to local markets and challenges while also helping the corporation capture the scale and scope benefits that result from integrating their operations with other business units. Because the decentralized units have multiple responsibilities, it is difficult to define a sound basis for performance and accountability.

For more than a century, companies expanding into new product lines, new market segments, and new regions have employed a variety of organizational design approaches, some of which we described in Chapter 2. Among the choices are organizing by function, by product, by customer and market segment, or by geography. None of these worked perfectly, so newer forms—including organization by matrix, technology, channel, network, and virtual—have also been tried. Despite all this innovation in organization structure and form, however, the problems of coordination, alignment, and accountability remain.

Several complex organizations have used a corporate-level Strategy Map and Balanced Scorecard to create alignment and integration among their diverse and dispersed units. Typically, these two documents enable the enterprise to articulate high-level strategic themes. These enterprises took their existing structure as given, feeling that tinkering by realigning authority, responsibility, and decision rights among operating units would not provide the magic they needed to achieve corporate-level synergies. Rather than continue to search for an ideal but never attainable structural solution, they articulated strategic themes in their corporate scorecard, believing that these would provide an informational solution for allowing decentralized units to seek local gains while also contributing to corporate-wide objectives.

Aligning disparate organizations through strategic themes is especially valuable for public-sector agencies and departments. The problems that the public sector is trying to solve are extremely complex and difficult: drug trafficking, illegal immigration, homelessness, poverty, welfare dependency, teenage pregnancy, environmental pollution, homeland security, crime, intelligence, structural unemployment, and many others. It would be highly unlikely that any single organizational unit, agency, or department had all the authority, resources, and knowledge to solve these problems by itself.

Also, in contrast to the private sector, realigning existing governmental agencies and departments so that they can address a particular problem is a Herculean effort, with progress typically measured in geological time. Each department or agency has its own constituency and, typically, its own band of supporters in the state or national legislature. Attempting to restructure or combine agencies to accomplish a mission more effectively runs into immediate, focused, and highly organized resistance.

Therefore, governments that want to create positive social impact must operate with their existing units, which were formed through a somewhat random, unmanaged, historical time path. Their challenge is how to mobilize diverse agencies—having different missions, different histories and cultures, and different support bases—to cooperate so that collectively they can achieve outcomes beyond what they would accomplish operating independently. Multiple agencies, often at various levels of government and in different jurisdictions, must coordinate their efforts—not a natural act for government bureaucracies—if they are to achieve positive social impact.

In this situation, the Balanced Scorecard provides an ideal mechanism to set high-level, interagency objectives that allow the multiple agencies to work together to accomplish the mission. Thus, we should expect to see public-sector scorecards developed for high-level, multiorganizational initiatives or strategic themes. The Balanced Scorecard provides the context and the process for engaging representatives from the multiple public-sector agencies in high-level discussions and cooperation.

We use three case studies to illustrate the role of corporate-level strategic themes in integrating the operations of diverse and dispersed organizational units. DuPont Engineering Polymers is a representative private-sector example, with its use of five time-sequenced strategic themes. Royal Canadian Mounted Police, a public-sector counterpart to DuPont EP, also used five strategic themes to align its international, national, provincial, and municipal operating units. The Washington State salmon recovery effort illustrates the role of building a high-level Balanced Scorecard to align agencies in different departments and governmental units to address a major public policy issue.

CASE STUDY:
DUPONT ENGINEERING POLYMERS DIVISION

The Engineering Polymers (EP) division of DuPont had $2.5 billion in annual sales and employed 4,500 people in thirty operating facilities around the world. EP, like many multinational, multiproduct organizations, experienced difficulties in implementing a coherent strategy throughout its eight related global businesses and six shared-service units.

Like many matrix organizations, EP experienced confusion about roles and responsibilities. People were starting initiatives that were not coordinated across the business, and other new initiatives were generally underfunded and understaffed, so business continued as usual. During the five years before adopting the Balanced Scorecard, EP had compounded annual earnings growth of 10 percent, but this was achieved mainly by cost-cutting and productivity improvements, because revenue growth was only 2.5 percent annually. Craig Naylor, group vice president and general manager, saw how to use the Balanced Scorecard to align all employees, business units, and shared services to a common strategy that featured revenue growth. Subsequently scorecard measures would provide feedback to continually test the strategy.[9]

The new strategy had an overarching objective to maximize shareholder value through a combination of productivity improvements and
growth opportunities. The improvements in productivity involved both
continuous and step changes in process capabilities. The company expected to generate growth opportunities by offering more integrated products and services to customers. DuPont EP's senior management team
built a divisional Balanced Scorecard Strategy Map around five time-
sequenced strategic themes that described how the units could align their
actions to deliver the revenue growth and cost-reducing financial objectives. The five themes were as follows:

Operational excellence: Deploy process improvement tools such as six
sigma and cost reduction to deliver significant productivity improvements.

Supply and service: Create differentiation for customers through logistics
excellence to reduce the order-to-cash cycle.

Manage the portfolio of products and applications: Focus on products and
applications having the highest margins, and introduce new products
and applications.

Customer management: Bring complete solutions to targeted customers,
offering a unique package of capable products, low cost, and excellence
in supply.

New business design: Devise entirely new ways of reaching and servicing
end-use customers.

The sequence of themes corresponded to the time frames required for
successful implementation: improving operating processes and logistics
would deliver near-term (nine to fifteen months) results. It would take two
to three years to create portfolios of products that would provide more
complete customer solutions. Realizing the benefits of developing and installing an entirely new business model with customers would take three to
four years.

EP developed Strategy Maps and assigned a manager to be accountable
for each of the five strategic themes. For example, Figure 4-10 shows the
Strategy Map for the first theme: operational excellence. This theme
stressed delivering existing products better, faster, and cheaper to customers. The theme's measures and targets related to specific improvements
in cost, quality, yield, and equipment availability. The theme's strategic

Figure 4-10 DuPont EP Operational Excellence Theme: Strategy Map, Measures, and Initiatives

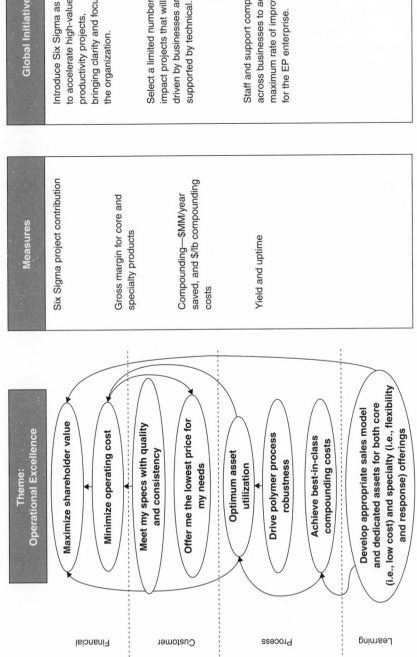

Theme: Operational Excellence

Financial
- Maximize shareholder value
- Minimize operating cost

Customer
- Meet my specs with quality and consistency
- Offer me the lowest price for my needs

Process
- Optimum asset utilization
- Drive polymer process robustness
- Achieve best-in-class compounding costs

Learning
- Develop appropriate sales model and dedicated assets for both core and specialty (i.e., low cost) and specialty (i.e., flexibility and response) offerings

Measures

Six Sigma project contribution

Gross margin for core and specialty products

Compounding—$MM/year saved, and $/lb compounding costs

Yield and uptime

Global Initiatives

Introduce Six Sigma as the tool to accelerate high-value productivity projects, bringing clarity and focus to the organization.

Select a limited number of high-impact projects that will be driven by businesses and supported by technical.

Staff and support compounding across businesses to achieve maximum rate of improvement for the EP enterprise.

initiatives included six sigma quality programs and best-practice sharing across business units to maximize the rate of learning and improvement throughout the division. Figure 4-11 shows the complete EP Strategy Map, which is built on the five sequenced strategic themes.

EP viewed the five themes as the DNA of its strategy, the genetic code that would be embedded in every business unit and shared-service unit. EP cascaded the high-level strategic themes by having its three major geographic regions and five product-line units build their own scorecards. These business unit scorecards highlighted how the five themes would be implemented in each region and product line as well as each unit's unique objectives and initiatives for its local strategy.

Similarly, the global functional units—manufacturing, IT, finance, HR, marketing, and R&D—constructed their own scorecards to ensure that functional excellence would be developed and deployed to assist the global, regional, and product-line strategies. The actual content of each theme could differ in each business unit, but all businesses built their individual strategies around the five themes (see Figure 4-12). This approach made opportunities for leverage and synergy across business units far more visible than ever before.

Note that only a few business units were expected to make a contribution to all five themes. Several focused on as few as two of the themes. In constructing its individual Strategy Map and Balanced Scorecard, each unit reflected how it could contribute to the division-level themes and also how it needed to cooperate and integrate with other business and support units to achieve cross-unit synergies. The structure shown in Figure 4-12 enabled EP senior management to know what was unique for each business unit and shared-service unit, and which objectives required integrated solutions across several units.

EP, like most organizations, faced a classic conflict. The local businesses and their employees wanted to focus on running their businesses efficiently day-to-day. It was difficult to get sufficient attention from them to align their businesses to divisionwide strategic initiatives. To get share of mind for initiatives relating to EP's five new strategic themes, amid all the other programs and initiatives already under way, managers forced out many local projects that were not contributing to one or more of the five themes. This made space for new initiatives and projects that would enhance the divisional strategic themes so that they became embedded in the ongoing day-to-day routines of employees.

An often fatal weakness of a matrixed organization is the endless debates that occur among business units, functional departments, and

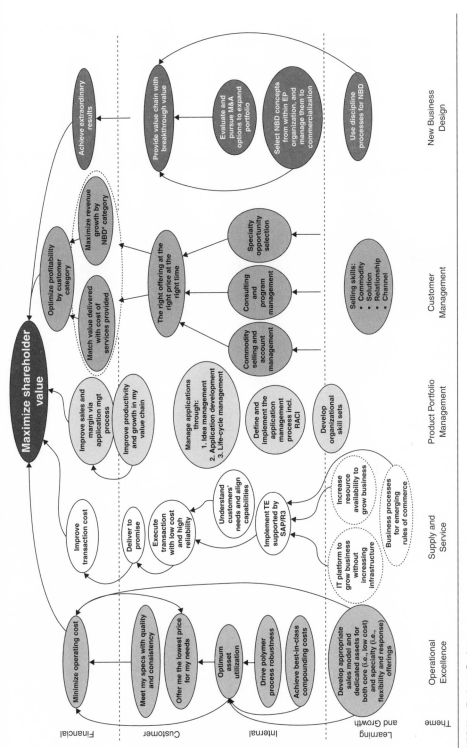

Maximize shareholder value

Financial
- Achieve extraordinary results
- Optimize profitability by customer category
- Maximize revenue growth by NBD* category
- Match value delivered with cost of services provided
- Improve sales and margin via application mgt process
- Improve productivity and growth in my value chain
- Improve transaction cost
- Minimize operating cost

Customer
- Provide value chain with breakthrough value
- The right offering at the right price at the right time
- Deliver to promise
- Meet my specs with quality and consistency
- Offer me the lowest price for my needs

Internal
- Evaluate and pursue M&A options to expand portfolio
- Select NBD concepts from within EP organization, and manage them to commercialization
- Specialty opportunity selection
- Consulting and program management
- Commodity selling and account management
- Manage applications through:
  1. Idea management
  2. Application development
  3. Life-cycle management
- Define and implement the application management process incl. RACI
- Execute transaction with low cost and high reliability
- Understand customers' needs and align capabilities
- Implement TE supported by SAP/R3
- Increase resource availability to grow business
- Business processes for emerging rules of commerce
- IT platform to grow business without increasing infrastructure
- Optimum asset utilization
- Drive polymer process robustness
- Achieve best-in-class compounding costs

Learning and Growth
- Use discipline processes for NBD
- Selling skills:
  - Commodity
  - Solution
  - Relationship
  - Channel
- Develop organizational skill sets
- Develop appropriate sales model and dedicated assets for both core (i.e., low cost) and specialty (i.e., flexibility and response) offerings

Theme
- New Business Design
- Customer Management
- Product Portfolio Management
- Supply and Service
- Operational Excellence

*NBD–New Business Designs

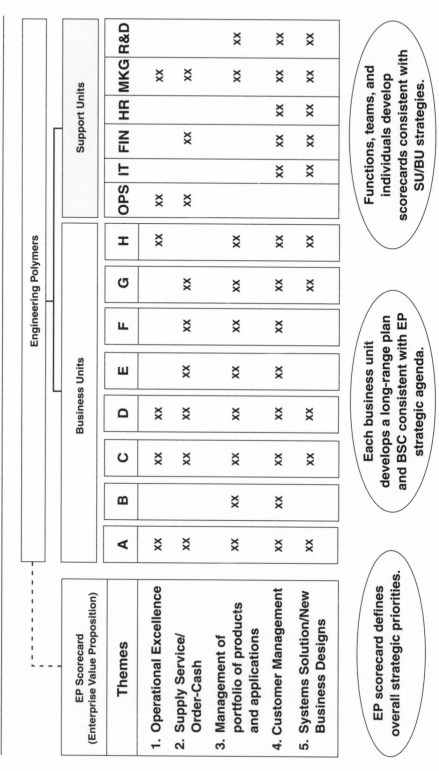

Figure 4-12 DuPont EP: Aligning Business, Regions, and Support Functions with Five Strategic Themes

geographical regions about resource allocation. EP reported that the clarity of the five strategic themes, cutting across business units, geographical regions, and shared-service functions, forced greater clarity about priorities and provided more transparency for resource allocation. This led to more productive discussions and dialogues based on a shared understanding of the fundamental drivers of overall business performance. Individuals used the scorecard architecture and measures to gain support for agendas and projects. Enthusiasm and constructive discussions pervaded the organization because of the shared understanding of strategy.

At DuPont Engineering Polymers, the strategic themes described a strategy that did not change even in its highly dynamic and competitive environment. Although tactics and initiatives may change bimonthly, EP's strategic themes emphasized fundamental objectives for the organization: improve the supply chain, work better and more closely with distributors, and build new business relationships with end-use customers. These themes were not ephemeral. They sustained organizational direction and focus for years—not weeks, months, or quarters.

CASE STUDY: ROYAL CANADIAN MOUNTED POLICE

The Royal Canadian Mounted Police (RCMP), with twenty-three thousand employees and a C$3 billion annual budget, is Canada's national policing service, and also provides contract policing services for Canadian provinces, territories, and municipalities. The RCMP operates at four levels—international, national, provincial/territorial (eight provinces and three territories), and local (over 200 municipalities and 190 First Nations communities). At the turn of the twenty-first century, the RCMP faced several challenges, not the least of which related to finances and resources required for a policing organization entering the new millennium. A new commissioner, Giuliano Zaccardelli, committed himself to continued management improvement at the RCMP. He had a vision that the RCMP could become a strategically focused organization of excellence. Even with his strong leadership and vision, Commissioner Zaccardelli faced the challenge of how to align all RCMP units, spread across an enormous land mass, to corporate-level priorities.

A senior-level project team at the RCMP launched a process to translate the vision and mission ("Safe homes, safe communities") into something operational that could be understood countrywide. The project team developed a Senior Executive Committee (SEC) Strategy Map (see Figure 4-13).

Figure 4-13 Case Study: Royal Canadian Mounted Police

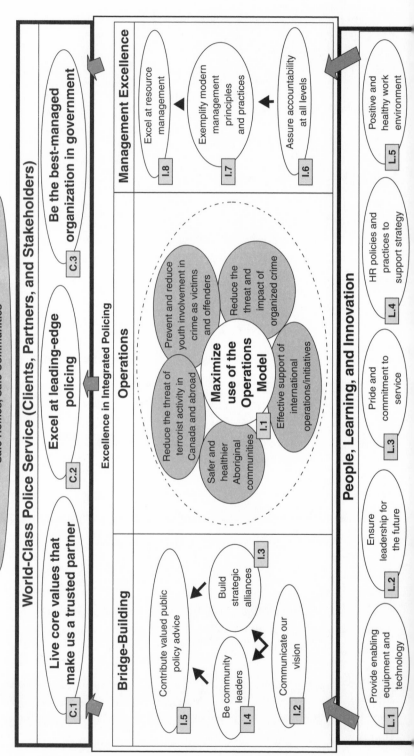

The top-level perspective (clients, partners, and stakeholders) captures the RCMP value proposition to the core groups it serves: funding agencies, other levels of government (both domestic and international), and citizens in direct receipt of policing services. For example, the value proposition for funding agencies was for the RCMP to "be the best managed organization in government," while the value proposition for its local partners was to "live core values that make us a trusted partner." Each of these objectives is tied together by a primary objective: "excel at leading-edge policing." In essence, the RCMP value proposition is to deliver world-class, leading-edge policing services, at a reasonable cost to partners, stakeholders, and citizens.

The internal process perspective is built around three themes, each containing objectives that support the three pillars of the RCMP value proposition. The bridge-building theme articulates the communication, partnership, and alliance processes that support the goal of becoming a trusted partner. The operations theme, on which we will focus more shortly, stresses the use of the Operations Model—an RCMP methodology for being intelligence led in all activities and conduct of investigations. At the heart of this theme is excellence in service to clients, since excelling at service will increase the quality of all the policing operations. Finally, the management excellence theme supports the requirements of the funding/oversight agencies.

The people, learning, and innovation perspective captures the importance the RCMP places on providing a stimulating and safe work environment for its employees, supported by advanced technology and leadership growth.

The heart of the new policing strategy is contained within the internal operations theme, which describes five overarching corporate-level priorities that go beyond day-to-day policing activities:

- Reduce the threat and impact of organized crime
- Reduce the threat of terrorist activity in Canada and abroad
- Prevent and reduce youth involvement in crime as victims and offenders
- Effective support of international operations
- Contribute to safer/healthier Aboriginal communities

Understanding that each of the five strategic priorities required national-level strategic coordination, the RCMP developed five "virtual" Strategy Maps for each priority (Figure 4-14 shows the Strategy Map for one of the five strategic priorities: contribute to safer/healthier Aboriginal communities). Each of the five priority maps had its own measures,

Figure 4-14 Strategy Map for "Safer, Healthier Aboriginal Communities"

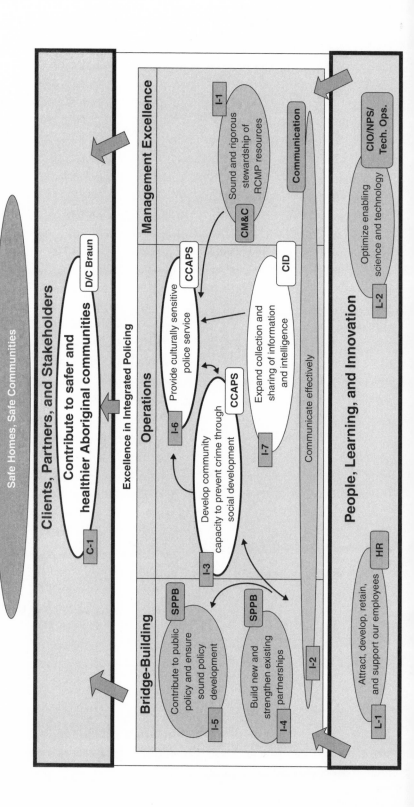

targets, and initiatives required to execute the strategic priorities. A senior RCMP executive was assigned as a priority champion for each strategic priority. The champion convened a panel of RCMP executives for periodic meetings to review progress against the priority's targets, an example of how Strategy Maps and Balanced Scorecards can be used to manage "virtual organizations," in this case a strategic priority for which no single organizational unit had ownership responsibility and accountability.

With Strategy Maps and scorecards for the corporate-level strategy and for the five strategic priorities in place, the cascading process to local units could commence. To ensure alignment and consistent execution of these strategic priorities, each objective on the "virtual" Strategy Maps was assigned to a business line—or corporate service line—and placed on the relevant Strategy Map. The local divisional units considered the relevance of the national priorities for their divisions, then customized these high-level strategic priorities to reflect the specific realities of their operations. In addition, the local Strategy Maps incorporated the division's normal policing responsibilities (see Figure 4-15 for an example of a division-level Strategy Map). Thus an RCMP unit in Canada's Northwest Territory, where terrorist activity, organized crime, or international crime are rare, would not necessarily incorporate objectives for those priorities. It would definitely include objectives relating to youth involvement in crime and contributing to safer/healthier Aboriginal communities. Conversely, an RCMP unit based in Toronto might not be able to make as great a contribution to Aboriginal communities as the Northwest unit, but would include objectives related to reducing threats from organized crime, international crime, and terrorist activity. In this way, all units played a role in delivering on RCMP strategic priorities beyond their day (and night) job of local policing.

With the BSC at the heart of RCMP's management system, the Senior Executive Committee could now stay focused on strategic priorities, knowing that the local units were responsible and accountable for day-to-day operations. Data on strategic objectives were updated every sixty days so senior executives could stay in touch with how their priorities were being implemented in the field.

CASE STUDY: SALMON RECOVERY IN WASHINGTON STATE

RCMP is an excellent example of achieving alignment within a large public-sector agency. But some issues are beyond the scope of any single governmental agency or authority. Consider the problem of salmon recovery in

Figure 4-15 "G" Division Strategy Map

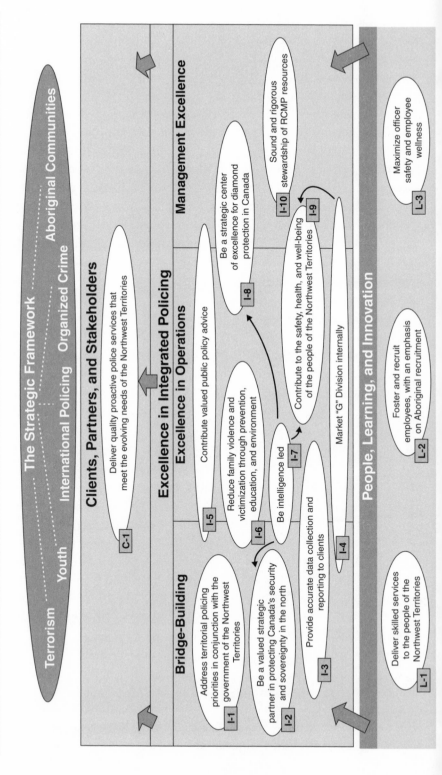

Washington State. The federal government, through the Endangered Species Act, had mandated that the state make dramatic improvements in the quantity of salmon in the ocean and rivers around the state. If the U.S. government was not satisfied with the state's recovery plan and its performance in meeting the plan, it could intervene by demolishing hydroelectric dams and stopping or severely curtailing all forestry, agriculture, hydropower production, transportation improvements, land use changes, and recreational activities, such as fishing and boating, until the state implemented a credible plan to restore salmon populations.

Governor Gary Locke had asked each agency to devise performance measures linked to salmon recovery, but he doubted that the sum of these individual, diffuse efforts would add up to the desired outcome of producing a coherent, credible, and acceptable plan to increase salmon populations. No single agency had complete control over all aspects of the environment that affected the supply of salmon. The governance structure was highly fractured and included 6 neighboring states, another country (Canada), 8 U.S. agencies, 12 state agencies, 39 counties, 277 cities, 300 water and sewer districts, 170 local water suppliers, and 27 autonomous Indian tribes whose members loved to hunt and fish. Left on their own, state agencies could set measurable objectives for outputs under their control that influenced salmon production. Yet the decentralized efforts would likely fail because the strategies of individual, decentralized agencies did not represent a coherent, comprehensive strategy.

Washington state already had an interagency strategic process under way to define an agenda for salmon recovery. From this initiative, it was a logical step to build a Balanced Scorecard for a strategic theme to preserve and enhance salmon, even though no czar of salmon existed and no single agency at any level had salmon recovery within its primary authority or responsibility. Assembling knowledgeable and interested senior managers to work on a common task enabled the salmon-recovery task force to pool the participants' collective knowledge to create a Balanced Scorecard that would express a comprehensive and integrated strategy for salmon recovery (see Figure 4-16). What's more, the open, transparent process built trust and commitment among the participants about how they could work within their agencies, and collectively across agency lines, to achieve the ambitious salmon recovery targets.

The agency representatives then went back to their agencies and identified performance measures, targets, programs, and initiatives that would contribute to the high-level strategic theme. The agency scorecards would include not only actions under their direct control but also, and perhaps

Figure 4-16 Salmon Recovery Scorecard Objectives

Goal: **Restore salmon, steelhead, and trout populations to healthy and harvestable levels and improve habitats on which fish rely.**

Customer: **To protect an important element of Washington's quality of life . . .**

- We will have productive and diverse wild salmon populations.
- We will meet the requirements of the Endangered Species Act and Clean Water Act.

Processes: **Our habitat, harvest, hatchery, and hydropower activities will benefit wild salmon.**

- Freshwater and estuarine habitats are healthy and accessible.
- Rivers and streams have flows to support salmon.
- Water is clean and cool enough for salmon.
- Harvest management actions protect wild salmon.
- Enhance compliance with resource protection laws.

Collaboration: **We are engaged with citizens and our salmon-recovery partners.**

- We will reach out to citizens.
- Salmon-recovery roles are defined and partnerships strengthened.

Financial and Infrastructure: **Our building blocks for success include . . .**

- Achieve cost-effective recovery and efficient use of government resources.
- Use best available science and integrate monitoring and research with planning and implementation.
- Citizens, salmon-recovery partners, and state employees have timely access to the information, technical assistance, and funding they need to be successful.

even more important, the links they would have to make with the other government agencies, with private citizens, and with other entities for the entire effort to be a success.

For each Balanced Scorecard measure, the salmon-recovery team identified an executive sponsor and supporting interagency workgroup that would ensure a good data collection and reporting process for that measure. The executive sponsor also had the authority to convene meetings to discuss the initiatives that should be funded to improve the measure, and to discuss the progress and problems on the measure's performance.

Used in this way, the Balanced Scorecard provided the mechanism by which individuals in diverse and dispersed agencies could reach a consensus about a common plan of action, and then implement the needed managerial actions: collecting and reporting data, allocating resources, conducting progress and problem-solving meetings, and adapting the strategy in light of experience and new knowledge.

While the process of strategy formulation came first, the Balanced Scorecard provided a way to begin discussions with the public about indicators of progress. More important, the scorecard provided the discipline to convene individuals from multiple organizational units to describe important strategic themes (in effect, a virtual organization). The scorecard included both the outcomes desired (how to measure success for the strategic theme) and the performance drivers, especially in the internal processes and learning and growth required for the group to achieve the desired outcomes of the strategic theme. Individual organizational units then defined their own strategies and scorecards, including their respective contributions to the objectives articulated in the strategic theme's scorecard. And the theme-based scorecard provided the mechanism to convene meetings in which representatives from diverse agencies and constituencies could solve problems collectively rather than from within agency silos.

SUMMARY

An enterprise can achieve significant economies of scale when it centralizes key processes—such as production, distribution, purchasing, human resource management, or risk management—to serve its diverse business units. The decision to centralize a shared process is made at corporate headquarters and becomes a component of the enterprise value proposition. The enterprise also creates value when it encourages business units to integrate their previously separate offerings to deliver complete solutions to targeted customers.

An enterprise can enhance its human capital and its employees' career development by providing opportunities for employment experience in diverse business units and geographic regions. It can also promote the sharing of knowledge and best practices throughout all its business and support units so that new ideas can be rapidly transmitted and assimilated within the enterprise far faster than if each unit had to develop or learn such ideas by itself.

Finally, the enterprise creates synergies when it articulates strategic themes that enhance links and coordination among multiple business units. The strategic themes are articulated on the enterprise Strategy Map and Balanced Scorecard. They provide an alternative to a matrix structure organization, because business unit managers now have objectives on their Strategy Maps and Balanced Scorecards that relate both to their own local objectives and to the enterprise priorities. In effect, business unit managers operate as dual citizens, serving both their local units and the corporate entity.

In the public sector, a Strategy Map and Balanced Scorecard can be developed for high-level objectives—such as improving salmon recovery, national intelligence, homeland security, or drug interdiction—that require the coordination and integration of the efforts of many entities if the public benefit is to be achieved.

NOTES

1. R. S. Kaplan and D. P. Norton, *Strategy Maps: Converting Intangible Assets into Tangible Outcomes* (Boston: Harvard Business School Press, 2004), 18–28.
2. For more information on the organization change agenda, see ibid., Chapter 10; and "Measuring the Strategic Readiness of Intangible Assets," *Harvard Business Review* (February 2004).
3. Talk given at North American Summit, Balanced Scorecard Collaborative, October 2003.
4. John Bronson, Speaking at BSCol Conference on Human Resource Alignment, Naples, Florida, February 2002.
5. "Motivate to Make Strategy Everyone's Job," *Balanced Scorecard Report* (November–December 2004).
6. R. S. Kaplan and D. P. Norton, "Measuring the Strategic Readiness of Intangible Assets," *Harvard Business Review* (February 2004).
7. Results of SHRM research (2002).
8. Correspondence with the Balanced Scorecard Collaborative.
9. "How to Mobilize Large, Complex Organizations Using the Balanced Scorecard: An Interview with Craig Naylor of DuPont Engineering Polymers," *Balanced Scorecard Report* (September–October 2000): 11–13.

CHAPTER FIVE

ALIGNING SUPPORT FUNCTIONS

CHAPTERS 3 AND 4 SHOW HOW ENTERPRISES create shareholder value by aligning their business units with the corporate strategy. But organizations also create value by aligning their support units with the business unit strategy. Consider the approach advocated by Larry Brady, president of FMC Corporation:

> *I doubt that many companies can respond crisply to the question, "How does staff provide competitive advantage?" . . . We have just started to ask our staff departments to explain to us whether they are offering low cost or differentiated services. If they are offering neither, we should probably outsource the function.*[1]

Support or shared-service units, such as human resources, finance, purchasing, and legal, have their origin in the nineteenth-century functional organization described in Chapter 2. The units contain employees who have specialized knowledge and expertise that can be productively deployed throughout the organization for tasks such as designing compensation and promotion systems, operating information systems, conducting international treasury operations, and managing regulatory and litigation matters. To achieve critical mass, support groups are typically centralized and, in the aggregate, incur operating expenses of between 10 and 30 percent of sales.

Senior executives have struggled for decades with the question of how to monitor and evaluate their support groups to ensure that they produce benefits in excess of their costs. Organizations such as The Hackett Group provide benchmarking information that compares the company's spending on its support services to that of similar organizations. But such benchmarking is not really useful unless the organization's goal is to spend the least amount possible on its support units and to not use these units as a source of competitive advantage.

The output of support groups—such as expert advice, a trained, motivated employee, a report, the design and operation of a key process, or a partnering relationship with a business unit—is often intangible. It is difficult to quantify these outputs when organizations attempt to evaluate a unit's effectiveness and efficiency. The traditional management control literature refers to support units as "discretionary expense centers," to contrast them with standard cost centers, where budgeted expenses can be linked, via tight causal mechanisms, to the production of standard products and services.[2]

Support groups are generally staffed with expert specialists whose culture is quite different from that of managers in line operating units. Consequently, support groups frequently become isolated from the line organization; executives of business units accuse them of living in headquarters-based functional silos and being incapable of responding to local operating needs. In two surveys we conducted, respondents reported that two-thirds of human resources and information technology organizations were not aligned with business unit and enterprise strategies. Correcting this misalignment and transforming the focus of support units—to one of meeting the needs of their internal customers—provide opportunities for substantial increases in shareholder value.

SUPPORT UNIT PROCESSES

Support units can follow a systematic set of processes to create value through alignment (see Figure 5-1). First, they align their strategies with business unit and corporate strategies by determining the set of strategic services to be offered. The process starts with a clear understanding of enterprise and business unit strategies, as revealed by line organization Strategy Maps and Balanced Scorecards. Each support function then determines how it can help business units and the enterprise achieve their strategic objectives. For example, as illustrated in Figure 5-1, the human resources, information technology, and finance organizations identify a portfolio of strategic services that will have the greatest impact on the successful implementation of strategy.

Figure 5-1 Aligning Support Units with Enterprise Strategy

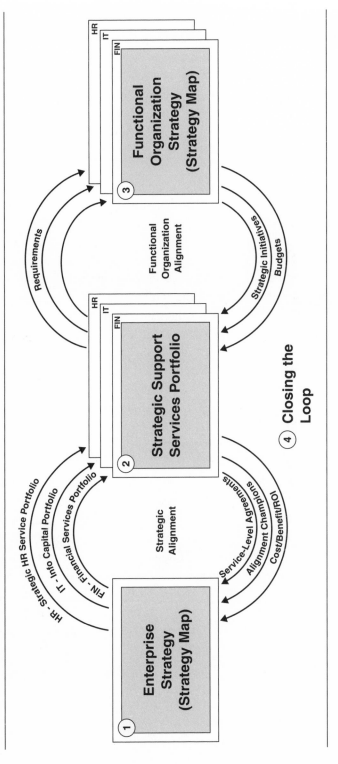

Second, support units align their internal organizations so that they can execute the strategy. They develop strategic plans that describe how they will acquire, develop, and deliver their strategic services to operating units. The plan becomes the foundation for the support units' Strategy Maps, Balanced Scorecards, strategic initiatives, and budgets.

Finally, support units close the loop by assessing the performance of their functional initiatives using techniques such as service-level agreements, internal customer feedback, customer ratings, and internal audits.

As a specific example of this process, Canon, USA—a leading manufacturer and distributor of cameras, copiers, and professional optical products—conducts an annual strategy discussion forum at which business units and support units coordinate their strategies for the upcoming year. Business units start by presenting their strategies to the support units and explaining how support units can contribute to their success. Support unit executives review their past performance and propose their objectives, targets, and initiatives for the future. Line and support unit executives then conduct an active dialogue, culminating in approved support unit functional plans, including Strategy Maps, Balanced Scorecard measures, targets, and approved initiatives. These forums are held during the budget process, enabling the approved resource levels for support units and their strategic initiatives to be incorporated into budget decisions.

SUPPORT UNIT STRATEGIES

Given the quotation from Larry Brady at the beginning of this chapter, what kinds of strategies make the most sense for support units? In principle, support units can create competitive advantage by excelling at any of the strategy archetypes used by business units: low cost, product leadership, or complete customer solutions. Undoubtedly, some of a support unit's activities should be performed at the lowest possible cost. These would be routine operational tasks such as payroll processing, benefits administration, and computer network maintenance. Such routine activities are necessary for the enterprise to function, but performing them in a world-class manner, other than at low cost, doesn't provide the organization with differentiation for competitive advantage.

Also, support units that attempt to follow a strategy based solely on low-cost delivery of *all* their services run a high likelihood of becoming outsourced. Internal groups are not likely to sustain a cost advantage for routine processes over an external outsourcing company. The latter often has advantages from scale economies and the option of producing and delivering services from low-cost regions of the world.

Product leadership is also a difficult strategy to sustain in a service business. New capabilities can be quickly imitated by others. Although product leadership remains a potential strategic option, no organization that we have worked with has asked its service functions to excel at innovation. Support units, in practice, invariably opt for a customer solutions or customer intimacy strategy. They strive to be operationally excellent at delivering basic services at low cost and high reliability, but they also identify a few critical services that they can excel at and that contribute to the differentiation and strategy of the business units they serve.

The customer intimacy or solutions strategy requires that support units build partnerships with their internal customers. This, in turn, leads to requirements for employee competencies in relationship management and for a culture of collaboration and customer focus that is quite new for support units that previously existed in centralized functional silos. Making this transformation from functional specialist to trusted adviser and business partner becomes the critical capability for a support unit's new strategy.

PORTFOLIO OF STRATEGIC SERVICES

Support units enhance business unit and corporate strategies through the portfolio of services they offer (see Figure 5-2). Each support organization develops a customized set of potential strategic programs. A typical strategic services portfolio contains ten to twenty initiatives. We illustrate the process of developing the strategic services portfolio with three important support units: human resources, information technology, and finance.

Human Resources Portfolio of Strategic Services

Our experience of working with several dozen human resources groups has indicated that the HR strategic services portfolio usually has three components:

1. *Strategic competency development programs:* These programs identify and develop personal competencies that are important to the success of the organization. The programs include identifying strategic job families, developing competency profiles for these families, analyzing the gaps between job requirements and existing

Figure 5-2 A Portfolio of Strategic Support Services Form the Bridge Between Enterprise and Functional Strategy

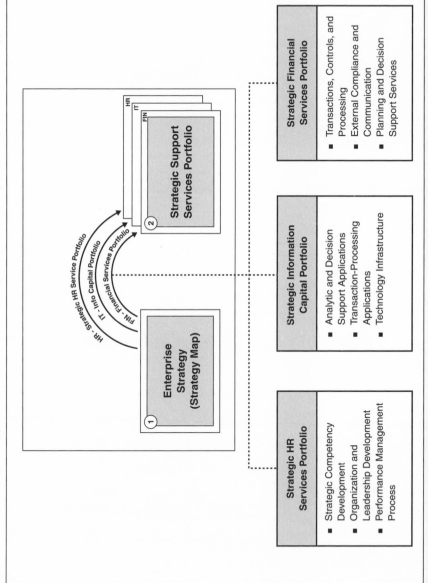

competencies, and developing the training programs for employees to close the gaps.

2. *Organization and leadership development:* These programs develop leaders, promote teamwork, foster organization synergy, and enhance the climate and values of the organization. The initiatives that can be included in this theme include developing the leadership competency model, conducting leadership development programs, succession planning, planning the rotation and development of key employees, developing culture and values, sharing best practices, and communicating strategy internally to all employees.

3. *Performance management process:* These programs define, motivate, appraise, and reward the performance of individuals and teams. In particular the programs include helping to set performance goals for individuals and teams, conducting appraisals of individual and team performance, aligning employees' incentive and reward systems with strategic objectives, and facilitating change management.

We illustrate how companies can develop their HR strategic services portfolio by using a case study from Handleman Company.

CASE STUDY: THE HANDLEMAN CORPORATION

The Handleman Corporation, with sales of $1.3 billion and more than 2,300 employees, operates as the music category manager and distributor for several leading retailers such as Wal-Mart and Best Buy. The music industry presents a range of business challenges, including technological change, piracy, customer concentration, and declining markets. Under the leadership of Chairman and CEO Steve Strome, Handleman adopted the Balanced Scorecard as the framework to clarify and execute its strategy.

The upper part of Figure 5-3 shows the Handleman corporate Strategy Map (excluding the learning and growth perspective). A key process is applying specialized knowledge of consumer demands to become the indispensable link between the artists and labels (which provide the music) and retailers (which sell the music to consumers). Excelling at the critical internal processes of relationship management and supply-chain management would enable Handleman to deliver higher-quality service than merchants could do for themselves. And it would use strategic transactions to diversify into businesses having growth opportunities that leverage Handleman's core capabilities and business expertise. Handleman cascaded its

Figure 5-3 Strategic HR Services Portfolio at Handleman

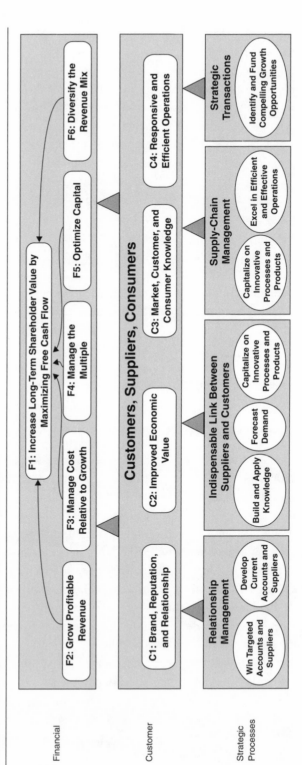

Strategic HR Services Portfolio

	Strategic HR Services Portfolio
Strategic Competency Development	(A) Strategic Job Family Identification (B) Competency Profiling (C) Training and Competency Development
Organization Leadership Development	(D) Succession and Development Planning (E) Organization Alignment
Performance Management Process	(F) Performance and Development Process (G) Compensation and Rewards (H) Strategic Communications

corporate Strategy Map to three geographic divisions—the United States, Canada, and U.K.—and to three shared-service units: human resources, information technology, and finance.

The lower half of Figure 5-3 shows how Handleman's human resources organization developed strategic initiatives to support the corporate strategy. Starting with initiative A in Figure 5-3, HR executives worked with their line counterparts to identify the one or two job families that would create the greatest impact on each of the four corporate strategic themes. This process produced the nine strategic job families shown in the lower panel of Figure 5-4. In the aggregate, the total number of staff in these nine job families represented fewer than 10 percent of the 2,300-person workforce, allowing the HR organization to focus its staff development efforts on the critical strategic personnel.

For each strategic job family shown in Figure 5-4, an HR executive interviewed key employees and managers to identify the core competencies that were necessary for staffers to be successful in their positions (initiative B in the lower panel of Figure 5-3). The lower columns in Figure 5-4 summarize the competency profiles for each job family. For example, an account executive must have good industry knowledge and must excel at relationship management, communications, and negotiations. A product manager must master technical competencies, such as pricing, product purchase, and inventory management, as well as interpersonal competencies, such as negotiations and vendor relationships. The competency profiles, coupled with an assessment of employees currently in each job family, provided a framework for identifying gaps within individuals and across the organization.

For initiative C in Figure 5-3, the training organization worked with the competency profiles to generate a consolidated list of training courses to close skill gaps in the strategic job families. It identified six global core competencies (see the column headings in Figure 5-5) that were common to all jobs: business acumen, planning and organizing, communications skills, teamwork, company values, and leadership skills. It also identified thirteen competencies that were specific to individual jobs: best practices; consumer, customer, and industry knowledge; financial analysis; innovation; merchant attitude; negotiation skills; process flow; project management; quality orientation; relationship management; a focus on results; strategic thinking; and technology knowledge.

The training organization then launched a series of nine management development programs to help employees obtain and strengthen the specific competencies required for their positions (see the row headings in

Figure 5-5). In this way, training programs were directly linked to the strategic requirements of the organization, and the training budget and resources were focused on areas with the greatest return on investment.

The human resources organization, along with the Center for Performance Management (the balanced scorecard group) also led the delivery of the remaining initiatives shown in the bottom panel of Figure 5-3:

Initiative D, succession and development planning: Identify and cultivate high-growth individuals and prepare succession plans for each key job.

Initiative E, organization alignment: Facilitate the design and cascading of scorecards at all levels of the organization.

Initiative F, performance and development process: Help supervisors and employees develop personal objectives, scorecards, development plans, and performance reviews linked to the strategy.

Initiative G, compensation and rewards: Develop new programs to reward top performers and motivate employees to achieve strategic financial and nonfinancial objectives.

Initiative H, strategic communications: Communicate and educate the organization about the strategy through a broad range of channels, such as off-site forums, newsletters, management meetings, and training programs.

Handlemen, after three years of using the Balanced Scorecard, was named to *Crain's* magazine list "Best Places to Work in Southeast Michigan in 2003" and included in "Metropolitan Detroit's 101 Best and Brightest Companies to Work For" over four consecutive years. Handleman was also named the National Association of Retail Merchants Wholesaler of the Year for three consecutive years. This award recognizes Handleman's outstanding achievements and continuing key role as an integral part of the music industry supply chain.

Information Technology Portfolio of Shared Services

The continued evolution and emergence of information technology offers every organization the opportunity for achieving performance breakthroughs and competitive advantage by effective alignment of this resource with corporate and business unit strategies.[3] Those who don't take

Figure 5-4 Strategic Job Families and Competency Profiles at Handleman

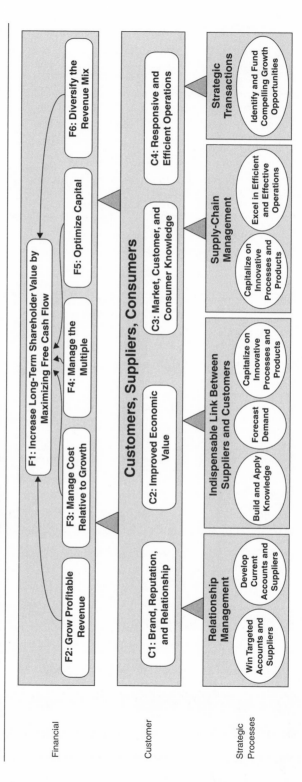

Account Executive	Field Salesperson	Product Manager	Internal Consultant	Analyst	Manager	Supply Chain Manager	Strategic Planner	Project Manager
Able to build and sustain internal and external relationships	Exhibits in-depth knowledge of consumer trends within market	Demonstrates knowledge of industry and genres with passion and enthusiasm	Proactive self-starter who exhibits a "can do" attitude	Able to utilize and identify modifications to required technology	Focuses on results and quickly resolves problems	Understands all product flow steps from artist to consumers	Able to see the "big picture" and identify opportunities	Able to see the "big picture" and focus on the organization's best interests
Exhibits a "can do" attitude in resolving customer problems	Demonstrates creative thinking to drive sales	Balances pricing deals with inventory limits for best business results	Able to see the "big picture" and recommend comprehensive solutions	Understands vendor pricing models	Able to quickly adapt to change	Identifies opportunities for continuous improvement within the supply chain	Applies understanding of financial analysis to evaluate opportunity viability	Gathers and shares information in a clear and unambiguous way
Uses professional communication skills	Uses professional communication skills	Able to analyze pricing models and develop product purchase scenarios	Demonstrates knowledge of internal and external best practices	Is detail oriented with a focus on quality	Able to analyze impact of changes in product flow	Demonstrates analytical thinking to identify innovative solutions	Demonstrates willingness to take innovative risks	Able to develop and maintain a workable project plan
Demonstrates competitive and industry knowledge	Able to calculate sales figure estimates	Has strong negotiation skills	Able to build and sustain internal and external relationships	Demonstrates industry and customer knowledge	Provides clear direction on expected outcomes	Exhibits problem-solving skills including proactive problem identification and resolution	Able to develop buy-in throughout management	Exhibits problem-solving skills including proactive problem identification and resolution
Has strong negotiation skills	Proactive self-starter who exhibits a "can do" attitude	Able to build and sustain vendor relationships	Has strong facilitation and influencing skills to drive solutions and resolve issues	Demonstrates knowledge of consumer trends across markets	Motivates and inspires culturally diverse people toward successful outcomes	Demonstrates knowledge of internal and external best practices	Has strong negotiation skills	Able to hold team members accountable for delivering quality results on time
							Able to build and sustain internal and external relationships	

Ⓑ Competency Profiles

Figure 5-5 Aligning Training Programs with Core Competencies Required by the Strategy at Handleman

Courses	Global Competencies						Job-Specific Competencies												
	Business Acumen	Plan/Organizing	Comm. Skills	Teamwork	Company Values	Leadership	Best Practices	C/C/I Knowledge	Financial Analysis	Innovative	Merchant Attitude	Negotiation Skills	Process Flow	Project Management	Quality	Relationship Mgt.	Results Focused	Strategic Thinking	Technology
Management Development Programs																			
Persuasion and Influencing for Success			X								X	X							
Finance for Nonfinancial Executives	X	X							X							X		X	
Introduction to Effective Project Management		X		X			X							X					X
Coaching and Mentoring Skills			X			X	X									X			
Leadership Ethics					X	X	X												
Mastering Business Writing			X												X				
Leading Diversity, Valuing Differences					X	X		X								X			
Instituting Change for Leaders				X		X						X				X		X	
Conflict Management			X	X													X		

a leadership position with IT run the risk that their competitors will. At the very least, an organization must be prepared to be a fast follower with respect to developing and deploying new IT capabilities.

Every organization must identify and deliver the portfolio of information technology initiatives required to execute its strategy. The information technology portfolio, like its HR counterpart, typically has three components:

1. *Business analytics and decision support:* applications that promote analysis, interpretation, and sharing of information or knowledge
2. *Transaction processing:* systems that automate the basic repetitive events of the organization
3. *Infrastructure:* the shared technology and management expertise required to enable effective delivery and use of information capital

Figure 5-6 illustrates the strategic portfolio approach at Sport-Man, Inc. (SMI). The top half of the figure shows a high-level image of the SMI Strategy Map, and the bottom half shows the company's portfolio of strategic applications. Because the retail industry is transaction intensive, significant operational economies can be achieved through effective automation of transaction systems.

Wal-Mart's rise to become the world's largest retailer came in part from redefining and restructuring the supply chain that linked customer point-of-sale purchases to supplier replenishment. SMI has identified three transaction-processing applications as strategic. Application B1 is a store management system that automates the point-of-sale information; application B2 is an inventory control system that ensures that SMI is always in stock on its core merchandise; and application B3 is a distribution system that provides rapid replenishment of store inventory from regional distribution centers.

Because of the data intensity generated by these transactions, retail organizations make effective use of business analytic and decision support applications to understand consumer behavior and quickly adapt to it. SMI has identified eight such applications to support each theme of its overall strategy. For example, two applications that model and track customer behavior support the "brand development" theme. The market research application (A1) analyzes various market segmentation and value proposition alternatives, and the customer analysis application (A2) looks at customer profitability, cross-purchasing, and the annual purchasing cycle.

Figure 5-6 Strategic Information Capital at Sport-Man, Inc.

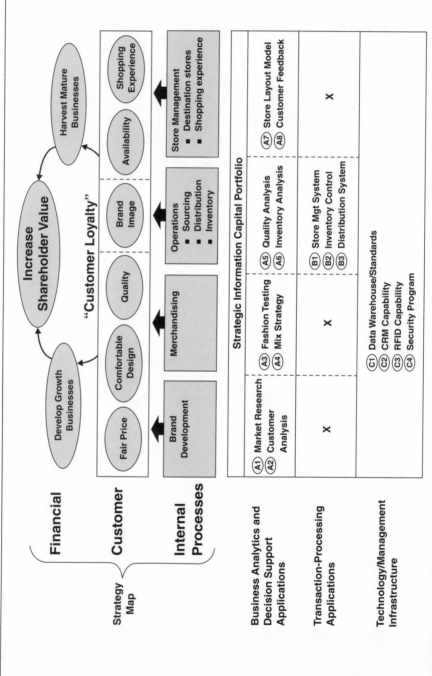

The ability to develop these transaction and analytic applications is based on the existence of a sound underlying infrastructure. More than one-half of the typical IT budget is invested in such infrastructure.[4] SMI has identified four infrastructure applications: C1, a data warehouse to support the analytic and decision support programs; C2, a customer relationship management (CRM) platform to support store-level management; C3, an investment in radio-frequency identification (RFID) micro-chip technology for supply-chain management; and C4, a data-center security upgrade.

As with the HR portfolio, the IT portfolio typically includes ten to twenty specific applications to support the enterprise strategy, plus additional initiatives to support strategies specific to each business unit. These initiatives must then be converted into a plan that defines how the applications will be developed and how their development will be managed.

Finance Portfolio of Strategic Services

The finance function has specific statutory and operating responsibilities for the corporation. These responsibilities include financial transaction management, such as accounts receivable, accounts payable, and payroll; regulatory reporting, including investor reporting, managing relationships with internal and external auditors, and board reporting; and managerial reporting, such as monthly financials and budget variance reports.

These responsibilities are necessary for all organizations to perform. But if the finance department does not attempt to define a value-creating strategy, the operational and statutory responsibilities will dominate its agenda. A finance department, while continuing to serve in its operational and statutory roles, can add value by building strategic partnerships with managers in the line organization. An example of a strategic support service is helping a senior line manager understand reports on customer and product-line profitability and working with the line manager to develop action plans that transform unprofitable products and customer relationships into profitable ones. An enterprise strategic service would be to incorporate cross-business initiatives and programs into the periodic budgeting and planning process.

In Figure 5-2, we identified three components of a typical finance portfolio of strategic services:

1. *Transaction controls and processing:* improvements in the structure and effectiveness of transaction systems, such as working capital management and risk analytics that facilitate business units' asset productivity and risk-management strategies

2. *External compliance and communication:* ensuring compliance with regulatory requirements and external communication, and ensuring that external reports and disclosures adequately reflect the company's strategy

3. *Planning and decision support:* analytics, consulting, and systems that improve the management of strategy across the organization

Figure 5-7 presents an example of the financial services portfolio development at Retail, Inc., a disguised organization that is structurally similar to our earlier case at Handleman. The top half of the figure shows a partial Strategy Map, clearly defining financial objectives, customer objectives, and four internal process themes. The finance organization, in a workshop with line executives, defined how its services could add value to the strategy. These objectives are shaded on the Strategy Map.

The strategic financial services portfolio is found in the bottom panel of the figure. The planning and decision support section of the portfolio contains three initiatives: A, a statistical model that processes historical data to improve forecast accuracy; B, activity-based costing analytics that calculate supplier and product-line profitability; and C, sophisticated financial planning software that supports the company's merger and acquisition process. The remaining initiatives are more like infrastructure and are not linked to specific Strategy Map processes.

Four strategic initiatives support transactions, controls, and processing: D, improving controls; E, transaction processing efficiency; F, tax management; and G, cash flow optimization. The external compliance and communication section of the portfolio has H, an initiative for compliance with Sarbanes-Oxley, and I, an initiative to better communicate the company message to investors, intended to impact financial objective F6, "manage the multiple." These nine initiatives constitute the portfolio of strategic services that will be managed and delivered by the finance organization.

ALIGNING THE SUPPORT ORGANIZATION

Once the strategic services for the support unit have been established, the unit must develop its strategy to deliver the promised services. This strategy, in turn, must be translated into a Strategy Map and Balanced Scorecard that communicate the strategy to all support unit employees and help to monitor the performance of the support unit in delivering its strategic objectives.

A support unit, like a business unit, has a mission, customers, services, and employees. Some support units, such as the information technology

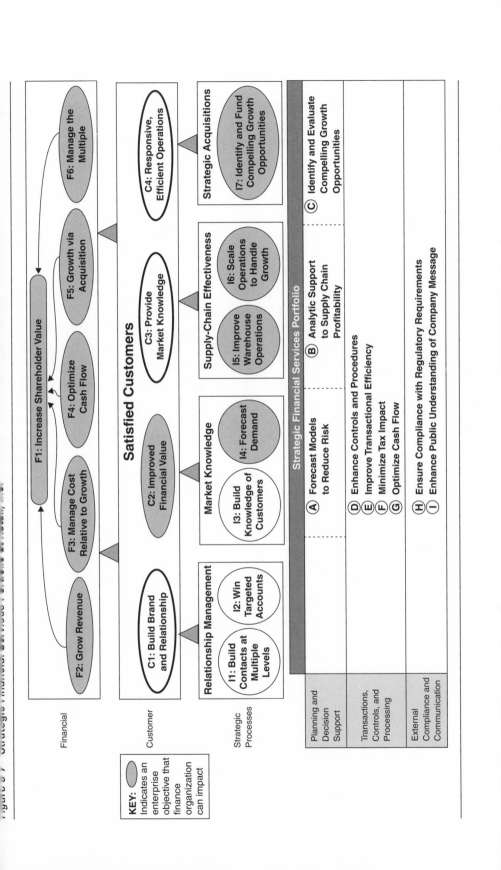

Figure 5-7 Strategic Financial Services Portfolio

departments of financial service organizations, have budgets that would place them on the *Fortune* 1000 list of largest companies. But support departments differ from business units in a couple of ways. Support units do not exist to make a profit; their purpose is to help business units in the line organization generate revenues and make profits. Also, the support unit's customers are almost always internal, not external; the customers are the internal business units and their employees, who use or benefit from the services provided by the support unit.

When constructing a support unit Strategy Map and Balanced Scorecard, it is useful to think of the support unit as a "business within a business." At the highest level, the support unit should have the same overarching goal as the enterprise—some measure of shareholder value (or its equivalent in nonprofits). It is essential that all the employees in the organization, whether in line units or support units, stay focused on the ultimate measure of success if they are to function as part of the corporate team.

The financial perspective of a support unit's Strategy Map is divided into two components: efficiency and effectiveness. *Support unit efficiency* deals with traditional issues such as the cost of services delivered and adherence to budget. *Support unit effectiveness* describes the impact that the support unit has on the enterprise strategy. Sometimes referred to as a "linkage scorecard," the effectiveness objectives should define the specific objectives and measures in the enterprise scorecard that the support unit directly impacts.

For example, an HR organization, through leadership development programs, might improve the enterprise's ability to grow through acquisition. "Successful growth through acquisition" would appear on HR's linkage scorecard. Even though HR does not have direct control over this objective—and, in addition, success might require the efforts of other departments—the HR organization is measured (and rewarded, in part) based on such linkage scorecard objectives. This ensures that the support unit always remembers and pursues the ultimate reason that it exists—to enhance enterprise and business unit strategies.

We have observed that some support units build their Strategy Maps as if they were nonprofit organizations, with the customer perspective on top, and the financial perspective—focusing on efficiency, productivity, and resource management—as a subsidiary perspective. Although we are sympathetic to this representation, most of the support units we have observed want to be thought of as contributing to value creation within their enterprises and therefore deliberately include some enterprise-level financial objectives at the top level of their Strategy Maps and Balanced Scorecards. They want to drive enterprise value creation, not just serve as a captive internal support function.

The support unit generally has two classes of customers: (1) the business unit managers to whom they provide services directly, and (2) the employees or external constituents who are beneficiaries and recipients of the services. Its typical customer intimacy or total customer solutions strategy calls for building business partnerships with its customers. Every support unit should understand its customers' strategy and use its functional expertise to create and deliver solutions that contribute to its customers' success.

The internal process perspective of a support unit scorecard has three themes. The first theme focuses on the function's operational excellence, which will drive the efficiency objective of the financial perspective. Key measures for this theme include cost per transaction, quality, and response time.

The second theme deals with how the function manages the relationship with its internal customers. Service companies, such as IBM, Accenture, and EDS, devote considerable time to defining the processes and skills required for effective relationship management. This is the heart of their account-development strategies. Internal support staff should be no different; they, too, are service companies. They should make a similar investment in defining a client management process. Techniques such as a designated relationship manager, integrated planning, service agreements, and customer reviews have all proven effective.

The third theme deals with strategic support of the business. This theme drives the effectiveness component of the strategy, providing customers with new capabilities that enhance their strategies. The structure of this theme varies from function to function. The architecture mirrors the categories and the specific requirements found in the strategic functional services portfolio discussed earlier.

The learning and growth perspective reflects the specific needs of the functional staff for training, technology, and a supportive work climate.

In summary, the support unit strategy must be aligned with enterprise and business unit strategies. The strategic services portfolio (recall Figure 5-1) defines how the support function aligns its objectives with those of the line organization. This link should be clearly reflected in the customer perspective of the support unit scorecard. Periodic customer reviews should measure the progress being made in delivering the initiatives in the strategic services portfolio. The internal process perspective of the scorecard defines the way in which strategic support will be provided to the business unit.

We now demonstrate how to apply this general architecture to the development of Strategy Maps and Balanced Scorecards for the human resources, information technology, and finance functions.

Aligning the HR Organization

Figure 5-8 presents a Strategy Map template for a human resources unit; Figure 5-9 is the corresponding template for a human resources Balanced Scorecard.[5] The two templates have proven to be effective starting points that HR organizations can customize to their actual situations.

The financial perspective of the HR scorecard has two components: HR efficiency and HR effectiveness. Efficiency generally deals with operational issues related to the relative cost of services. Benchmarks relative to external norms are frequently used here. For example, to maintain a focus on productivity, "benefits management cost per employee" can be compared to proposals from external providers.

HR effectiveness can be measured through the linkage scorecard—a small set of measures taken directly from the enterprise scorecard that the HR organization can influence although not directly control. For example, if the corporate strategy is growth through acquisition, the HR linkage scorecard might measure "key staff retention," "sales created through cross-selling," or "merger benefits achieved."

A human resources organization has two kinds of customers: the line business units that HR partners with to deliver its services, and the employees themselves, who are the direct recipients of a full array of HR services. Business units look to HR to provide a professional partnership of knowledgeable support. Some companies, reflecting this professional partnership, rename the customer perspective the client perspective.

The HR organization, in turn, delivers and is held accountable for the solutions negotiated in its strategic services portfolio. Scorecard measures for the business unit partnerships include feedback relative to deliverables in the jointly developed plan (the deliverables are often described in service agreements between a support unit and its business unit customers), and the business unit managers' assessments of the professional capabilities and service orientation of the HR employees they work with directly. HR's relationship with its other set of customers—employees—can be measured by a survey of employee satisfaction with the programs and services provided by HR.

The internal process perspective generally is built around three themes. Theme 1, "achieve operational excellence," focuses on the efficiency with

Figure 5-8 HR Organization Strategy Map Template

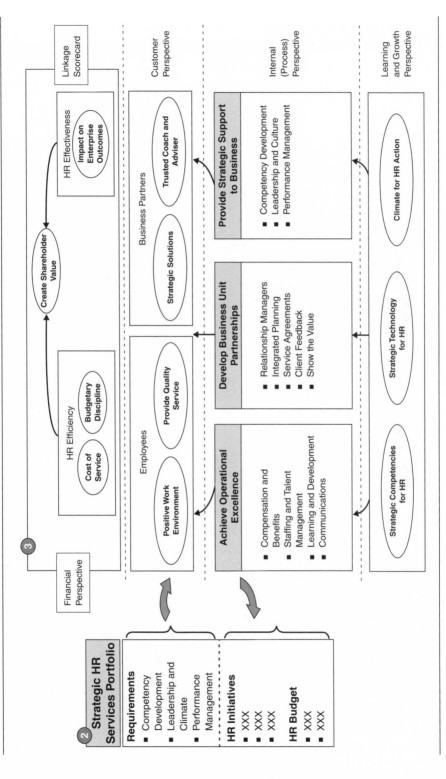

Figure 5-9 HR Organization Balanced Scorecard Template

Business Linkage	Strategic Objectives	Strategic Measures	Targets	Strategic Initiatives	Budget
Financial	M1. Create Shareholder Value	Stock Price Multiple	Competitive Norms		
	M2. M3. M4. } Objectives on Enterprise Scorecard Impacted by HR	Measures on Enterprise Scorecard Impacted by HR			
	F1. Improve HR Efficiency	■ Budget Cost vs. Actual ■ HR Cost/Employee	■ 100% ■ 90% of Norm		
Customer	C1. Create a Positive Work Environment	■ Employee Satisfaction Survey	■ 80% Rating	■ Employee Survey	$CCC
	C2. Build Strategic Partnership	■ Service Agreement Feedback	■ 85% Rating	■ Account Review Program	$BBB
	C3. Ensure Human Capital Readiness	■ Human Capital Readiness	■ 75%	■ Human Capital Readiness Report	$AAA
Internal	I1. Achieve HR Operational Excellence	■ Cost per Transaction ■ Cycle Time ■ Error Rate/Complaints	■ 5% Reduction ■ 21 Days ■ 50% Reduction	■ Activity-Based Costing ■ Process Reengineering ■ TQM for HR Processes	$NNN $OOO $PPP
	I2. Develop Business Unit Partnerships	■ Service Agreements in Place (%) ■ HR Strategic Plans in Place (%) ■ Time with Customer	■ 90% ■ 90% ■ 10 Hrs/Week	■ Service Agreements Program ■ HR Strategic Planning Process ■ Relationship Management Program	$KKK $LLL $MMM
	I3. **Provide Strategic Support to Business**				
	(a) **Build Strategic Staff Competencies**	■ **Human Capital Readiness**	■ **100%**	■ **Strategic Job Family Identification** ■ **Competency Profiles** ■ **Training and Development**	**$DDD** **$EEE** **$FFF**
	(b) **Develop Leaders and Supportive Culture**	■ **Leadership Alignment** ■ **Cultural Alignment**	■ **100%** ■ **100%**	■ **Leadership Development** ■ **Mission, Vision, Values**	**$GGG** **$HHH**
	(c) **Create a High-Performance Organization**	■ **Staff Alignment**	■ **100%**	■ **Strategic Communications** ■ **Performance Management Program**	**$III** **$JJJ**
Learning and Growth	L1. Provide Strategic HR Info	■ HR Application System Readiness	■ 100% (vs. Plan)	■ HR Systems Plan	$QQQ
	L2. Develop Strategic HR Competencies	■ HR Competencies: Readiness	■ 100% (vs. Plan)	■ HR Competency Plan	$RRR
	L3. Fill HR Leadership Pipeline	■ Key Position Depth Chart	■ 80%	■ HR Leadership Development Program	$SSS
	L4. Increase Best-Practice Sharing	■ Best Practices Transferred (Number)	■ 50%	■ Knowledge Management Program	$TTT
	L5. Ensure Strategic Alignment	■ Personal Goals Linked to BSC (%)	■ 80%	■ BSC Cascade	$UUU
	L6. Create Shared Vision and Culture	■ Strategic Awareness (%)	■ 80%	■ Strategic Education and Communication	$VVV
				Total	**$XYZ**

which the many enterprise-level HR programs are delivered. It influences HR's financial objective to stay within budget while delivering the expected mix and quality of services. This generally means measuring the cost per transaction and the quality and timeliness of HR services, such as compensation and benefits programs, recruiting, training, and annual performance reviews.

Theme 2, "develop business unit partnerships," is often overlooked in practice. It involves developing a formal process for managing relationships with business units. HR should adopt the same kinds of formal customer management processes (planning, account management, and feedback and reviews) that business units use with their external customers. Scorecard measures for this theme might include a status indicator of the level of professional relationships, such as percentage of business units with HR strategic support plans, as well as an account development measure, such as time spent consulting with customers.

Theme 3, "strategic support of business units," links the HR organization to its strategic services portfolio. Objectives are generally found for the three major areas shown in Figure 5-8: building strategic staff competencies; developing leaders and improving organizational culture; and instilling a commitment to performance management. Responding to the specific requirements to deliver the HR portfolio of strategic services, the HR organization defines specific programs and initiatives to satisfy business strategy requirements (including a budget for initiatives) and a service agreement that defines the specifics of schedules, deliverables, and staffing.

The learning and growth perspective of the HR Strategy Map corrects a typical problem in many HR organizations: the shoemaker's children going barefoot. Human resources professionals, like all other employees, have specific needs for training, information systems, alignment, and performance management. Particularly as the HR organization shifts its value proposition to providing customized consulting relationships with business units, HR employees must acquire entirely new skill sets. Internal programs for the HR staff should be subjected to the same standards of excellence as those for its business unit customers. HR employees should be viewed as customers of the HR organization for these services, including strategic plans, relationship managers, and feedback processes.

The fourth column in the HR Balanced Scorecard (Figure 5-9) shows the strategic initiatives that support the HR unit's strategic objectives, measures, and targets. These initiatives are the actions and interventions that lead to successful strategy execution. The initiatives must be budgeted so that informed economic trade-offs can be made. Although most of the initiatives shown in Figure 5-9 support the internal management of the HR organization, those associated with internal processes (I3) comprise the strategic support for business units. This process and associated initiatives produce the deliverables to HR's customers. The business units must approve the budget for these initiatives as part of the annual plan for the HR unit.

CASE STUDY: HUMAN RESOURCES AT INGERSOLL-RAND

We introduced the Ingersoll-Rand (IR) enterprise strategy and Strategy Map in Chapter 3 (recall Figure 3-4). IR's corporate-level strategy was to move from being a highly diversified company organized in numerous stand-alone product divisions to becoming a more integrated solutions company that would go to market as a team, integrating the products of several business units to meet a customer's unique needs. The implications for organization and cultural change were profound. Its strategic theme, "leverage the power of our enterprise through dual citizenship," spoke to the need for new competencies, new values, the sharing of knowledge, and the expansion of employees' views beyond the boundaries of their product companies to the IR enterprise as a whole.

Ingersoll's CEO asked the human resources organization to help implement the dual citizenship theme. Don Rice, senior vice president for human resources and global services, led the effort, starting with developing a Strategy Map for this agenda (see Figure 5-10). The first three process excellence themes—"develop leaders," "drive organization performance," and "build strategic employee competencies"—specifically address the corporate strategy agenda. The fourth theme, "achieve HR process excellence," focuses on the quality and efficiency of HR operational services such as delivery of compensation and benefits.

Collectively, the four process excellence themes deliver the human resources value proposition to its two sets of customers: "enhance leadership effectiveness" of business unit partners and "be the employer of choice" for Ingersoll's employees. The impact of the HR strategy on financial results would yield results reported in the financial perspective:

- Business growth enabled by better leadership
- Acquisition effectiveness enabled by a team-oriented culture
- Improved efficiency enabled by better management of the HR processes

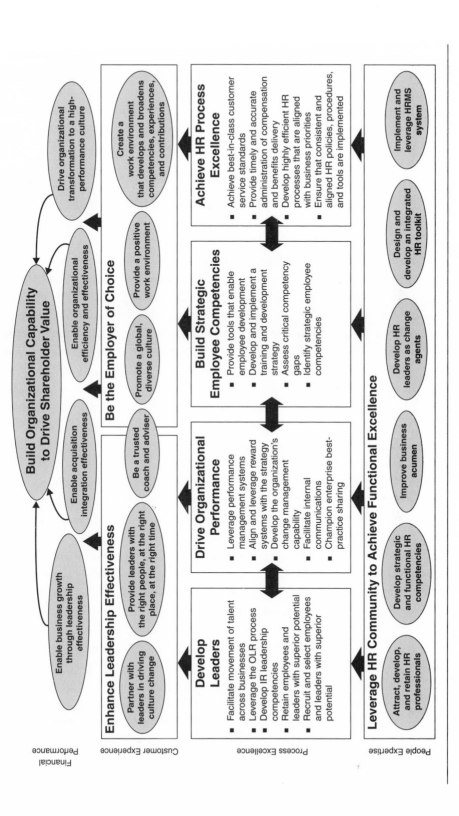

Herb Henkel, Ingersoll-Rand's CEO, commented on the approach taken by IR's human resources group: "I have never seen anything that so clearly articulates the value that a support function adds to the business. We should use this as a recruitment tool for HR professionals. If anyone couldn't sign up for this, then we wouldn't want them in the company."[6]

Aligning the Information Technology Organization

Based on our experience with dozens of information technology organizations, we have prepared the generic IT department strategy template shown in Figure 5-11.[7] This map illustrates the balance that IT organizations must maintain: be competent at basic, necessary services while developing the capabilities to collaborate with business units, offering them customized services, solutions, and technologies that advance their strategies. This strategic positioning shifts the debate from how much to spend on information technology to how much to invest in IT to advance the organization's strategic agenda.

The financial perspective reflects objectives to lower the unit costs of supplying basic IT services while also enhancing the enterprise's outcomes through effective deployment of IT products and services. The IT unit's strategy gets aligned with the enterprise strategy through the portfolio of strategic IT services, which is derived from the enterprise strategy and negotiated with the business units.

Success in delivering the portfolio of infrastructure and applications is measured, in the customer perspective, at two levels: (1) the basic competency level: the supply of reliable, high-quality IT services at a competitive cost, and (2) the value-adding contribution level, where the IT organization helps business units become more productive and profitable and, ultimately, becomes a vital component in the success of the business units' differentiation strategies.

The internal process is organized by three strategic themes:

1. *Achieve operational excellence through* access to timely and accurate information and computing resources reliably at reasonable cost. The IT unit provides a cost-effective portfolio of core technology infrastructure—the shared technology and managerial expertise required to deliver computing services to employees—and basic technology applications, including enterprise resource planning (ERP) and other transaction-processing systems, that automate the basic repetitive transactions of the enterprise.

Figure 6-11 Information Technology Organization Strategy Map Template

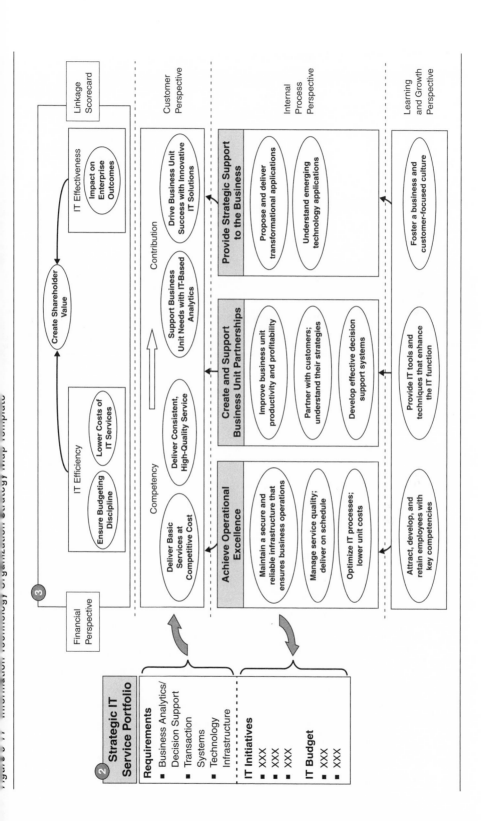

2. *Create and support business unit partnerships.* The IT unit becomes the trusted adviser to operating managers on how to deploy information technology to improve business unit profitability and external customer satisfaction. The technology includes analytic applications: the systems and networks—such as customer relationship management and activity-based costing (ABC)—that promote analysis, interpretation, and sharing of information and knowledge.

3. *Provide strategic support to the business.* The IT unit supplies innovative and emerging technology-based solutions that help business units position themselves for competitive advantage. It introduces transformational applications, the systems and networks that change the prevailing business model of the enterprise.

The first theme helps to demonstrate the group's ability to supply basic IT capabilities to business units at competitive costs, along with reliable service delivery and consistent quality. The second theme enables the group to develop solutions customized to the needs of each business unit. In this way, the IT department becomes a strategic partner of the business unit and participates with it in creating and executing its strategy. With the third theme, solutions leadership, the IT group offers product-leadership computing that supports the business units' differentiation strategy by offering innovative information-based solutions to customers and suppliers.

Information technology support units might opt only for initiatives in the first theme: supplying basic IT infrastructure and applications at low cost and with high reliability and availability. The parent organization, however, might then decide that these basic IT products and services can be obtained most efficiently by outsourcing the function to an external supplier that enjoys tremendous scale and global economies in acquiring and operating IT resources. Internal IT groups will likely want to differentiate themselves from external providers by offering the themes of strategic partnership and solutions leadership to its business unit partners. These require higher spending on IT resources but offer more than commensurate returns through high-value-added products, services, and solutions.

Our colleague Robert S. Gold argues that the typical IT organization follows a sequential strategy of successively satisfying a business unit's hierarchical needs.[8] The IT organization starts by demonstrating its competency in the consistent, reliable, low-cost supplying of basic information capabilities and services, such as those listed in theme 1. Success along these dimensions is necessary but usually is not sufficient to meet all of a business unit's IT needs. It eliminates dissatisfaction but does not by itself contribute to value creation for the business unit.

Once the IT organization's competency has been established, it earns the right to move to the capabilities identified in the second and third themes. First, it develops alliances with business units, contributing to their productivity and profitability strategies by offering customized initiatives and applications. The highest level of IT support occurs when IT customizes emerging technology capabilities that position the business unit for distinctive competitive advantage.[9]

The employee objective in the learning and growth perspective identifies the critical skills required for the IT unit's people to deliver on the three-pronged strategy of operational excellence, business partnerships, and industry-leadership solutions. The IT unit, of course, needs its own technology support to manage and deliver its offerings. It often must shift the culture away from being a sandbox in which technology mavens happily play by themselves. It must instill a new culture of customer focus in which IT professionals understand the operations and strategies of business units and supply an appropriate mix of products, services, and solutions that create success for their customers, the internal business units.

We illustrate the development of an IT Strategy Map and Balanced Scorecard for the large information systems group at Lockheed Martin Corporation.

CASE STUDY: LOCKHEED MARTIN ENTERPRISE INFORMATION SYSTEMS

Lockheed Martin Corporation became the country's largest defense contractor after the merger of Lockheed and Martin Marietta in 1995. Sales in 2004 were $35.5 billion, and the company had a backlog of $76.9 billion. Its largest customer (62 percent) is the U.S. Department of Defense, with other customers including nondefense government (including homeland security), 16 percent of revenues; international sales, 18 percent; and domestic commercial, 4 percent.

Lockheed Martin's enterprise information systems (EIS) organization has more than four thousand employees working in its Orlando, Florida, headquarters and in several dozen decentralized units around the United States, including Washington, D.C.; Fort Worth; Sunnyvale, California; and Denver. "We're trying to make strategy a part of everyone's job," says Ed Meehan, vice president of operations for Enterprise Information Systems.

Business unit leaders, especially since the 1995 merger, were concerned because the company's IT units operated in stovepipes and silos. This problem was especially acute because IT capabilities were at the heart of the company's strategy to be the leader in "Net-centered" capabilities. Lockheed Martin expects its technology to be at the center of how the military will organize and fight in the information age, linking various systems and sensors to exponentially increase the military benefit of those systems that otherwise operate independently.

To meet its new challenges as a value-added IT provider to the corporation, EIS adopted a complete customer solutions strategy to become the supplier of choice for internal IT services for the corporation. It also wanted to serve external customers by helping Lockheed Martin businesses win large IT-related contracts from the government, such as those expected from the U.S. Department of Homeland Security.

EIS launched a Balanced Scorecard program to align its various operating departments with the overall EIS strategy and also with the strategies of the corporation. The BSC would help EIS become the credible innovator and supplier of cutting-edge, net-centric capabilities. Figure 5-12 shows the EIS Strategy Map. The language reading upward along the left side of the map ("Our diverse, empowered workforce . . .") provided what one EIS leader called a *Reader's Digest* version of the map: a way to quickly both introduce the structure and set up the content when the map is presented to audiences new to the Strategy Map concept.

EIS leadership identified business and technology leaders within Lockheed Martin as their key customers and used the voice of the customer to describe five customer objectives. Reading from left to right, these objectives move from "table stakes" ("Guarantee secure, reliable, high-quality solutions," "Show me the value," and "Deliver on commitments . . .") to objectives that more fully realize potential value from Lockheed Martin ("Understand my unique business and customer" and "Innovate with me to win business and keep it sold"). EIS leadership understood that the credibility EIS would establish following its success in the table stakes objectives was a prerequisite to EIS being seen by its internal customers as a contributing partner in winning business, and not merely as a service provider.

Building on objectives for an "energized, strategy-focused workforce," the four-themed structure of the internal process perspective reflected this left-to-right movement from competency to contribution. The

Figure 9-12 Lockheed Martin Enterprise Information Systems Strategy

Magnify the Power of Lockheed Martin Through IT

to

Realize the Real-Time Net-Centric Strategy

That

Focused Actions

Executes

Our Diverse, Empowered Workforce

Serve the National Interest and Increase Shareholder Value

Improve margins | Leverage investments | Grow revenue

Business and Technology Leaders say:

"Guarantee secure, reliable, high-quality solutions"

"Show me the value"

"Deliver on commitments to enable my mission success"

"Understand my unique business and customer"

"Innovate with me to win business and keep it sold"

Run the Business

Continuously improve solutions, performance, and responsiveness

Drive process improvement through innovative information access

Build the next-generation infrastructure and business systems

Understand and manage unit costs

Earn Trusted Partnerships

Anticipate, influence, and deliver on expectations

Strengthen communication, interactions, and relationships

Aggressively pursue knowledge of business strategies

Advance the LMC Business

Transform LMC through effective collaboration, Net-centric capabilities, and innovative solutions

Accelerate horizontal integration

Achieve Operational Excellence Through Disciplined Performance

Drive standardization and consolidation

Effectively select and leverage suppliers

Excel at program management and system engineering

Optimize portfolios of assets, initiatives, and service offerings

Attract, develop, and retain a talented, energized, strategy-focused workforce

Live our values and demonstrate SPIRIT

Promote creative thinking and innovative solutions

"disciplined performance" theme contained objectives and broad efforts throughout EIS to enable continuous improvement in overall EIS performance; efforts to drive standardization and consolidation, to manage the use of external suppliers, to employ the disciplines of program management and systems engineering, and to optimize portfolios served as a foundation for the objectives in the themes "run the business," "earn trusted partnerships," and ultimately "advance the business."

To run the business, EIS recognized that its customers cared primarily about quality and cost. By understanding and managing unit costs, EIS sought to isolate costs from demand and to better manage their impact on total IT cost. Development and enhancement of next-generation infrastructure, process improvement, and improved solutions, performance, and responsiveness were highlighted as key objectives. But satisfying these objectives was only the beginning.

By aggressively pursuing knowledge of business strategies, EIS leadership sought to strengthen relationships with its partners and to anticipate and deliver on their expectations. With this improved relationship, EIS expected to empower horizontal integration within Lockheed Martin and better realize the corporation's net-centric capabilities. "We're trying to magnify the power of Lockheed Martin through information technology," Meehan says. "We're making people's ability to get information more seamless."

Placing the value perspective at the top of the Strategy Map, EIS leaders reinforced the financial contribution that the EIS organization enables in the Lockheed Martin enterprise: to improve margins by managing cost, to leverage investments in existing IT capabilities, and to grow revenue.

By mid-2005, EIS had cascaded this Strategy Map into its ten functional areas and was already seeing heightened awareness and engagement with the EIS strategy among its workforce.

Aligning the Finance Organization

Finance, the third unit we profile, is perhaps the most powerful of all support units.[10] It measures and controls the organization's financial resources, and it interprets and enforces numerous accounting standards and compliance requirements imposed by external regulatory authorities. It also communicates with the enterprise's diverse constituencies, including shareholders, analysts, the board of directors, tax authorities, regulators, and creditors.

The finance function has encountered dramatic changes in the past decade. Corporate reporting scandals triggered the Sarbanes-Oxley legislation, which forced increased scrutiny of organizations' reporting, internal processes, and controls. Electronic technologies, such as the Internet, revolutionized payments, billing, inventory, and supply-chain processes. The new knowledge-based economy, where 80 percent or more of corporate value is derived from intangible assets, required measurement and management systems that go beyond traditional budgets and financial reporting. Moreover, new measurement approaches, such as economic value added, rolling forecasts, activity-based cost management, and Balanced Scorecards, were introduced. Contemporary finance organizations must cope with the newly imposed external constraints and requirements while simultaneously applying new measurement and management methodologies that help drive the organization's strategy implementation into the future.

Finance groups are responding to these challenges by extending their historic scorekeeping function to forge new partnerships with business units and corporate executives. A recent study described the CFO's new role as "chief performance adviser."[11] A Booz Allen Hamilton study found that "chief financial officers are viewed by their CEO as their primary aides in driving company-wide transformation efforts."[12] Clayton Daley, CFO of Procter & Gamble, described the dual roles for today's CFO: "I consciously think of myself as wearing two hats. I am responsible for traditional accounting issues: cash flow, capital, and cost structures. But my role is increasingly linked with strategy and operations."[13]

We can capture these multiple responsibilities using a generic finance function Strategy Map, as shown in Figure 5-13. The financial objectives are to operate the finance function efficiently and stay within the budget authorized for its mix of regulatory, compliance, control, and decision support activities. The efficiency theme also incorporates assisting the enterprise in achieving its cost-reduction and productivity objectives through an effective, adaptive budgeting process, disciplined resource allocation and investment processes, and operational reports and feedback that support employees' continuous improvement and productivity programs. Its effectiveness objective, derived from objectives on the enterprise Balanced Scorecard affected by the finance function, will share enterprise success measures such as revenue growth, return on equity, and economic profit.

The finance Strategy Map reflects two types of customers: external constituents and internal business partners. External constituents—including shareholders, the board of directors, analysts, and regulators—

Figure 5-13 Finance Organization Strategy Map Template

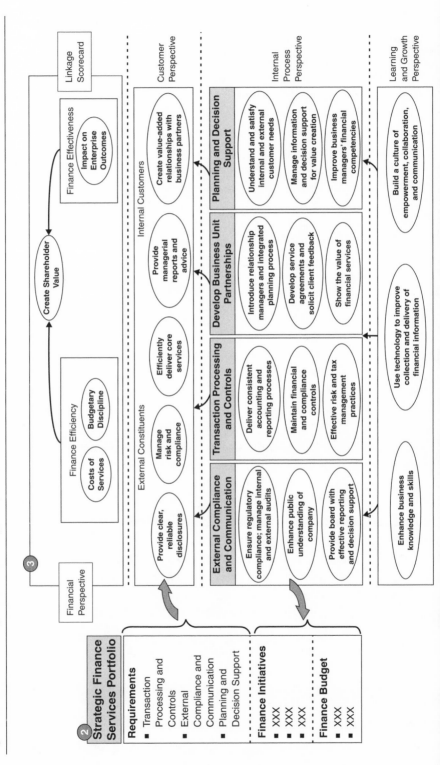

look to the finance function to provide high-quality quarterly and annual financial reports and disclosures, corporate risk management, and controls and compliance that ensure that the enterprise is operating well within legal and ethical boundaries. The internal business customers want consistent, low-cost execution of basic accounting and finance processes—payroll, accounts receivable and payable, monthly closings, and consolidation—as well as informative reports to management and financial advice and support for its strategies.

The internal processes that deliver these benefits to internal and external customers are built around four themes.

External compliance and communication: Address the needs of external constituents through regulatory compliance, effective communication of the company's economics and strategy, board reporting and decision support, and oversight of internal and external auditing processes.

Transaction processing and controls: Become operationally excellent in delivering reliable transaction processing, record keeping, financial reporting, tax and risk management, and internal controls and compliance. These are the necessary processes that any enterprise expects its finance function to perform well.

Develop business unit partnerships: Build an understanding of business unit requirements for financial management support, and install a professional process to deliver this understanding.

Planning and decision support: Deliver the strategic support plan developed jointly with the business units; become business unit managers' trusted financial advisers by supplying and interpreting financial and nonfinancial information and by providing a portfolio of analytic tools that supports business decisions, management control, and strategy implementation.

The finance function's learning and growth objectives describe the transformation requirements of its new role. Finance must maintain its historic competencies in accounting, financial reporting, compliance, and controls. But it must build on these competencies to develop new competencies among its employees that enable them to understand operations and strategy and to work effectively with business unit line managers. Many companies now require that all finance managers spend time working in operating units, often in line positions. Johnson & Johnson sends its new finance function hires through a two-year training program to enable financial managers to have a focus on customers, an understanding of the marketplace, an aptitude for teamwork, and the ability to be positive change agents.[14]

Almost all routine processing and reporting of transactions are now automated, requiring finance personnel to have strong capabilities in information technology. They must ensure the validity and integrity of financial systems and must enhance transaction-processing systems, such as ERP, with higher-level analytic applications that transform raw data and transactions into information and knowledge for managers.

To excel at the internal process theme of planning and decision support, the finance function cannot be only an objective, independent scorekeeper on the sidelines. It needs a new culture and climate where its professionals become the value-added financial advisers to managers and executives. But while they are transforming into this "chief performance adviser" role, finance managers must be prepared, as a former Federal Reserve chairman once said was his job, to take away the punch bowl when the party becomes a little too exuberant. Finance managers must have a strong value system that helps them achieve a balance between being contributing and loyal team members and representing the needs and expectations of external constituencies for integrity, control, risk management, and long-term shareholder value creation.

CASE STUDY: HANDLEMAN FINANCE DEPARTMENT

We illustrate a finance department Strategy Map (Figure 5-14) and Balanced Scorecard (Figure 5-15) by continuing with the Handleman example, introduced earlier in this chapter. Its finance unit Strategy Map provides a comprehensive overview of a corporate finance department that includes advice as well as audit, investor relations, tax, controllers group, treasury, and internal financial services within one scorecard.[15]

The Handleman finance group defined four key customer objectives:

C1: Responsive and efficient finance operations. The finance group will be responsive and efficient. It will focus on reducing the time that is spent on daily transactional tasks and increase the time spent on analytical functions to enhance decision making while maintaining a very high standard for accuracy and controls.

Figure 5-14 Handleman Finance Division Strategy Map

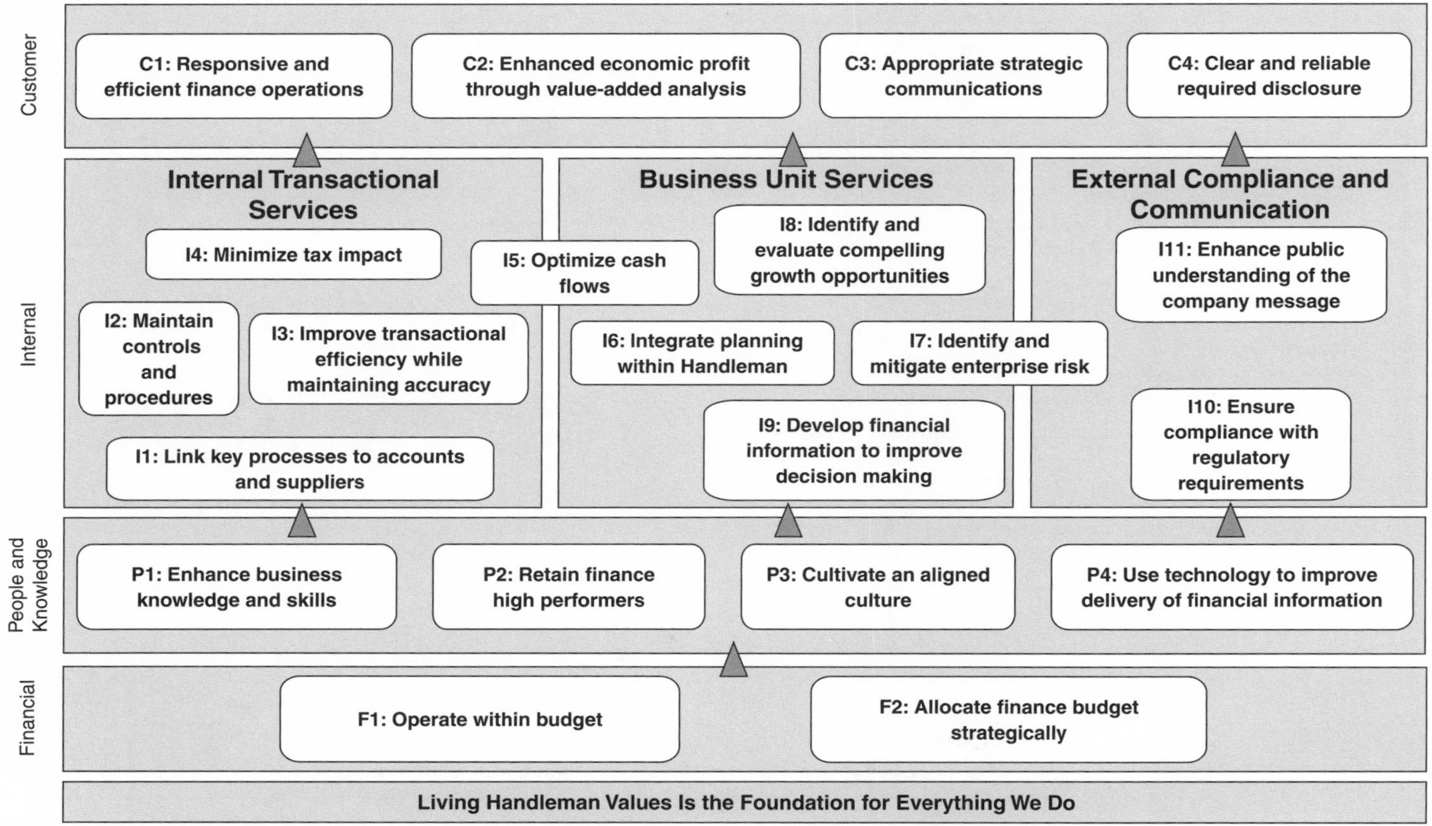

External Compliance and Communication

C4: Clear and reliable required disclosure

I11: Enhance public understanding of the company message

I10: Ensure compliance with regulatory requirements

P4: Use technology to improve delivery of financial information

Business Unit Services

C3: Appropriate strategic communications

C2: Enhanced economic profit through value-added analysis

I8: Identify and evaluate compelling growth opportunities

I7: Identify and mitigate enterprise risk

I6: Integrate planning within Handleman

I9: Develop financial information to improve decision making

P3: Cultivate an aligned culture

F2: Allocate finance budget strategically

Internal Transactional Services

C1: Responsive and efficient finance operations

I5: Optimize cash flows

I4: Minimize tax impact

I3: Improve transactional efficiency while maintaining accuracy

I2: Maintain controls and procedures

I1: Link key processes to accounts and suppliers

P2: Retain finance high performers

P1: Enhance business knowledge and skills

F1: Operate within budget

Living Handleman Values Is the Foundation for Everything We Do

Customer

Internal

People and Knowledge

Financial

Figure 5-15 Handleman Finance Division Balanced Scorecard

	Strategic Objectives	Strategic Measures
Customer	C1 Responsive and Efficient Finance Operations C2 Enhanced Economic Profit Through Value-Added Analysis C3 Appropriate Strategic Communications C4 Clear and Reliable Required Disclosure	C1A Business unit satisfaction survey C1B Total finance SG&A per to total revenue C2A Divisional economic profitability versus plan C3A % of execution to communication plan C4A Composite rating measure
Internal Transactional Services	I1 Link Key Processes to Accounts and Suppliers I2 Maintain Controls and Procedures I3 Improve Transactional Efficiency While Maintaining Accuracy I4 Minimize Tax Impact I5 Optimize Cash Flows	I1 % Completion against initiatives plan I2 % Processes, controls, and procedures documented I3A Closing timetable and accuracy I3B Number of transactions per FTE I4 Effective tax rate I5 Actual cash flow compared to budget
Business Unit Services	I6 Integrate Planning Within Handleman I7 Identify and Mitigate Enterprise Risk I8 Identify and Evaluate Compelling Growth Opportunities I9 Develop Financial Information to Improve Decision Making	I6A Progress on integrating governance recommendations I6B Total number of work days to complete annual plan I7 % of completion against enterprise risk mitigation plan I8 Number of qualified opportunities in the pipeline I9 Number of new models developed
External Compliance and Communications	I10 Ensure Compliance with Regulatory Requirements I11 Enhance Public Understanding of Company Message	I10 % of timely filings of all documents I11 Progress to plan on developing the communication program
People and Knowledge	P1 Enhance Business Knowledge and Skills P2 Retain Finance High Performers at Handleman P3 Cultivate an Aligned Culture P4 Use Technology to Improve Delivery of Financial Information	P1A % Completion of skills gap plan P1B Number of finance staff to complete mini-rotation P2A Retention rate of high performers P3A % of personal accountabilities aligned across finance P4A Improved due date delivery of top deliverables P4B % of strategic requests implemented
Financial	F1 Operate Within Budget F2 Allocate Finance Budget Strategically	F1 $ Variance to budget F2 % of SG&A dedicated to analytical versus transactional activities

C2: Enhanced economic profit through value-added analysis. Finance will support the business customers in their efforts to maintain and grow the profitability of the company. This support is provided through the thorough investigation and useful analysis of business-related information to facilitate proactive business initiatives. Finance must focus its limited resources in areas that capitalize on enhanced value for its customers.

C3: Appropriate strategic communications. The finance communications plan will increase the company's price/earnings multiple by employing disciplined practices of clear and visible external communications of the company's strategy.

C4: Clear and reliable required disclosure. Finance will provide reliable financial information for investors and creditors to make decisions. This information must meet regulatory standards for accuracy and timeliness.

The second customer objective, C2, links the finance group to the success of the business units. With this objective, the finance group commits to working closely with the business units, as their economic partner, to help them increase their economic profits.

The four customer objectives are driven by eleven internal process objectives, organized by three themes: internal transaction services, business unit services, and external compliance and communication. The key internal processes, within the business unit services theme, for becoming an economic partner are as follows:

I8: Identify and evaluate compelling growth opportunities. Finance will play the leading role in helping Handleman grow by acquisitions or partnerships with other firms that can provide quicker and more effective access to new customers, new markets, or new content and suppliers. In addition, finance will identify strategic transactions that expand the company into new businesses, such as rebundling existing offerings, growing the online business, or entering other entertainment or nonentertainment product lines.

I9: Develop financial information to improve decision making. Finance, to enhance business managers' decision making, will migrate from a primarily transactions-based organization to one that is analytical. This will allow finance to provide the delivery of timely, useful, and fact-based financial information.

The first two "people and knowledge" objectives in the finance Strategy Map are to develop the competencies necessary for the new finance strategy to be implemented, and to retain the experienced, trained, high-performance members of the finance staff. The third objective, "cultivate an aligned culture," links to the business partnership theme by highlighting the need for those in the finance function to work together to help the business achieve its growth and profitability objectives:

P3: Cultivate an aligned culture. To make the maximum contribution to achievement of the corporate and finance strategy, the finance organization needs to be focused in the same direction. Silos within the functional finance areas need to be eliminated. We are a team, with each individual playing a part in achieving our strategy. We must all understand how we contribute to the finance Strategy Map and must take accountability for our part of the plan. To create this alignment, we will, when necessary, modify our processes, including our compensation systems, internal communications processes, and organizational structure.

The Handleman Strategy Map and accompanying Balanced Scorecard provide an excellent example of the challenges facing a twenty-first-century finance organization. It must continue to excel at its traditional roles of transaction processing, internal controls, external communications, and compliance while also developing the skills and a new culture to forge strategic partnerships with business units, helping them create and sustain higher shareholder value.

CLOSING THE LOOP

We have illustrated how to develop Strategy Maps and Balanced Scorecards that align support units with business units and the enterprise. Alignment, however, must be actively managed as an ongoing process, and not just described with maps and scorecards. As illustrated in Figure 5-16, an effective alignment process for a support unit includes the following components.

- A *relationship manager* from the support unit, responsible for the alignment
- An integrated planning process, in which the support unit participates, that defines the unit's role to support business unit objectives

Figure 5-16 Closing the Loop: A Process to Achieve Support Unit Alignment

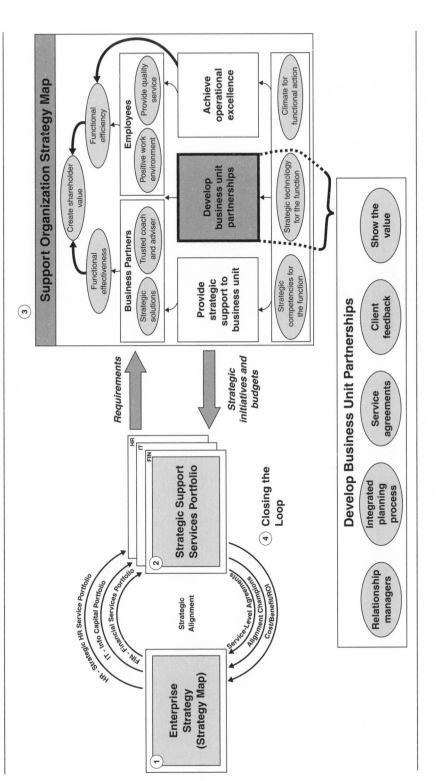

•. *Service agreements* that define the support unit's deliverables, service levels, and costs, including *initiative owners* to ensure that each initiative in the strategic services portfolio is delivered effectively to the client, the business units

• *Internal customer feedback* sessions based on the service agreement

• *Assessment of costs and benefits* to validate the contribution of the support unit

Relationship Managers

The first step in building a business unit partnership is to assign someone to lead and manage the relationship. It's impossible to conceive of human resource consultants from Hewitt or information technology consultants from Accenture attempting to manage a client relationship without identifying a relationship manager. Yet, according to our research, only 33 percent of IT organizations and 43 percent of HR organizations follow the practice of assigning relationship managers to the business.[16]

IBM Learning (described in Chapter 4) started its alignment process with business units by appointing *learning leaders* to work with each major business unit. A *learning* leader had to understand the business unit strategy, translate that strategy to a Strategy Map, and educate the client on how training would enhance the strategy. The learning leader facilitated a planning process that identified learning solutions and coordinated their development and delivery. Through these activities, learning leaders forged a strategic partnership with their business unit counterparts.

J. D. Irving, a diverse family-owned conglomerate headquartered in New Brunswick, Canada, identified *alignment champions* that it assigned to each of eight major business groups. The alignment champions owned the process for developing, communicating, and reviewing business unit plans, measures, and incentives. These change agents helped business unit managers develop their leadership behavior, share best practices, and align their business units with corporate objectives.

Integrated Planning Process

Steps 1, 2, and 3 in Figure 5-17 describe an effective, integrated planning process for support units. The process assumes that business units already have Strategy Maps. If business units do not have a clear articulation of their strategies—one that can be translated into a Strategy Map—then alignment with support functions is considerably more

Figure 5-17 Service-Level Agreements and Customer Feedback Process

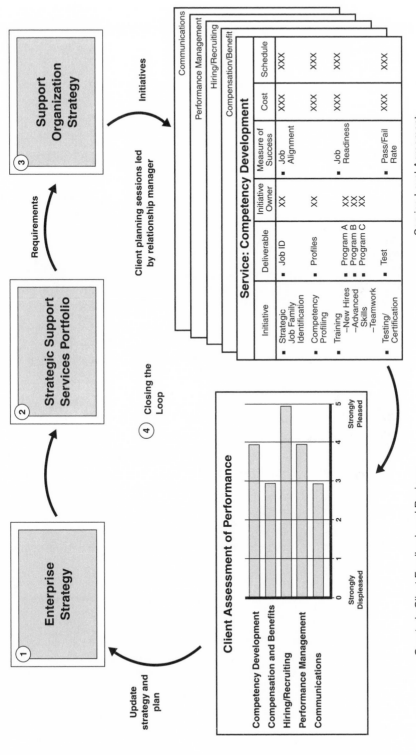

difficult. Relationship managers can be consultants to their business units, helping them to create Strategy Maps when they don't have one. Building Strategy Maps is an analytic, structured process that relationship managers can learn.

After a member of the human resources department of one organization helped a business unit manager build a Strategy Map of his business, the manager observed, "This is the best description of my strategy that I've ever seen. I never expected to learn something like this from our human resources department." The planning exercise was a clear step in establishing a professional partnership based on mutual respect.

Service Agreements and Client Feedback

The strategic planning process produces a set of initiatives for the support unit to develop and deliver for the business unit. These deliverables are the essential drivers of results in the business unit; for example, if an effective training program isn't prepared in time, employee skills will not be developed and the results of new programs, such as quality or sales, will be delayed.

The commitments to deliver the services or programs associated with the initiatives are frequently translated into *service agreements* that precisely define the support unit's deliverables. The service agreement provides the basis for managing the relationship between the business unit and the support unit and provides an explicit basis for accountability for results.

An *initiative owner* is assigned to help keep the support unit focused on delivering each approved initiative in its portfolio and fulfilling the service agreement. The initiative owner works with an assigned sponsor (or customer) from the line organization. The support unit's executive team manages its portfolio of strategic initiatives as an integrated portfolio, just as venture capital managers actively manage their portfolios of strategic investments. The executive team reviews the status of its strategic services portfolio each month and conducts detailed reviews of specific initiatives at least quarterly.

These monthly meetings promote a professional dialogue about the support unit's performance and about its shared responsibility with business units. One business unit manager commented, "These quarterly reviews allow us to see problems coming much sooner than in the past. We're working much better as a team, with less finger-pointing. This has pointed out that good performance from purchasing is a shared responsibility."

Costs and Benefits

Relationship managers must ultimately ensure that the services provided by their support units meet the objectives established by the business units they partner with. This goes beyond simply showing that initiatives, agreed to by both parties, were delivered on time and on budget. The support unit, led by the relationship manager, must accept shared responsibility for results with the line organizations. If the services don't produce results, then the support unit bears some of the responsibility.

We generally recommend that when organizations design an incentive compensation system, they base half of the bonuses of support unit staff on results achieved in the businesses they serve. This approach keeps everyone focused on success, as defined by the enterprise.

EXTENSIONS

We have described the strategic services portfolio and Strategy Maps of three key support units that virtually all organizations contain. Rather than a single chapter, we could devote a book to this subject to reflect the alignment of many other support units—such as purchasing, research and development, legal, treasury, real estate, environment, safety, quality, and marketing—with business unit and enterprise strategy. Even the big three we've covered in this chapter—human resources, information technology, and finance—typically have multiple departments that work on specialized functions.

For example, an enterprise IT group might include departments having specific responsibility for operations, technology, systems, applications, and security. Therefore, large support units need to use their group-level strategy as the basis for cascading strategy and scorecards down to their operating departments, just as the corporate strategy is cascaded down to business unit strategies.

SUMMARY

Support units contribute to organizational synergies when they align their activities with business unit and enterprise priorities. Although this statement may seem obvious, most organizations do a poor job of creating such alignment. Internal support units need to build new ways of managing that create partnerships and alignment with their internal customers. Such alignment constitutes the principal economic justification for retaining internal shared-services units rather than outsourcing their services to lower-cost providers.

In this chapter, we articulate the basic principles involved in aligning support units with enterprise and business unit strategies. Start by understanding and identifying the specific parts of the strategy that the support unit can influence. These objectives should appear as high-level objectives on the support unit scorecard (the linkage scorecard); they form the common thread between the business and the support unit.

Customer strategies build partnerships with the client (the customer solutions strategy most typically adopted by support units) and feature client objectives as high-level outcomes on the unit's Strategy Map. Internal process objectives can typically be represented via three strategic themes. One represents the low-cost, reliable, high-quality supply of basic, nondifferentiated services. Another addresses the building of business unit partnerships, and the third emphasizes the creation and delivery of innovative services that help business units succeed with their strategies.

The learning and growth objectives include providing support employees with the new skills, knowledge, and experience they need so that they can become trusted advisers to business unit managers. In this role they exploit new IT services and applications to deliver services more efficiently and effectively; to transform the culture from one focused on functional excellence to one focused on customers; and to deliver solutions that add value to business partner customers. With these guidelines in mind, organizations should be able to align their internal support units to participate in activities that create additional value and synergies for the enterprise.

NOTES

1. "Implementing the Balanced Scorecard at FMC Corporation: An Interview with Larry D. Brady," *Harvard Business Review* (September–October 1993): 146.
2. See "Responsibility Centers: Revenue and Expense Centers," Chapter 3 in R. Anthony and V. Govindarajan, *Management Control Systems*, 8th edition (Chicago: Irwin, 1995), 107–123.
3. At least one critic, however, would dispute this statement; see N. Carr, "IT Doesn't Matter," *Harvard Business Review* (May 2003).We, with others, respectfully disagree and believe that effective alignment of the IT resource with strategy can be a distinctive source of value creation.
4. P. Weill and M. Broadbent, *Leveraging the New Infrastructure: How Market Leaders Capitalize on Information Technology* (Boston: Harvard Business School Press, 1998), 37–39.
5. Cassandra Frangos, a colleague of ours at the Balanced Scorecard Collaborative, has been a major contributor to our knowledge of building human resources Strategy Maps and Balanced Scorecards.

6. "Motivating Cross-Boundary Thinking at Ingersoll-Rand," Balanced Scorecard Report (March 2005).

7. Robert S. Gold, a colleague of ours at the Balanced Scorecard Collaborative, has been a major contributor to our knowledge of building information technology Strategy Maps and Balanced Scorecards.

8. The motivation for this work comes from F. Herzberg's adaptation of the hierarchical needs model of A. Maslow, *Motivation and Personality,* 3rd edition (New York: HarperCollins, 1987). The concept of first satisfying hygiene factors (i.e., competency) before addressing motivation (i.e., contribution) was articulated in F. Herzberg, B. Mausner, and B. Snyderman, *The Motivation to Work,* 2nd edition (New York: Wiley, 1959).

9. R. S. Gold, "Enabling the Strategy-Focused IT Organization," *Balanced Scorecard Report* (September–October 2001).

10. Arun Dhingra and Michael Nagel, colleagues of ours at the Balanced Scorecard Collaborative, have been major contributors to our knowledge of building finance unit Strategy Maps and Balanced Scorecards.

11. "The CFO as Chief Performance Adviser," report prepared by CFO Research Services in collaboration with PriceWaterhouseCoopers LLP, CFO Publishing Corporation, Boston, March 2005.

12. V. Couto, I. Heinz, and M. Moran, "Not Your Father's CFO," *Strategy + Business* (Spring 2005): 4.

13. Ibid., 4.

14. Ibid., 10.

15. Observe that Handleman's finance unit has chosen to place its financial perspective at the base, and not the pinnacle, of its Strategy Map. This illustrates our earlier discussion of the option to treat support units as nonprofit organizations, stressing service to clients and customer objectives as the top-level objectives.

16. SHRM/Balanced Scorecard Collaborative, "Aligning HR with Organization Strategy," survey research study 62-17052 (Alexandria, VA: Society for Human Resources Management, 2002); "The Alignment Gap," *CIO Insight,* 1 July 2002.

CHAPTER SIX

CASCADING
THE PROCESS

PREVIOUS CHAPTERS ARTICULATE theory and discuss examples of how to align business and support units with a corporate strategy. Corporations follow different paths to achieve enterprise-wide alignment. Some start at the top, at the corporate level, and then cascade sequentially down the organizational hierarchy. Others start in the middle, at the business unit level, before building a corporate scorecard and map. Some launch an enterprise-wide initiative right at the start, and others conduct a pilot test at one or two business units before extending the scope to other enterprise units.

In our experience, there is not a single correct answer. We have seen multiple approaches used, each of which ended up with a successful implementation. In this chapter we describe the principles we have learned about the cascading process and illustrate it with examples from successful adopters.

We start with two simple and polar examples: franchise operations, for which the decentralized units deliver a common value proposition; and holding companies, in which the individual operating companies are autonomous, each having its own strategy and value proposition. We then consider the more complex situation in which decentralized operating units have strategies that simultaneously reflect corporate priorities and local situations.

We close the chapter with an extended example from Bank of Tokyo-Mitsubishi. This implementation seemingly breaks the rules but was still highly successful. This case study illustrates that the cascading process, although informed by general principles, can and should be customized to each organization's culture and situation.

FRANCHISE OPERATIONS:
TOP-DOWN COMMON VALUE PROPOSITIONS

Consider first the scorecard development in corporations consisting of homogeneous retail or geographic units, such as quick service restaurant outlets, hotels and motels, branch banks, and regional distribution centers (as discussed in Chapter 3). For these enterprises, a corporate-level project team develops the scorecard that will be used at each decentralized unit. The common scorecard reflects the financial metrics for each outlet, including the mix between revenue growth and cost improvement; the customer measures of satisfaction, retention, and unit sales growth; the customer value proposition; the metrics for critical internal processes and for employee satisfaction, retention, and capabilities; information systems deployment; and organization culture. Once determined, the common scorecard is communicated to all units and embedded in their reporting and incentive systems.

The benefits of deploying a common value proposition and scorecard across homogeneous units are apparent. First, the process is simple. Once the corporate project team has determined the Strategy Map and associated Balanced Scorecard of measures and targets, these can be quickly deployed throughout the organization. No further analysis or work at local, decentralized levels is required.

Second, the company can easily communicate the common message through speeches, newsletters, Web sites, and postings on bulletin boards. Every employee in every location receives the same, consistent message.

Third, the common measures foster a spirit of internal competition. They facilitate internal benchmarking and best-practice sharing. With every unit following the same strategy and using the same metrics to measure the success of the strategy, the company can identify the leaders and the laggards in any particular measure and then share the information from the best to raise the performance of everyone else.

But there are some downsides in deploying a common corporate value proposition across the organization. Inevitably, the process will feel top-down and authoritarian because little discretion is left to local units. The initial response from many units, long suffering from having to react to short-lived corporate improvement initiatives, will be denial: "This too will pass; let's wait it out." The units will be skeptical that the corporate headquarters is truly committed to its new Balanced Scorecard initiative.

Assuming, however, that the corporate executives sustain the initiative, many units will move from the denial stage to the "medicinal" stage: when forced to consume bad-tasting medicine that our parents and doctor insist is good for us, let's do it quickly and get it over with. At this stage, the units are in compliance mode. They do the reporting mechanically, at the end of each period, to satisfy the corporate desire for more performance measures. The units see this as a no-win initiative. If their performance is viewed as acceptable, then they will be left alone for another period, but they will still have incurred the cost to produce data about the new performance measures. If, however, their performance is viewed as substandard, then they will be found out, asked to supply explanations, and forced to take corrective actions.

In both the denial and the medicinal stage, the decentralized units are not using the Strategy Map and Balanced Scorecard to generate benefits within their local organizations. They are not mobilizing their employees to achieve the corporate goals, not aligning their departments and functions with the common strategy, not educating and motivating their employees to support the strategy, and not embedding strategic focus on the recurring management processes of planning, budgeting, allocating resources, reporting, evaluating, and adapting.

Corporate executives face the challenge of getting the managers of all the decentralized units to appreciate how they can use the common Strategy Map and Balanced Scorecard to align their processes, departments, and people to deliver the common value proposition. Corporate leaders need to persuade local managers about the benefits of having each unit reinforce the value being created at every other unit in the corporation.

At Ann Taylor, a women's fashion apparel retail chain, each unit had employees create and perform skits relating to the strategic objectives and measures on the common scorecard. Some employees wrote poems, others staged miniplays that portrayed the targeted customer and her buying experience, and still others composed and performed rap songs in ensemble groups. In this way, each employee studied the strategy, internalized it in his or her own way, and had fun performing and watching the creative talents of other employees and supervisors. Even though the common value proposition had been determined at the corporate level, the local performances and games mobilized supervisors and employees and created energy for contributing to the common value proposition.

HOLDING COMPANIES: BOTTOM-UP

In contrast to the top-down cascading process used by corporations with homogeneous retail outlets, scorecard projects in diversified corporations typically start at the operating company level, at least one level below corporate. For example, at the diversified FMC Corporation, senior corporate executives initiated the project by identifying six of FMC's operating companies to "volunteer" to be the pilots. Corporate provided resources for consultants, but each company developed its own independent scorecard.

Several months later, at a corporate meeting attended by executives from all the FMC companies, the presidents of the pilot companies reported on what they had learned from their projects, generating enthusiasm among all the other operating companies for implementing the new management system. By the end of the year, each operating company had its own scorecard that had been approved by senior corporate management.

Once developed, the FMC operating company scorecards became the accountability contract between corporate headquarters and the operating companies. BSCs provide the agenda and content for discussions at the quarterly meetings of headquarters executives and management of each operating company.

Before the scorecard was introduced, discussions between FMC corporate and operating company executives were about financial measures only, such as return on capital employed (ROCE) and its components. If operating company executives were hitting their ROCE targets, discussions were pleasant and relatively short. If executives fell short on ROCE targets, discussions were longer and more difficult. With the scorecard, in contrast, executives still discussed financial performance, but they also discussed nonfinancial measures that predicted future profitability and growth.

Each operating company scorecard was different. The different scorecards could not be aggregated together into a corporate scorecard, except for the financial measures, which tended to be common across the operating companies. Despite the variety in scorecards, corporate executives found it easy to prepare for a meeting with each operating company. They reviewed the unit's approved strategy and scorecard and then assessed its current performance against approved targets.

Also, the corporate executives now felt they "owned" the strategy at each operating company. If the company CEO left, voluntarily or involuntarily, the replacement CEO did not have free rein to introduce an entirely new strategy for the unit. The baseline case was for the new CEO to continue to execute the strategy that had been previously proposed by and approved for the unit. New business unit CEOs who wanted to modify the strategy or introduce an entirely new one would first develop a new Strategy Map and BSC with their organizational units and then take these to corporate for approval. This process provided a more systematic way throughout the organization for the autonomous units to have the initiative and responsibility for their strategies while still giving the corporate parent a tool to control and assess operating company performance in formulating and implementing their strategies.

FMC operated for several years in this manner before finally producing a corporate-level scorecard that, not surprisingly, contained mostly financial and employee (learning and growth) measures. It also included several internal process measures, primarily related to safety, that each organizational unit would include in its local Balanced Scorecard.

In summary, scorecards in highly diversified corporations rarely start at the corporate level because no corporate-level strategy typically exists. Each operating company develops its own strategy and accompanying scorecard, which corporate executives approve and subsequently use to monitor operating company performance. At some point, the corporate parent develops a corporate-level scorecard to aggregate the financial and employee measures of the autonomous units, and also to articulate corporate-level themes—such as excelling at safety, quality, or the environment—that are then incorporated into scorecard measures at each operating company.

HYBRID CASCADING PROCESSES

Most organizations, operating between the two polar cases of identical decentralized units and highly diversified corporations, can choose from two implementation paths. One is a classic top-down process in which the initial Strategy Map and Balanced Scorecard are done at the corporate level, followed by scorecards at each business and support unit that implements the corporate-level strategy and scorecard measures.

The second approach is more bottom-up, with pilot projects performed at the business unit level to develop local Strategy Maps and BSCs. These projects build knowledge and confidence about the management tool, and only subsequently is the project taken up to the corporate level for an explicit articulation of the corporate value proposition.

TOP-DOWN CASE STUDY: U.S. ARMY

The prime example of an effective top-down cascading process, not surprisingly, was done at a large, hierarchical, and highly integrated organization: the U.S. Army. The Army Balanced Scorecard, which it called the Strategic Readiness System, was launched in early 2002, after approval at the highest organizational level: the chief of staff of the Army (CSA) and the secretary of the Army (SA).

The first scorecard, referred to as the level 0 scorecard, reflected the global Army strategy (see Figure 6-1). The scorecard defined the mission in terms of two core competencies: "train and equip soldiers and grow leaders" and "provide relevant and ready land power capability to the combatant [field] commanders and the joint team." Instead of customers, the U.S. Army had stakeholders—U.S. citizens, Congress, and the executive branch—for which it identified six key capabilities: shape the security environment, execute prompt response, mobilize the army, conduct forcible entry, sustain land dominance, and support civil authorities.

The internal process perspective was organized by four strategic themes:

- Adjust the global footprint.
- Develop a joint interdependent logistics structure.
- Build the future force.
- Optimize reserve component contributions.

The learning and growth perspective emphasized objectives for people that would sustain a capable, all-volunteer force. And, instead of a financial perspective, the Army used a resources perspective to reflect its ability to obtain the people, funds, infrastructure, installation, and institutions, within a reasonable time period, to carry out its mission.

The Army project team completed the level 0 scorecard within three months, and the CSA and SA approved it in April 2002. In the next step (see Figure 6-2), the level 0 scorecard was cascaded out to level 1 units that reported directly up to the CSA. Level 1 units consisted of thirty-five major Army commands and staff directorates, such as medical, personnel, and logistics. The level 0 scorecard provided the strategic framework and guidance to these thirty-five units. Each command and directorate defined its strategic priorities in support of the Army as well as those that fulfilled its local mission.

A new headquarters unit, the SRS Operations Center (SRSOC), led the cascading process and served as a centralized consulting unit for the

Figure 6-1 U.S. Army Strategy Map

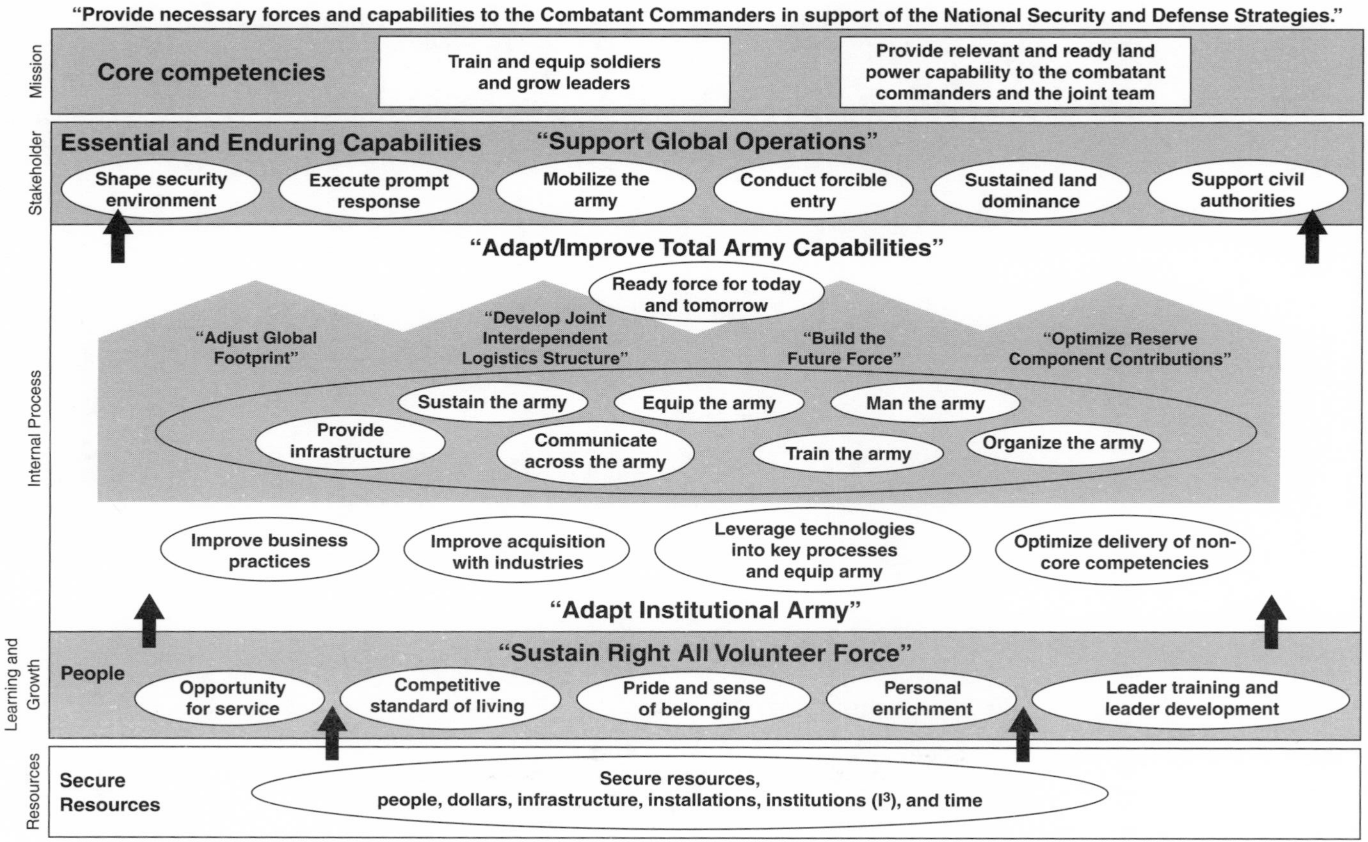

"Provide necessary forces and capabilities to the Combatant Commanders in support of the National Security and Defense Strategies."

Core competencies	Train and equip soldiers and grow leaders	Provide relevant and ready land power capability to the combatant commanders and the joint team

Essential and Enduring Capabilities "Support Global Operations"

- Shape security environment
- Execute prompt response
- Mobilize the army
- Conduct forcible entry
- Sustained land dominance
- Support civil authorities

"Adapt/Improve Total Army Capabilities"

"Adjust Global Footprint"

"Develop Joint Interdependent Logistics Structure"

- Provide infrastructure
- Sustain the army
- Communicate across the army
- Equip the army

"Build the Future Force"

Ready force for today and tomorrow

- Train the army
- Man the army
- Organize the army

"Optimize Reserve Component Contributions"

- Improve business practices
- Improve acquisition with industries
- Leverage technologies into key processes and equip army
- Optimize delivery of non-core competencies

"Adapt Institutional Army"

"Sustain Right All Volunteer Force"

- Opportunity for service
- Competitive standard of living
- Pride and sense of belonging
- Personal enrichment
- Leader training and leader development

People

Secure Resources — Secure resources, people, dollars, infrastructure, installations, institutions (I3), and time

Mission

Stakeholder

Internal Process

Learning and Growth

Resources

Figure 6-2 Cascading the Balanced Scorecard Throughout the Army

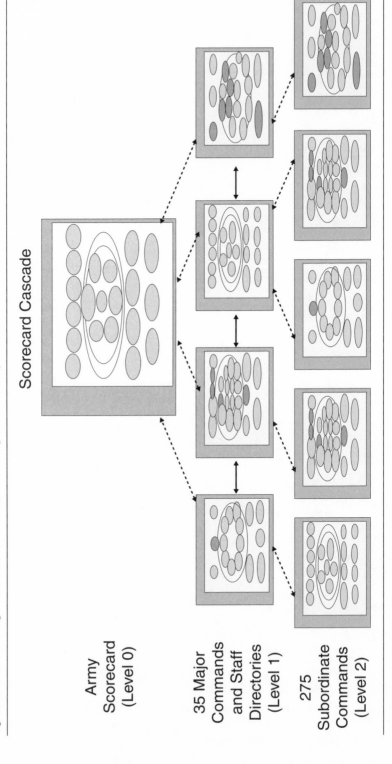

Scorecard Cascade

Army
Scorecard
(Level 0)

35 Major
Commands
and Staff
Directories
(Level 1)

275
Subordinate
Commands
(Level 2)

project. Consisting of a core team of Balanced Scorecard experts, the SRSOC provided guidance, expertise, training, technology support, and quality control for the BSC rollout throughout the Army. The SRSOC led a two-day training class, which eventually reached four hundred BSC project leaders, on the basics of BSC methodology and the Army level 0 scorecard.

Each major command BSC team worked with its leadership to capture strategic priorities and built the Balanced Scorecard using an online tool, the SRS Design Center Express. This design support tool provided multimedia instruction, templates, and alignment with Army objectives and measures. Status reports generated by the Design Center enabled the SRSOC to keep level 1 teams working within specified time frames. The SRSOC held weekly conference calls that included question-and-answer sessions, and it established two checkpoints at which each unit had to submit its Strategy Map and Balanced Scorecard measures for peer review.

The senior officers in each major operating command and staff directorate approved their unit's Balanced Scorecard and then submitted it to the CSA for review. The CSA used this as an opportunity to discuss strategic direction with commanders undergoing organizational change.

The next cascade, down to the 275 level 2 organizations, was executed in a similar manner as with the level 1 organizations. The key difference was that level 2 organizations received their support from operations centers established at each level 1 organization. The level 1 operations centers were responsible for quality control, questions and answers, Design Center support, time-line monitoring, and general program oversight. The headquarters (level 0) SRSOC provided support when a level 1 operations center required assistance. By establishing individual level 1 operations centers, the project accelerated knowledge transfer and generated buy in at the field level. The training and online SRS Design Center Express enabled all 275 level 2 organizations to develop their Balanced Scorecards in parallel. One further cascading level still remained. Eventually, individual divisions and separate brigades, consisting of around ten thousand soldiers, would have their own scorecards.

Army officers now use the Balanced Scorecard to conduct regular strategic resourcing review meetings with their general officers, senior civilian leaders, and other team members. The SRS BSC enabled each team to evaluate recent unit performance in a way that cut across organizational silos (e.g., logistics, operations, medical, training, and other staff areas). People from different organizations within the Army had easy access to scorecard data and aligned quickly around issues that connected the various organizations. Put simply, the scorecard enabled the Army to "get the right people in the room" when issues cropped up.

The Army Balanced Scorecard gives the leadership accurate, objective, predictive, and actionable readiness information to dramatically enhance strategic resource management. For the first time in its history the Army has an enterprise management system that integrates readiness information from active and reserve field and staff, thereby enabling the Army to improve support to combatant commanders, to invest in soldiers and their families, to identify and adopt sound business practices, and to transform the Army. By gathering timely information with precision and expanding the scope of the data considered, this reporting system markedly improves how the Army measures readiness. The Army is further developing this system to leverage leading indicators and predict trends, avoiding issues that affect readiness before they become problems.

In addition to the benefits realized at the top level of leadership, individual commands have extracted tremendous value from the BSC. The individual units have been able to more effectively meet their mission-essential task lists and simultaneously focus on readiness and overall transformation toward the objective force of the future.

TOP-TO-MIDDLE AND MIDDLE-TO-TOP CASE STUDY:
MDS CORPORATION

A slightly different process was followed by MDS Corporation, a diversified enterprise. MDS also followed an initial top-down process but because its operating units were autonomous, the corporate-level strategy was not fully developed in the first formulation of the corporate Balanced Scorecard. Once operating units developed their maps and scorecards, the corporate team updated its scorecard and selected measures that then became common throughout all units.

MDS Corporation, headquartered in Toronto, is an international health and life sciences company that provides products and services for the prevention, diagnosis, and treatment of disease. With locations in twenty-three countries, MDS employs more than ten thousand people and had fiscal 2004 revenues of $1.8 billion. MDS is a diversified company operating through four major business sectors: MDS Isotopes supplies imaging agents for nuclear medicine, material for sterilization systems, and therapy systems for planning and delivery of cancer treatment; MDS Diagnostics provides laboratory information and services to prevent, diagnose, and treat illness; MDS Sciex supplies advanced analytic instruments, such as mass spectrometers; and MDS Pharma Services provides contract research and drug development services to the pharmaceutical industry, along with pioneering the development of functional proteomics in finding completely new ways to discover drugs.

From 1973 to 2002, sales increased at a 20 percent cumulative annual growth rate, and earnings increased at a 16 percent CAGR. Clearly, MDS was not a company in crisis; it did not have a burning platform. MDS launched a Balanced Scorecard project to transform itself from "good to great" by focusing on the most important value-creating activities and achieving more alignment throughout its diverse business units. The MDS corporate team started by asserting what it would not change. It would retain its core values—"integrity, commitment to excellence, mutual trust and a genuine concern and respect for people"—and referenced the importance of embedding the core values in all aspects of corporate life as the foundation of its Strategy Map.

MDS placed its vision—"to build an enduring global health and life science company"—at the pinnacle of its corporate Strategy Map. MDS's goal of going global required expanding well beyond its historic Canadian and North American base. MDS also included a statement of its values— "passionate about the kind of company we are building together"—within its financial perspective (see Figure 6-3). These statements of vision, values, and purpose would endure even with the new strategy MDS wanted to define to stimulate organizational growth and change.

The enterprise Strategy Map incorporated explicit financial measures and targets to maintain MDS as a profitable, high-growth company. The learning and growth objectives also reflected corporate-wide priorities about people and systems. MDS corporate selected four general customer themes, each supported by several customer and internal process objectives. To allow its diverse business units the freedom and initiative to individually define how they created value, MDS deferred selecting measures for customer and internal process objectives. This by itself was a corporate revelation because it was the first time that the corporate management process recognized that business units, and not the corporate headquarters, created most of the value.

In cascading the enterprise Strategy Map, MDS identified eleven business units as its most strategic. These units had direct contact with customers and clients. Corporate asked those business units to develop Strategy Maps and Balanced Scorecards and to cascade these down to their departments and people. Corporate BSC coordinator Bob Harris selected a BSC process owner in each business unit and worked with these process owners to maintain consistency in format and terminology and to share learning throughout projects. Each business unit developed its own

Figure 6-3 Original MDS Corporate Strategy Map

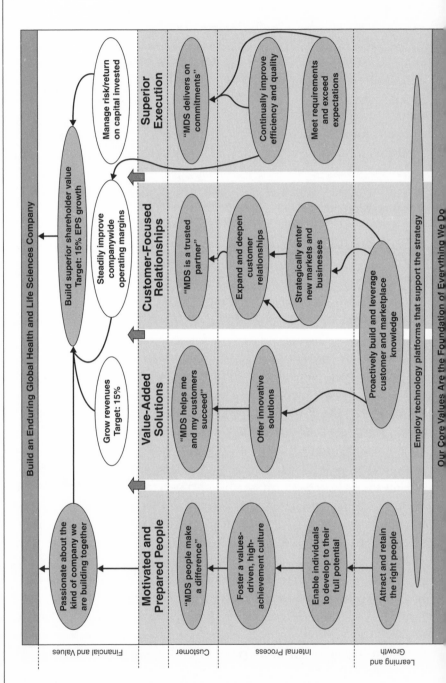

customer value proposition, choosing between low cost, customer intimacy, and product leadership.

The corporate headquarters initially struggled to define how it and the rest of the organization added value beyond that created by the eleven strategic business units. Eventually it concluded that the headquarters added value by top-down leadership and direction using its structure of four operating divisions (isotopes, diagnostics, late and early stage pharmaceutical services), by direct corporate support of basic R&D, and by an infrastructure of shared services.

With the basic alignment structure now in place (see Figure 6-4), the corporate project team revisited the corporate Strategy Map. During this revision, corporate reduced the number of objectives on its map from eighteen to twelve (see Figure 6-5).

The first corporate map was too specific, and several of the business units had adopted the four high-level corporate customer objectives without defining the specific customer value proposition that created differentiation for their unit. The new corporate map reflected the understanding that corporate headquarters did not have customers; only business units had customers. Corporate therefore selected only one highly generic customer objective for its map, "build enduring relationships," making it clear that each business unit had to select the specific customer value proposition that would enable it to build enduring customer relationships.

The corporate leadership also now selected measures for each corporate objective and assigned a corporate executive to be responsible and accountable for achieving targeted performance for that measure. The corporate measures and targets provided clear guidance for common measures and associated targets for each business unit scorecard. The corporate role was not to treat its business units as "customers." The corporation owned the business units; it would set priorities and targets for the business units and would provide support to help the business units achieve targeted performance. Occasionally, corporate would intervene when it saw that a corporate priority—say, for innovation—required corporate funding for cross-unit or basic research beyond what an individual business unit could justify solely for its own performance. The corporate business development unit would find and fund acquisitions that it felt would benefit multiple business units. These interventions were based on objectives either on the corporate Balanced Scorecard or those of its shared-service units, such as corporate business development.

These two case studies illustrate two quite different approaches, yet each worked well for its organization and culture. The U.S. Army used a

Figure 6-4 Complete MDS Alignment

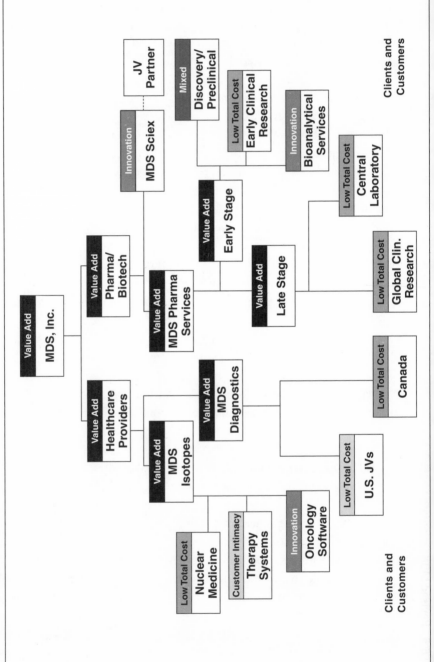

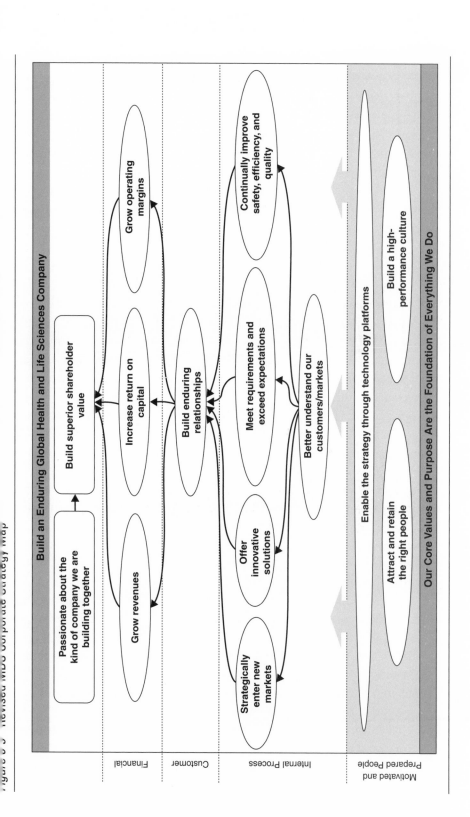

Figure 8-3 Revised MBO Corporate Strategy Map

Build an Enduring Global Health and Life Sciences Company

Financial

- Passionate about the kind of company we are building together
- Build superior shareholder value
- Grow operating margins
- Increase return on capital
- Grow revenues

Customer

- Build enduring relationships

Internal Process

- Strategically enter new markets
- Offer innovative solutions
- Meet requirements and exceed expectations
- Better understand our customers/markets
- Continually improve safety, efficiency, and quality

Motivated and Prepared People

- Attract and retain the right people
- Enable the strategy through technology platforms
- Build a high-performance culture

Our Core Values and Purpose Are the Foundation of Everything We Do

classic top-down approach. The corporate strategy was determined at the top and then cascaded down to lower-level operating units, where the maps and scorecards of the decentralized units simultaneously reflected corporate themes and priorities as well as their local missions and challenges. MDS used a more iterative approach. Headquarters first framed a preliminary corporate Strategy Map, and then operating and support units developed their own maps and scorecards. After this first round of scorecard development, headquarters revisited and revised the corporate Strategy Map and BSC and then cascaded common measures back down to local operating and support units.

CAN BUSINESS UNITS GO FIRST?

Many implementations of the BSC and Strategy Map do not start at the corporate level. The first scorecard might be built at a division or business unit level for two reasons. First, the corporation may want to pilot the concept at a local unit to gain knowledge, experience, credibility, and enthusiasm before launching a major project to develop and cascade scorecards across the entire enterprise.

Second, and more typically, the zeal to build and use a Balanced Scorecard as a strategy management system may not exist at the corporate headquarters. The enthusiasm for the concept may originate at a local business, geographic, or support unit. Following the ideas presented in the book so far, the local missionary may feel that she should first convince the senior corporate executive team of the benefits of the scorecard system so that it can be launched and sponsored at the top. Such a conversion to a new measurement and management concept, however, may take years if not decades. Few of us have the patience to wait for insight to burst forth spontaneously from the executive suite.

Our recommended course is to build the initial scorecard where the leadership and enthusiasm for it exist. Often this is at a local unit. But this approach may lead to a suboptimal local strategy. The unit's strategy may reflect the best thinking about how it can create value through exploiting competitive opportunities in its local markets, but it may not be the strategy that adds the highest value to the corporation because it ignores links and opportunities for integration with other units in the organization.

The solution to this apparent dilemma, however, is simple. Early in the formative stages of the local project, representatives from the team should travel to corporate headquarters and meet with, say, the chief operating officer and the chief financial officer. The team members describe the project they have just launched and ask for guidance from the COO and CFO using some version of the following script:

Where do we fit within the corporate-level strategy? As we develop our strategy, our map, and our scorecard, what corporate priorities should we consider? Which corporate-level themes should we be sure to incorporate? Are there links or integration with other business units that we should be aware of as we develop our strategy and performance measures?

The answers to these questions do not require that a corporate-level Strategy Map and BSC exist. They require only that the senior executive team have a clear corporate-level strategy that provides a framework to describe how local business units should operate to create synergies across the organization.

So the hoped-for reply to the questions might describe the nature of the customer value proposition that the local unit should be attempting to deliver, important global customers to be featured, the need for cross-selling to shared customers of other units, and the importance of leveraging a central resource or capability, developing people, or creating databases and knowledge that can be shared with other units. The response might include corporate-level themes for excellence in quality, safety, environmental impact, or e-commerce. Informed by this corporate-level response, the project team members can return to the local unit and embed the corporate priorities, links, and opportunities for integration into their unit's Strategy Map and Balanced Scorecard.

Of course, an alternative response from the senior executives would be to dismiss the question as irrelevant:

Don't bother us with all this jargon about corporate-level strategy and common customer value propositions. We're not populated at headquarters with a lot of MBAs or ex-consultants. Just go out there and make money. That's what corporate wants.

The team members conclude, "OK, no corporate strategy here. We are free to adopt any strategy we want, as long as it delivers the financial results." In this case, the local unit develops its own Strategy Map and BSC without explicit guidance from corporate (other than "The strategy had better work"). But at least they tried to identify synergy opportunities, even if rebuffed.

We hope that in either case, the local unit will develop a great scorecard that helps it implement its strategy rapidly and effectively and soon enjoys considerable financial success. As knowledge and confidence grow about how the scorecard facilitates effective strategy execution, the concept can migrate horizontally to other business units and vertically to the division and eventually the corporation. The key guiding principle, when people are developing the first scorecard at the local level, is to incorporate, as best they can, the opportunities for value creation by linking with other business units and shared services in ways that enhance the value created by the local unit by effective execution of its strategy.

We have seen examples where the first scorecard was built in a shared-service unit, such as human resources or information technology. This can certainly be a successful approach, but only when the shared-service unit understands the strategies of the operating units and the corporation sufficiently well that it can articulate a strategy for itself that directly helps the corporation and business units achieve their strategic objectives.

In one international automobile company, the first scorecard in the company was built for the IT group for European operations. The IT group played a central role in the operations of the eight independent product-line units in the region, so it felt confident it understood the strategies of these eight operating units. When the eight product-line units learned about the IT scorecard initiative and observed it in practice, they decided they wanted Balanced Scorecards, too. The IT BSC project team soon became the lead project team for the projects in the eight European units.

Eventually, news of the initiative drifted to corporate headquarters, and the person from IT who had helped to launch the project in his local department got the assignment to be the corporate-level resource for worldwide deployment of a Balanced Scorecard management system. Although this is not necessarily the recommended sequence for cascading scorecards throughout the organization, it certainly is a feasible one and one that allows enthusiasm and commitment to develop from the grass-roots level rather than being imposed from the top.

MIDDLE-TO-TOP-DOWN:
THE BANK OF TOKYO-MITSUBISHI, HEADQUARTERS
FOR THE AMERICAS

Our final example seemingly breaks the rules, but eventually it worked out fine. The Bank of Tokyo-Mitsubishi, Headquarters for the Americas (BTMHQA), based in New York, focuses on wholesale banking in North and South America. It has offices in twenty-three cities in nine countries in the region. It contains four major business units—treasury, global corporate banking, investment banking, and the corporate center—each with multiple divisions and groups. Each major business unit has a dual reporting relationship; it reports directly to a business unit headquarters in Tokyo and to the regional (Americas) headquarters in New York City.

BTMHQA adopted the Balanced Scorecard to provide a common strategic framework that would overcome differences between the Japanese and American cultures (see Figure 6-6). The BSC would also create horizontal alignment across the four major business groups, and vertical alignment up to regional headquarters and down to the geographical branches throughout the Americas.

At the start of the project, in the third quarter of 2001, senior executives at BTMHQA headquarters resisted articulating a corporate-level strategy and developing a corporate Strategy Map and Balanced Scorecard. Even though the various divisions and groups within BTMHQA shared customers and processes, the executives explained that in a Japanese company strategy is done bottom-up, not top-down. The BTMHQA senior executives told the project team, "If you want to know the strategy, go directly to the people."

The headquarters project team proceeded by directing and assisting personnel in each of the more than thirty BTMHQA groups and departments to build their own Strategy Maps. The exercise typically took a unit about thirty days, and in many cases only one or two individuals, working independently, performed the task.

Upon completion of the more than thirty Strategy Maps, the headquarters project team observed that beyond all scorecards having four perspectives, no unifying structure existed. On most of the maps, the internal process objectives did not identify the processes necessary for successful delivery of the customer value proposition. And, given the way they were constructed, few interdependencies were recognized across individual group Strategy Maps. Also, a key corporate priority—risk management—appeared in only a few group scorecards.

During the fourth quarter of 2001, the headquarters project team worked to synthesize the common ideas in the multiple Strategy Maps. The implicit strategy existed within them, but important features needed to be extracted and presented in a standardized format. The team developed a high-level template, a 4×3 matrix, to provide a common language that could be used to organize objectives in the four perspectives (see Figure 6-7). To remedy the insufficient attention paid to risk management in the initial maps, the team included, in the new template, an explicit financial perspective category related to risk outcomes, such as reduced credit and litigation losses; in the internal process perspective, it included an operating theme focused on risk-management processes.

Figure 6-6 Bank of Tokyo-Mitsubishi, Americas, Had to Bridge Two Distinct Cultures

Japanese Companies		American Companies
Vague	Mission and Vision	Defined
Incremental	Strategy Formulation Process	Grand Design
Operational Efficiency	Competitive Edge	Differentiation, Uniqueness
Bottom-Up (or Middle-Up-Down)	Decision Making	Top-Down
Implicit, Nonverbal, Closed	Communication Style	Explicit, Verbal, Open
Process Orientation	Performance Evaluation	Outcome Orientation
Single Culture, Cooperative	Work Culture	Diversified Culture, Competitive

Source: Adapted from I. Nonaka, "Essence of Failure," Tokyo: Diamond-Sha, 1984

Figure 6-7 Bank of Tokyo-Mitsubishi, Americas, Corporate Strategy Map Foundation

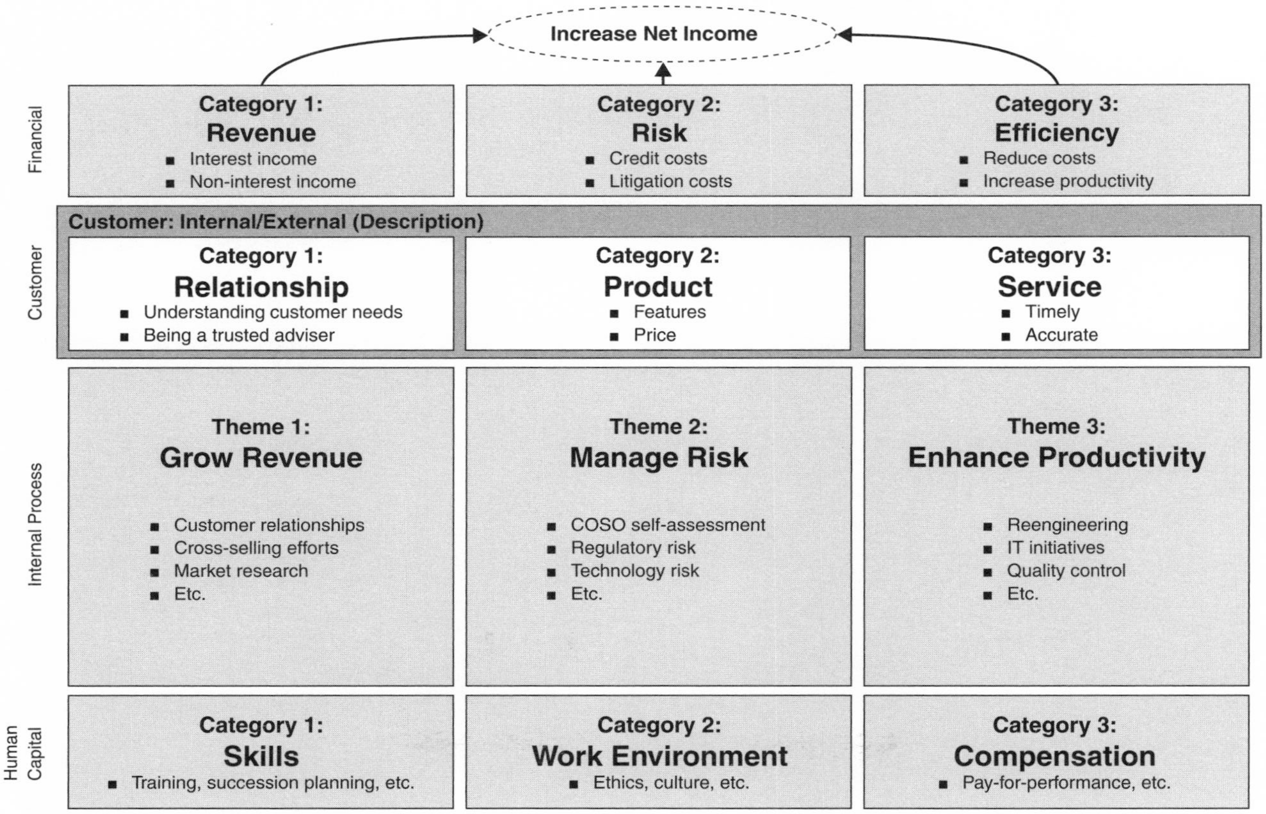

Increase Net Income

Financial

Category 1: **Revenue**	Category 2: **Risk**	Category 3: **Efficiency**
■ Interest income ■ Non-interest income	■ Credit costs ■ Litigation costs	■ Reduce costs ■ Increase productivity

Customer: Internal/External (Description)

Customer

Category 1: **Relationship**	Category 2: **Product**	Category 3: **Service**
■ Understanding customer needs ■ Being a trusted adviser	■ Features ■ Price	■ Timely ■ Accurate

Internal Process

Theme 1: **Grow Revenue**	Theme 2: **Manage Risk**	Theme 3: **Enhance Productivity**
■ Customer relationships ■ Cross-selling efforts ■ Market research ■ Etc.	■ COSO self-assessment ■ Regulatory risk ■ Technology risk ■ Etc.	■ Reengineering ■ IT initiatives ■ Quality control ■ Etc.

Human Capital

Category 1: **Skills**	Category 2: **Work Environment**	Category 3: **Compensation**
■ Training, succession planning, etc.	■ Ethics, culture, etc.	■ Pay-for-performance, etc.

The team introduced one more feature to ensure that each group recognized interdependencies with other units and to incorporate these on their revised scorecards. Each unit would code each objective in its revised Strategy Map as falling into one of three categories:

Type	*Definition*	*Example*
Common	Bankwide objectives, mandated throughout the organization on every scorecard	"Enhance cost efficiency" (financial perspective objective)
Shared	Interdivisional objectives shared between two or more units that were expected to cooperate to achieve the result	"Streamline credit approval process" (internal perspective operational efficiency objective)
Unique	Intradivisional objectives describing an activity expected to be fulfilled independently by that group	"Maintain knowledge of your customer files" (internal risk management theme objective for treasury)

For example, the shared objective "streamline the credit approval process" required the credit analysis group to work closely with the business development group. In the past, these two groups had operated independently. The credit analysis group saw as its objective, naturally, the need to minimize credit losses. Consequently, the credit approval group systematically turned down the new business being generated by the business development group. The new objective, shared between the two groups, communicated that the proper goal was to manage risk, not to eliminate it. For effective risk management, both business development and credit approval had to agree on criteria for acceptable risks so that new business could quickly and predictably be approved.

Each group used the strategic foundation of Figure 6-7 as a starting point to create a customized version for its situation. Each group rebuilt its Strategy Map so that its objectives now corresponded to the strategic themes in the corporate template, with each objective coded as to whether it was common across the corporation, shared with one or more other units, or unique to its own operations.

Figure 6-8 shows an example of a revised Strategy Map for the global corporate banking unit. The corporate template facilitated use of a

Figure 6-8 Redesigned BTMHQA Strategy Map (Example Banking Unit)

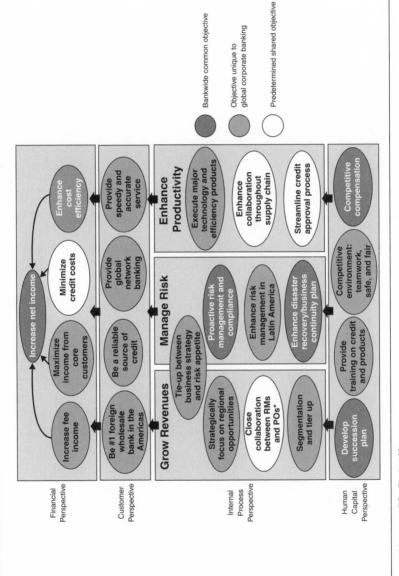

*RM - Relationship Managers, PO - Product Managers

centralized risk-management process across all units (as discussed in Chapter 4). The groups completed this process during the third quarter of 2002, and by the fourth quarter, the Balanced Scorecard management system was in place and operating.

By doing the project in the unusual sequence of business groups → corporate → business groups, the organization increased the time to reach an operational system to fifteen months. But the project sequence corresponded well with the corporate culture—which favored strategy emerging from the business groups, rather than corporate—so by the time the system was up and running, it was well accepted throughout the corporation.

News of the success of the Balanced Scorecard project in the Americas soon reached Tokyo, and in 2004 the worldwide corporate headquarters of Bank of Tokyo-Mitsubishi launched its own Balanced Scorecard project.

SUMMARY

An organization can cascade the Balanced Scorecard and Strategy Map management system top-down or bottom-up, but ultimately scorecard reporting, analysis, and decision making should be flowing in both directions. Starting with an enterprise Strategy Map and BSC is the textbook approach for aligning middle- and lower-level organizational units with corporate-level strategy. But many enterprises choose to start the scorecard at a business unit level to test and validate the concept and gain support from line and functional managers before deploying it enterprise-wide.

Most organizations eventually use an iterative process, starting with corporate guidelines for business unit Strategy Maps and scorecards but using the ideas emanating from the business units to revise the corporate map and scorecard. Pushing the scorecard down through the organization too hard and too early could lead to resentment and a backlash. Most organizations have found that flexibility is the key ingredient during the early stages of cascading. Once an organization is using the tool—following a process of regularly reporting on and talking about strategy—imposing corporate priorities from the top down becomes more acceptable.

CHAPTER SEVEN

ALIGNING BOARDS AND INVESTORS

IN PREVIOUS CHAPTERS, we discussed how Balanced Scorecards help to align and create synergies across internal business and support units (see the arrow at the left in Figure 7-1). With the increased emphasis on corporate governance, executives are now creating additional corporate value by using the Balanced Scorecard to enhance governance processes and to improve communication with shareholders (see the arrow at the right in Figure 7-1). As Jeff Immelt, CEO of General Electric, stated, "I want investors to know that they can trust us to govern our Company effectively. Then, they can judge GE by the quality of our business, our strategy, and our execution."[1]

Effective governance, disclosure, and communication reduce the risk that investors face when they entrust their capital to company managers. In this chapter, we show how companies can use the Balanced Scorecard to enhance their corporate governance and disclosure processes. Before illustrating this new application of the Balanced Scorecard, we introduce fundamental concepts in corporate governance.

GOVERNANCE 101

All market systems require intermediaries to help direct capital to its most productive opportunities and to monitor the performance of managers who have been granted capital by external investors.[2] Not all business ideas proposed by managers and entrepreneurs are "good" ideas that deserve funding. In the absence of valid information about business

Figure 7-1 The Balanced Scorecard Helps Organizations Manage the Value Creation Process at Each Level

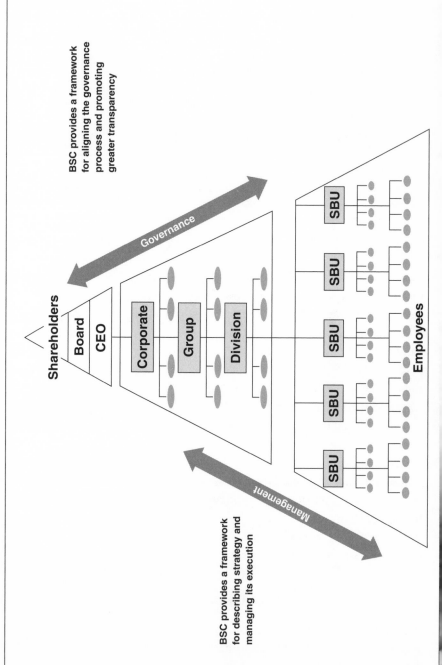

opportunities, investors cannot sort the good ideas proposed by company managers from the bad ideas.

This problem of hidden information—in which sellers (company managers) have much better information about their investment opportunities than buyers (potential investors)—arises in other markets as well. Consider the market for used cars. Prospective buyers often cannot get valid information from the seller about the condition of the car, and they do not have access to independent information about its quality. In this situation, sellers have superior information about the quality of the product or service being offered (called the *adverse selection* problem by economists).

Consequently, the used car buyer rationally assumes that the car is in bad condition and offers a price based on having to pay the cost to repair a lemon. Potential sellers of used cars that have been maintained in an excellent fashion will not be able to get full value for their vehicles and hence will not offer their cars for sale in such a market. The result is a poorly functioning market in which only low-quality products and services are offered for sale.

Extending this example to the capital market setting, if managers cannot credibly communicate the underlying value of their proposed projects, investors will not be willing to provide funds at a price that managers with excellent projects find attractive.[3] Thus, many high-return investment opportunities will not get funded.

Capital markets must also monitor how managers use the money that investors have provided them. Managers and investors do not have identical interests. Managers may make investments that increase the size of the company but not its profitability. Or, rather than pay dividends when good investments are not available, managers may retain cash to shield themselves from the discipline of justifying investments for future new projects.

Managers also can consume some portion of "other people's money" by occupying plush office space, operating a fleet of corporate jets, and taking excessive compensation. Managers may also distort the financial statements and disclosures they make to their investors to portray a better picture of company health than the economic reality warrants. Such distortion generates higher bonuses and helps them avoid the potential loss of their jobs if the true picture of their underperformance were revealed. These are all examples of managers' hidden actions, or *moral hazard*— when managers act according to their self-interest rather than in the interest of the company's owners.

Dispersed investors find it costly to monitor and sanction the disclosures and decisions taken by managers, especially when the managers' actions are not fully disclosed to them. If the consequences of managers' hidden actions cannot be mitigated, then investors will be reluctant to put their capital at risk by investing in corporations.

Advanced market economies have evolved a variety of institutions to mitigate such adverse selection and moral hazard problems in capital markets. Economies that are better at mitigating these problems grow faster and produce higher standards of living for their citizens than those that cannot attract and allocate private capital to attractive domestic investment opportunities.

Among the institutions that play a role are information and capital market intermediaries, such as analysts and professional money managers (see the top row in Figure 7-2). Analysts interpret companies' financial statements and disclosures, analyze companies' prospects, and make recommendations about which companies represent attractive or unattractive investment opportunities. Professional money managers—including mutual funds, venture capital investors, and private equity investors—

Figure 7-2   Capital Market Intermediation Chain

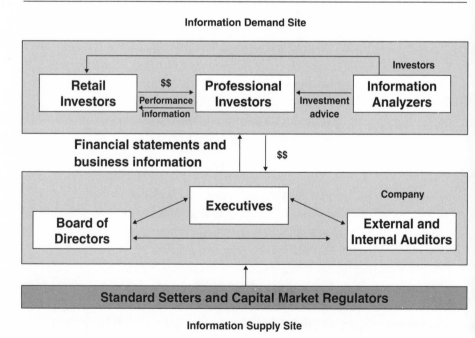

pool savings from diverse retail and institutional clients and, based on their own financial and business analysis and that of external analysts, provide capital to the most attractive investment opportunities.

The analysis, interpretation, and actual investing decisions made by retail investors and their professional managers are informed by the financial statements and disclosures prepared by company managers. To ensure that these financial statements and disclosures are reasonably representative of the operations of the companies, external auditors examine and test the validity of the reports, thereby mitigating the moral hazard problem that arises when managers report on their own performance.

Perhaps the most important component of this entire system of intermediation and governance is a company's board of directors. An active and engaged board is an essential part of shaping and executing a successful strategy. Boards contribute to organizational performance when they fulfill the following five major responsibilities:

1. Ensure that processes are in place for maintaining the integrity of the company, including
   - Integrity of financial statements
   - Integrity of compliance with law and ethics
   - Integrity of relationships with customers and suppliers
   - Integrity of relationships with other stakeholders.
2. Approve and monitor the enterprise's strategy.
3. Approve major financial decisions.
4. Select the chief executive officer, evaluate the CEO and senior executive team, and ensure that executive succession plans are in place.
5. Provide counsel and support to the CEO.

We elaborate on these five responsibilities next.

Ensure Integrity and Compliance

Directors must ensure that corporate reporting and disclosure represent the underlying economics of company performance and its key risk factors. Integrity and compliance in financial reporting include conforming with legal, accounting, and regulatory requirements, such as the Sarbanes-Oxley Act of 2002 in the United States. Internal and external auditors help a board gain assurance that the company's reporting, disclosure, and risk-management processes comply with these rules and regulations.

Directors must also monitor the risk taken by the company and must verify that managers have installed adequate risk-management processes to mitigate the adverse consequences should unanticipated events occur. The board must ensure that the company has adequate systems of internal controls to prevent loss of the company's assets, information, and reputation. And it must ensure that company managers are operating ethically, within the company's code of conduct, in the company's dealings with suppliers, customers, and communities as well as with employees. The board verifies that employees have not violated laws and regulations that would risk the company's assets and even its right to operate.

Approve and Monitor Enterprise Strategy

Board members do not generally participate in the creation and formulation of strategy. This is the responsibility of the CEO and the executive leadership team. But board members ensure that the company's leaders have formulated and are implementing a strategy for long-term creation of value for shareholders. And board members approve or reject major management decisions related to implementing the strategy.

To carry out this responsibility, board members must fully understand and approve the company's strategy. Once the strategy is approved, directors continually monitor its execution and results. For these purposes, directors must know the key value and risk drivers of the business.

Approve Major Financial Decisions

The board ensures that financial resources are being used effectively and efficiently to achieve strategic objectives. The board approves the annual operating and capital budgets and authorizes large capital expenditures, new financing or repayments, and major acquisitions, mergers, and divestitures.

Select and Evaluate Executives

Directors hire the chief executive officer and determine his or her compensation. The board also generally approves the hiring of other members of the senior executive team. Annually, the board assesses the performance of the CEO and the executive team and approves appropriate compensation and incentives.

To protect the company from the unexpected death, illness, injury, or voluntary departure of any key executive, the board must ensure that a succession plan exists for all members of the executive team.

Counsel and Support the CEO

The board counsels and advises the CEO. Individual board members use their specific knowledge of the industry and their functional and management expertise to provide guidance based on the company's history and competitive positioning. Directors share their knowledge, experience, and wisdom as the executive team describes strategic opportunities and impending major decisions.

LIMITED TIME, LIMITED KNOWLEDGE

To carry out their multiple responsibilities, board members need to know a great deal. They must know about financial results, the company's competitive position, its customers, its new products, its technologies, and its employees' capabilities. They must be aware of the performance and capabilities of the top managers as well as the broader talent pool.

And boards must know whether the company is complying with legal, regulatory, and ethical standards.[5]

Edward Lawler is a scholar of human capital, organizational effectiveness, and, more recently, corporate boards.[4] He writes, "A board should be focused on lead indicators. The challenge is to know what the right lead indicators are—which ones are unique to the organization and its business model . . . Boards need to review information about the culture of the organization. They need indicators of how customers and employees feel they're being treated."[6]

Boards often fall short in carrying out their responsibilities because of the limited time they have available and the inadequate information provided to them. The boards of failed companies, such as Enron, World-Com, and Adelphia, did not have adequate information to understand what was transpiring.[7] Some 90 percent of directors are not members of the executive team; they are part-time, outside directors. Many companies now consider an outside director as "not independent" if the director's company represents more than 1 percent of the company's financing, supplies, or sales.

As a consequence, "independent" directors now have far less specific knowledge of the company and its industry. Although such "independence" may offer some protection to investors, it limits the depth of knowledge independent directors can acquire and maintain about the company's industry and competitive position, especially if most of the information they receive consists of quarterly and annual financial statements.

Outside and independent board members also usually hold significant leadership positions in their own organizations. They find it difficult to dramatically increase the amount of time they can spend on board matters. Companies must find ways to use board members' available time more effectively. Such effective time management includes streamlining the information board members receive and evaluate before meetings and the information presented during meetings. It also includes focusing board meetings on matters that are of the highest strategic importance for the company. As a leading board scholar, Jay Lorsch indicates, "If directors were regularly getting a Balanced Scorecard, they would be much more likely to be informed about their companies on an ongoing basis. The scorecard's emphasis on strategy (linking to all activities, day-to-day and long-term) could help directors stay focused."[8]

A governance system built on the Balanced Scorecard helps the board of directors meet the two critical board challenges of limited time and limited information.

USING THE BALANCED SCORECARD
IN BOARD GOVERNANCE

The use of the Balanced Scorecard by boards of directors is an emerging new application, although one that we feel will increase over time. An increasing number of companies are including Balanced Scorecards in the board packet and are reserving time for their discussion during board meetings.

First Commonwealth Financial Corporation, a regional bank holding company based in central and western Pennsylvania, has been a leader in making the Balanced Scorecard the central document for board review and deliberations. In the next sections, we draw heavily upon the First Commonwealth experience.[9]

The Enterprise Scorecard

A board's Balanced Scorecard program starts with approving the organization's Strategy Map of linked strategic objectives and the associated enterprise Balanced Scorecard of performance measures, targets, and initiatives. This enterprise scorecard, of course, would have been created primarily for its traditional role of helping the CEO communicate and implement the corporate strategy throughout the organization.

For example, consider the Strategy Map in Figure 7-3 for First Commonwealth Financial Corporation, which adopted the Balanced Scorecard to implement a new strategy focused on lifetime customer relationships. The Strategy Map clearly portrays the high-level financial objectives of revenue growth and productivity enhancements; the customer objectives of lifetime relationships and excellent service delivery; the critical internal processes of leveraging client information and selling bundled financial products and services tailored to individual customer needs; and the learning and growth objectives of motivating and training employees in the new strategy and new way of selling. The Strategy Map has an accompanying Balanced Scorecard of measures, targets, and initiatives.

CEOs can use the enterprise scorecard for interactive discussions with their boards about strategic direction and performance in strategy execution. Used in this way, the Balanced Scorecard plays a central role in governance by providing board members with essential financial and nonfinancial information to support their responsibilities for overseeing performance.

For example, Wendy's International, one of the world's largest restaurant operating and franchising companies with more than 9,500 total systemwide restaurants, uses its BSC to communicate with its board of directors. The board does an intensive annual review of the financial results, process redesign benefits, new store growth, market share, customer satisfaction, taste and value-for-money comparisons against key competitors, and employee satisfaction and turnover. The board is updated quarterly on specific leading indicators, especially consumer-attributes feedback and market share changes.[10]

Initially, the executive team brings its enterprise Strategy Map and Balanced Scorecard to the board for review and approval. Ideally, the review should be done before these documents have been finalized, so that board members can contribute to discussions about strategic direction and positioning. The Strategy Map and Balanced Scorecard are the single most succinct and clear representations of the organization's strategy. They enable the board to understand the strategy, and they provide the basis for the board's evaluation of whether the strategy is capable of delivering long-term shareholder value at acceptable levels of business, financial, and technological risk.

Once approved by the board, the enterprise Strategy Map and Balanced Scorecard, with supporting documents of the scorecards of the primary business and support units, become the primary documents distributed to the board in advance of meetings. For example, at First

Figure 7-3 The First Commonwealth Financial Corporation Enterprise Strategy Map

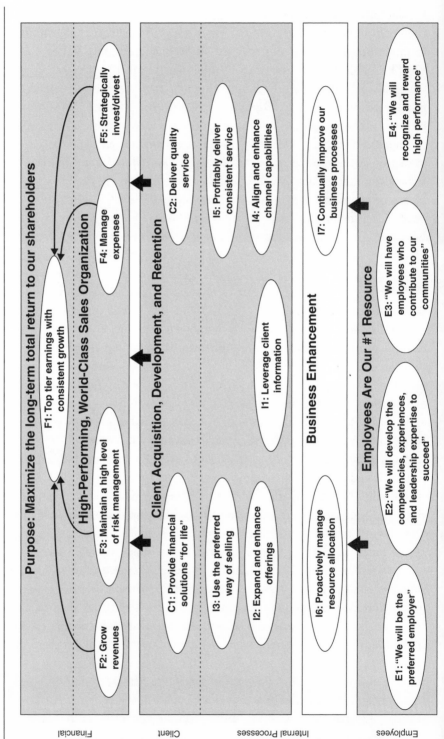

Purpose: Maximize the long-term total return to our shareholders

High-Performing, World-Class Sales Organization

Financial

- F1: Top tier earnings with consistent growth
- F2: Grow revenues
- F3: Maintain a high level of risk management
- F4: Manage expenses
- F5: Strategically invest/divest

Client Acquisition, Development, and Retention

Client

- C1: Provide financial solutions "for life"
- C2: Deliver quality service

Internal Processes

- I1: Leverage client information
- I2: Expand and enhance offerings
- I3: Use the preferred way of selling
- I4: Align and enhance channel capabilities
- I5: Profitably deliver consistent service
- I6: Proactively manage resource allocation
- I7: Continually improve our business processes

Business Enhancement

Employees Are Our #1 Resource

Employees

- E1: "We will be the preferred employer"
- E2: "We will develop the competencies, experiences, and leadership expertise to succeed"
- E3: "We will have employees who contribute to our communities"
- E4: "We will recognize and reward high performance"

Commonwealth Financial, the first page of the board package is a color-coded Strategy Map indicating those strategic objectives that are performing ahead of plan, at plan, and those that are falling significantly short of plan. These results become the agenda for board meetings, as the CEO engages directors in an interactive discussion about the company's recent experiences in implementing the strategy. Through a process of continual reforecasting, board members are kept informed of management's expectations for future performance of key financial measures and the company's key value drivers. Members of the audit committee become familiar with the risk factors underlying the company's operations and strategy, and this awareness helps to guide their decisions on financial reporting and disclosure.

Executive Scorecards

The second component of a board Balanced Scorecard program consists of executive scorecards that the full board and the compensation committee can use to select, evaluate, and reward senior executives. Executive compensation has been identified as an area where board performance has been most inadequate.[11] Many observers of board processes now believe that board compensation committees fail to set executive compensation at levels appropriate to their responsibilities and performance. These observers argue that board compensation committees have been captured by CEOs and the compensation consultants hired by CEOs to "assist" the board in setting executive compensation levels.

Clearly, for boards to perform their responsibilities for executive oversight and evaluation, they need a tool to provide them with a valid, objective assessment of executive performance. The board should design and approve a compensation and incentive system that rewards executives when they create short- and long-term value. The compensation plan should produce below-average compensation when executive performance falls short of industry averages.

Executive scorecards describe the strategic contributions of key executives. They help the CEO and the board to isolate the performance expectations of an individual executive from the performance expectations of the entire enterprise. The process of developing an executive scorecard starts with the enterprise scorecard. The CEO and the executive team come to an agreement about those enterprise objectives that are the primary responsibility of each member of the executive team.

For example, the chief information officer will likely have responsibility and accountability for objectives relating to information technology capabilities in the learning and growth perspectives, and also for the internal and customer objectives whose success is driven by excellent databases and information systems. The chief human resources officer will have primary responsibility and accountability for ensuring that employees have the requisite skills and experience to execute the strategy, that an effective communication process has made all employees aware of the enterprise and business unit strategy, and that each employee has personal objectives, a personal development plan, and an incentive plan based on contributing to the strategic objectives of the business and the enterprise.

In the case of First Commonwealth, Figure 7-4 shows the highlighted Strategy Map objectives for the CEO of the bank, and Figure 7-5 shows the associated executive scorecard with representative measures and targets for the bank CEO. Notice that the bank CEO has primary responsibility for the new marketing and sales strategy, but that other executives—the COO and the CIO—have primary responsibility for the cost, quality, and responsiveness of daily operations. The bank CEO also is expected to play the leadership role in establishing First Commonwealth's visibility and contributions in every community in which it operates.

By developing executive scorecards for each member of the senior leadership team, the CEO aligns the executive team with the strategy and gains an explicit mechanism for holding them accountable for their performance and contributions. The CEO can then reward them based on objective measures of their performance. Executive scorecards provide the board's compensation committee with information it can use to assess how well the CEO is evaluating and rewarding individual executive performance.

The CEO scorecard can be derived in the same way, highlighting those aspects of the enterprise scorecard that he or she has the primary responsibility for implementing. The CEO scorecard, and perhaps that of other senior executives, can be supplemented by key performance indicators that relate to the CEO or other senior executive roles beyond successful strategy implementation and increased shareholder value. For example, the CEO may have specific accountabilities for instituting effective governance processes, ensuring environmental and community performance, and maintaining relationships with key external constituencies such as investors, strategic customers and suppliers,

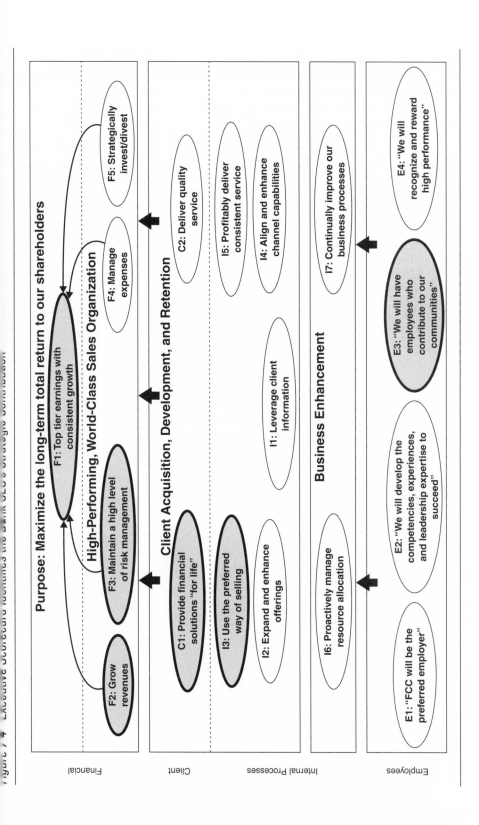

Figure 7-5 The Executive Scorecard Clarifies and Measures the Strategic Contribution

Strategic Role: The CEO of the Bank will grow revenues, transition the organization into a sales-driven culture, and ensure that the Growth Unit has the right management team to execute the FCFC strategy.

Executive Scorecard Framework: Bank CEO

Strategic Objectives (from Enterprise Strategy Map)	Individual Objective	Measure (per Enterprise BSC)	Target(s)	Rating
Financial F2: Grow Revenues	Enable *key* sources of revenue growth: (1) investment offerings for the affluent segments and (2) loan offerings for the commercial market.	■ Revenue Growth	■ <u>2003</u> 10%	
Stakeholder C1: Provide Financial Solutions "for Life"	Oversee the execution of the "one-name" initiative and new brand image campaign.	■ Acquisition, Development, and Retention by Segment	■ TBD	
Internal I2: Expand and Enhance Offerings I3: Use the Preferred Way of Selling	Identify targeted affluent and commercial relationships. Ensure account profiles are developed.	■ Sales Rate on Profiled Clients	■ <u>2003</u> 40%	
Learning and Growth E3: We Will Have Employees Who Contribute to Our Communities	Take an active leadership role in high-profile civic organizations.	■ Personal Involvement in Civic Activities	■ TBD	

regulators, and political leaders. Figure 7-6 shows a broader set of indicators that the board might draw on when establishing CEO and executive scorecards.

The board compensation committee should use the CEO's executive scorecard when designing its performance contract, thereby providing an objective and defensible basis for the CEO's compensation arrangement. Performance targets for the CEO's scorecard measures can be established based on explicit growth targets and performance relative to the industry.

The governance committee can also use executive scorecards as strategic job descriptions that provide the basis for executive succession plans and for identifying succession candidates. Cohn and Khurana express concern about the typical process used by boards to select CEOs: "CEOs are

Figure 7-6 Structure and Measures for Another Type of CEO Scorecard

The CEO Scorecard		
	Strategic Objectives	Typical Measures
Financial	■ Sustain Growth in Shareholder Value	■ Increases in Economic Value Added or Shareholder Value ■ Price/Earnings Ratio (vs. Peers) ■ Return on Equity (vs. Peers) ■ Investment Portfolio ROI
	■ Invest Strategically	■ Earnings Growth Rate ■ Revenue from New Sources
	■ Manage Productivity	■ Revenue per Employee ■ Cash Flow
Stakeholder	■ Build Effective Board/CEO Relationships	■ Board Assessment of Relationship
	■ Maintain Shareholder Relations	■ Number of Meetings with Shareholders ■ Shareholder Satisfaction Survey
	■ Satisfy Regulatory Requirements	■ Number of Violations ■ External Stakeholder Survey
	■ Grow Customer Value	■ Market Share (Key Markets) ■ Customer Satisfaction (Key Markets)
Governance Processes	■ Develop and Communicate Strategy	■ % of Workforce That Understands the Strategy (Employee Survey)
	■ Oversee Financial Performance	■ Quality of Earnings Rating ■ % of Investment Projects That Meet Targets
	■ Implement Performance Management Process	■ % Staff with Objectives Linked to Strategy (BSC) ■ % Staff with Incentive Compensation Linked to Strategy (BSC)
	■ Implement Risk Management Process	■ Process Quality (External Audit) ■ Risk Issues Closed (%)
	■ Manage Strategy Execution	■ Strategic Initiatives (vs. Plan)
Learning and Growth	■ Ensure Technology	■ R&D Investment/Sales (vs. Peers) ■ Number of Patents, Number of Patent Citations ■ New Product Development Cycle
	■ Ensure Human Capital Readiness	■ Human Capital Readiness (Strategic Jobs) ■ Key Positions with Leadership Succession Plans (%) ■ Key Enterprise Turnover
	■ Develop Corporate Culture	■ Employee Satisfaction Survey ■ Code of Conduct—Awareness

often selected, compensated, and held in awe more for the charisma and confidence they exude in their pinstriped Brooks Brothers suits than for their actual skills and competencies . . . [O]ften boards are at a loss to evaluate the real skills, experiences, and competencies that an individual needs to lead a particular company in a particular environment."[12]

When openings develop at the executive team level, the enterprise and executive Balanced Scorecards can help the board search for rising stars within the organization who have the experience and capabilities required for senior-level strategy implementation. The scorecards also provide guidance to the board in recommending specific training and job positions to high-achieving individuals so that they can become better prepared to assume senior-level leadership positions in the future.

When senior-level positions cannot be filled via internal promotions, the board's search committee can use the Strategy Map and Balanced Scorecard measures to create a position profile that will guide external searches, typically assisted by an executive search firm. Cohn and Khurana urge boards to use the quantified objectives on a Strategy Map to guide succession planning and execution: "[S]earch committees will stay focused on identifying and recruiting talent that meets their specific implementation challenges, and not succumb to the charisma of leaders who lack the relevant skills."[13]

Board Scorecard

We believe that most boards will find using an enterprise Balanced Scorecard in their periodic meetings, and using Balanced Scorecards to monitor senior management performance, as straightforward applications of their responsibilities for strategic oversight. In fact, a leading Canadian accounting organization has advocated that this practice become standard for all companies.[14]

A novel application is to develop a Strategy Map and Balanced Scorecard for the board itself. The U.S. Sarbanes-Oxley Act requires that boards make an annual assessment of their performance. What better tool for such a performance evaluation than an explicit statement of the board's strategic objectives? A board Balanced Scorecard provides the following benefits:

- Defines the strategic contributions of the board
- Provides a tool to manage the composition and performance of the board and its committees

- Clarifies the strategic information required by the board

Consider the generic board Strategy Map shown in Figure 7-7, and a segment from the associated board Balanced Scorecard in Figure 7-8. The board Strategy Map typically uses financial objectives identical to those articulated in the enterprise Strategy Map, because ultimately the board's success for shareholders is measured by its ability to guide the management team toward superior financial performance.

Rather than use the traditional customer perspective, however, the board scorecard introduces a stakeholder perspective, reflecting the board's responsibilities to investors, regulators, and communities. As discussed earlier in this chapter, the board's responsibilities to these stakeholders include the following:

- Approve, plan, and monitor enterprise performance
- Strengthen and evaluate executive performance
- Ensure enterprise compliance with regulations, laws, and community standards and use of adequate systems of internal control

These are the critical responsibilities that boards carry out to mitigate the moral hazard problems of managers acting in their self-interest rather than in the interests of their shareholders. The validation of financial reports and disclosures also provides investors with reliable information about investment opportunities and risks, thereby reducing the impact of hidden information.

The board is the single most important component in the entire system of capital market governance. It must ensure that managers are providing shareholders and regulators with valid financial and nonfinancial information, and that managers are using shareholders' capital to advance the shareholders' long-term interests. These board responsibilities are central to the effective functioning of capital markets. Unless investors can be assured that boards are carrying out these responsibilities objectively and independently, they will be reluctant to entrust their capital to enterprise managers.

The internal process perspective of the board's scorecard contains the objectives for board processes that enable the board to meet its shareholder and stakeholder objectives. Figure 7-7 shows three strategic themes for board processes: performance oversight, executive enhancement, and compliance and communication. These themes provide the architecture for defining the specific internal process objectives of the board.

Figure 7-7 The Board Strategy Map Clarifies How the Board Contributes

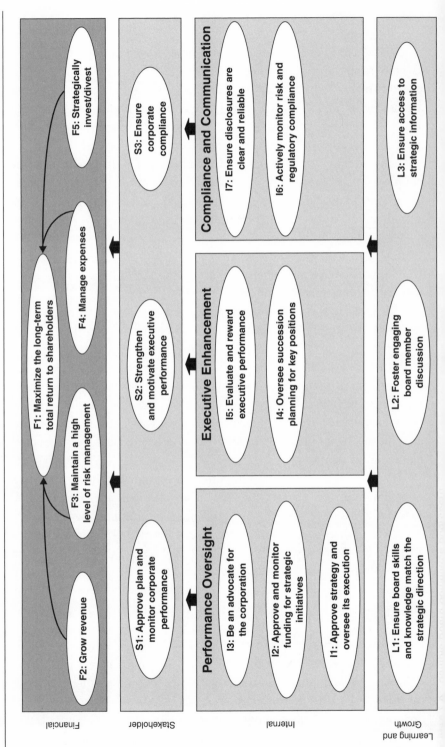

Board Scorecard Framework

Executive Enhancement Theme	Objective	Measure(s)	Target(s)	Owners
Financial Maximize the Long-Term Total Return to Shareholders (Maintain a high level of risk management) (Grow revenue)	■ Maximize the Long-Term Total Return to Shareholders	■ ROE Relative to Peers	■ 2003 75th Percentile	■ Executive Management
Stakeholder Strengthen and Motivate Executive Performance	■ Strengthen and Motivate Executive Performance	■ Are Executive and Affiliate CEOs on Track with Development Plans?	■ Yes	■ Compensation Committee
Internal Oversee Succession Planning for Key Positions (Evaluate and reward executive performance)	■ Oversee Succession Planning for Key Positions	■ Share of Executives with a Current Succession Plan in Place	■ 75% Year 1 ■ 100% Year 2	■ Governance Committee
Learning and Growth Ensure Access to Strategic Information	■ Ensure Access to Strategic Information	■ Board Member Survey on Relevance of Information Presented	■ Above Avg. Year 1 ■ Excellent Year 2	■ Full Board

The three strategic themes also link to the board's most important committees. The governance committee has primary responsibility for performance oversight. The compensation committee has primary oversight for evaluating and motivating the senior executive team. The audit committee has primary responsibility for enterprise compliance and communication with external constituencies.

The learning and growth perspective of the board's scorecard contains objectives for the skills, knowledge, and competencies of the board; the board's access to information about the enterprise's strategy and results; and board culture, especially the dynamics of productive board meetings that feature discussions and interactions among board members and the executive leadership team. The measures for the board's learning and growth perspective can be generated from board member surveys, completed after each meeting, that assess the quality of the meeting, board processes, and information supplied in advance and during the meeting.

David Dahlmann, the vice chairman of First Commonwealth, commented on the importance of the board scorecard's learning and growth objectives: "The board surveys help us determine if we have the right skills to help the company in its strategic direction, the right strategic information at the right time, and the right climate to encourage discussion and dissent."[15]

In summary, as shown in Figure 7-9, a three-component Balanced Scorecard program—with an enterprise scorecard, executive scorecards, and a board scorecard—provides the information and the structure to help boards to be more effective and accountable for their vital responsibilities in an effective capital market governance system. The enterprise scorecard, supplemented by the scorecards for business units and key support units, informs the board in a succinct and powerful way about the strategies being implemented by the enterprise.

As it monitors, counsels, approves, and decides strategic direction, the board will operate with a much deeper understanding of the enterprise's strategic context, and without its members being overloaded with excessive quantities of detailed information. Executive scorecards provide a clear basis for monitoring the management team's performance, for compensating executives based on performance in meeting strategic targets, and for assessing the adequacy of executive succession plans. The board scorecard informs all board members of their responsibilities and facilitates periodic assessment of board performance using well-understood criteria.

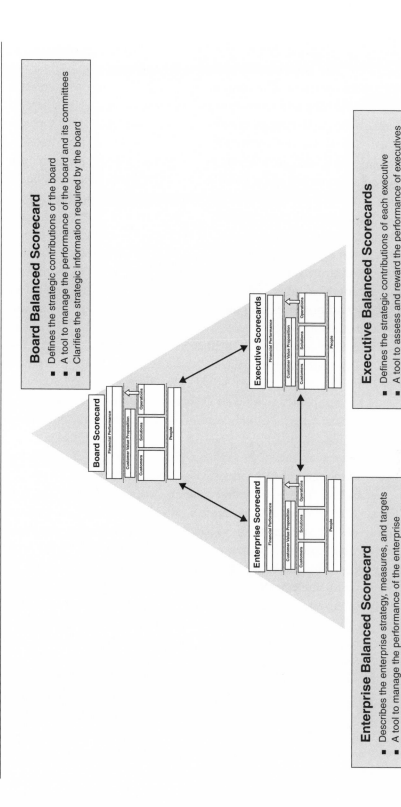

Board Balanced Scorecard

- Defines the strategic contributions of the board
- A tool to manage the performance of the board and its committees
- Clarifies the strategic information required by the board

Executive Balanced Scorecards

- Defines the strategic contributions of each executive
- A tool to assess and reward the performance of executives
- A key information input to the board

Enterprise Balanced Scorecard

- Describes the enterprise strategy, measures, and targets
- A tool to manage the performance of the enterprise
- A key information input to the board

ALIGNING INVESTORS AND ANALYSTS

Once the board approves and actively uses the enterprise's Balanced Scorecard of financial and nonfinancial measures, the natural progression is to communicate some of this key information to the company's owners. Several oversight committees, in fact, have advocated that Balanced Scorecard–type information about a company's strategy and execution be communicated to investors. Fifteen years ago, a high-level committee of the American Institute of Certified Public Accountants (generally referred to as the Jenkins Committee, after its chairman, Edward Jenkins) investigated the information needs of investors and creditors.[16] Among its recommendations were that companies provide, in addition to financial statements and measures, high-level operating data about a company's business activities and performance measurements of a company's key business processes. Such measures include the quality of the company's products or services, the relative cost of its activities, and the time required to perform key activities, such as new product development.

The committee's study indicated that analysts and owners were as interested in a company's business activities, business processes, and events affecting the company as they were in financial measures. The committee report emphasized that high-level operating data would help analysts and owners understand the business—in particular, the link between events and activities and their impact on the company's financial performance. The committee recognized that, in response to changes in their businesses, companies were changing their information systems and the types of information they use to manage their businesses, such as the performance of key processes for total quality management (TQM) and customer satisfaction measures. The committee concluded, "Users would benefit from greater access to the high-level performance measures management is using to manage the business."

Ernst & Young studied the information used by financial analysts. It concluded that earnings are *decreasingly* important in predicting stock price and that "35 percent of a company's valuation is attributable to nonfinancial information."[17] Analysts with the best track record for accuracy claimed to use the most nonfinancial measures. And in a more detailed investigation of four industry sectors—computer hardware, food, oil and gas, and pharmaceuticals—the study concluded that the nonfinancial metric most valued by investors was a company's ability to execute its strategy.

A 1999 Harvard Business School study also concluded that leading sell-side analysts wanted more nonfinancial data from corporations' external reports, including information about the competitive strategy of business units and the corporate strategy.[18] Marc Epstein, in two coauthored studies, provided examples of several companies that included nonfinancial metrics in their annual reports.[19]

But despite all the studies documenting analysts' desire to see information relating to a company's strategy and its execution, the reporting of nonfinancial performance measures by corporations remains ad hoc and intermittent. Even with widespread adoption of the Balanced Scorecard for managing strategy within corporations, virtually no corporation has chosen to use the Balanced Scorecard framework for external reporting and disclosure.[20]

In the mid-1990s, after the success of several early adopters of the Balanced Scorecard—Mobil US Marketing & Refining, Cigna Property & Casualty, and Chemical Retail Bank—we spoke to the senior division executives about whether they used their Balanced Scorecard indicators in their communications with analysts and investors. Several had spoken to analysts about the recent success of their divisions. None actually presented the division's Balanced Scorecard to the analyst community, but all structured their presentations to the analysts using the BSC framework. They reported that the analysts were highly enthusiastic about the presentation because the executives, instead of just discussing earnings per share growth rates and forecasts, actually described the underlying strategy that had led to recent and substantial improvements in financial performance.

For example, in one presentation, the executive explained how a major investment in new information technology had led to significant improvement in a customer-facing process, which in turn had led to higher customer retention and customer volume growth, a major contributor to recent growth in revenues and margins. The analysts could see that current results were not just luck; the executive had a specific strategy for value creation that his division was implementing successfully and was likely to sustain.

Ingersoll-Rand, a company discussed in Chapter 3, disclosed its high-level corporate strategy map in its 2002 annual report (see Figure 7-10). The Strategy Map shows high-level strategic objectives for all its businesses, but the report does not provide measures or data on the objectives. The disclosure was part of IR's strategy to brand the company as capable of achieving economies of scope from its seemingly diverse businesses through an integrated corporate strategy. In IR's 2003 annual report, the CEO's letter described accomplishment in the corporate

Figure 7-10 Ingersoll-Rand Strategy Map in 2001 Annual Report

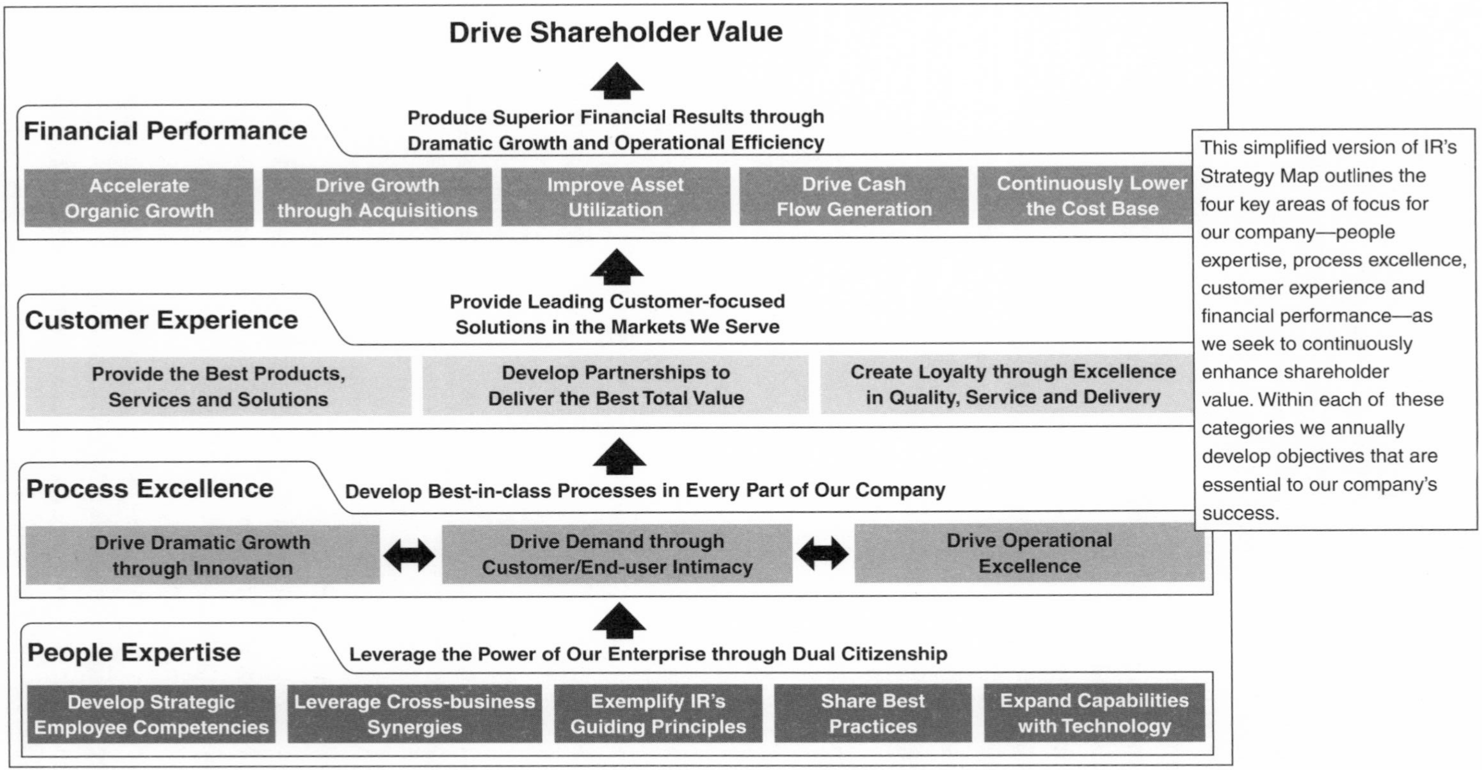

This simplified version of IR's Strategy Map outlines the four key areas of focus for our company—people expertise, process excellence, customer experience and financial performance—as we seek to continuously enhance shareholder value. Within each of these categories we annually develop objectives that are essential to our company's success.

Drive Shareholder Value

Financial Performance

Produce Superior Financial Results through Dramatic Growth and Operational Efficiency

| Accelerate Organic Growth | Drive Growth through Acquisitions | Improve Asset Utilization | Drive Cash Flow Generation | Continuously Lower the Cost Base |

Customer Experience

Provide Leading Customer-focused Solutions in the Markets We Serve

| Provide the Best Products, Services and Solutions | Develop Partnerships to Deliver the Best Total Value | Create Loyalty through Excellence in Quality, Service and Delivery |

Process Excellence

Develop Best-in-class Processes in Every Part of Our Company

| Drive Dramatic Growth through Innovation | Drive Demand through Customer/End-user Intimacy | Drive Operational Excellence |

People Expertise

Leverage the Power of Our Enterprise through Dual Citizenship

| Develop Strategic Employee Competencies | Leverage Cross-business Synergies | Exemplify IR's Guiding Principles | Share Best Practices | Expand Capabilities with Technology |

Source: IR 2001 Annual Report, page 9.

Balanced Scorecard themes: dramatic revenue growth through innovation and customer solutions, operational excellence, and dual citizenship. Similarly, each of IR's four major sectors described its accomplishments using these corporate themes. In 2004, CEO Herb Henkel continued to use the framework in his quarterly presentation to analysts, providing specific examples of innovation-driven growth, cross-business customer solutions, operational excellence, and dual citizenship.[21]

Wendy's, the leading quick-service restaurant, also uses the scorecard framework in its presentations to analysts, although without explicitly mentioning that the metrics being reported come from the four perspectives in its Balanced Scorecard.[22] Companies, like Wendy's, that apply the same metrics for every business unit, of course, have more standardized metrics to report than companies consisting of diverse operating units, which may have few metrics in common. Quarterly, Wendy's reports to analysts include the following measures:

Financial	• Sales growth per store
Customer	• Customer satisfaction
	• Taste comparison versus competition
	• Value to customers versus competition
Internal Process	• Service excellence (average drive-through time)
	• Order accuracy, drive-through service
	• Cleanliness
Learning and Growth	• Friendly, courteous employees
	• Employee turnover

Wendy's believes it has gotten benefits from its consistent disclosure of key nonfinancial metrics related to its strategy. In January 2005, Wendy's was named by Institutional Investor Research Group as having one of the best U.S. investor relations efforts. John Barker, vice president, investor relations and financial communications, stated, "Wendy's stock price is up 75% since it started its [Balanced Scorecard], due in part to increased disclosure."[23] Barker's remark suggests that companies' enhanced disclosure may increase their valuations by giving analysts confidence that recent earnings improvements are due to effective strategy execution that can be sustained into the future.

In summary, external reporting of Balanced Scorecard measures is at a preliminary stage. Several companies have used the structure of their Balanced Scorecards to frame their presentations to analysts, although they have not explicitly incorporated the data reporting into their quarterly or annual reports. External reporting in the United States is done in an environment of extensive regulation and high litigation risk. Consequently, despite the apparent keen interest from investors and analysts in having greater information about corporate strategy and its execution, corporate executives seem reluctant to be entrepreneurial or innovative in their disclosure practices. Perhaps as corporations become more comfortable using the Balanced Scorecard to communicate strategic performance internally with business units, employees, and their boards of directors, they may, at some point, become more proactive in embedding Balanced Scorecard data in reports to investors and analysts.

SUMMARY

Although still in its early stages, the Balanced Scorecard is beginning to be used in corporate governance and reporting processes. Directors' responsibilities are increasing, but the time they have available to perform their functions is not easily expanded. Directors must be able to do their jobs better and smarter, and not by working longer and harder.

A three-part BSC-based governance system offers directors streamlined and strategic information. In this way, board members have relevant information for their decisions about the company's future directions and its reporting and disclosure policies. Preparation and meeting time focuses on the company's strategy, its financing, and its most important drivers of value and risk. Executive scorecards inform the board's processes for executive selection, evaluation, compensation, and succession. And the board itself has a scorecard to guide decisions about board composition, board processes and deliberations, and board evaluation.

For corporate reporting, various studies have documented the keen interest in having supplementary nonfinancial measurements that would help analysts and investors understand and monitor a company's strategy. Several companies have started to use their Balanced Scorecard frameworks to structure their external communications. But this movement is still in its infancy, and more experimentation is required before most senior executives will become comfortable with supplying data to communicate and evaluate their strategies.

NOTES

1. J. Immelt, "Restoring Trust," speech, New York Economic Club, November 4, 2002.

2. This analysis of the problems of adverse selection and moral hazard in capital markets is taken from K. G. Palepu, P. M. Healy, and V. L. Bernard, *Business Analysis and Valuation Using Financial Statements: Text and Cases,* 3rd edition (Mason, OH: Thomson Southwestern), 2003.

3. The breakdown in markets when buyers cannot get valid information about the product or service being offered for sale was described in a Nobel Prize–winning paper: G. A. Akerlof, "The Market for Lemons: Quality Uncertainty and the Market Mechanism," *Quarterly J. Econ.* 89 (1970): 488–500. Groucho Marx, in a much earlier publication than Akerlof's, captured the essence of the adverse selection problem when he stated, "I don't want to join any club that would accept me as a member."

4. J. Conger, E. Lawler, and D. Finegold, *Corporate Boards: New Strategies for Adding Value at the Top* (New York: Jossey-Bass/Wiley, 2001).

5. J. Lorsch, "Smelling Smoke: Why Boards of Directors Need the Balanced Scorecard," *Balanced Scorecard Report* (September–October 2002): 9–11.

6. E. E. Lawler, "Board Governance and Accountability," *Balanced Scorecard Report* (January–February 1993): 12.

7. Ibid., 11.

8. Ibid., 10.

9. Details can be found in R. S. Kaplan, "First Commonwealth Financial Corporation," Case 9-104-042 (Boston: Harvard Business School Publishing, 2004).

10. J. Ross, "The Best-Practice Hamburger: How Wendy's Enhances Performance with Its BSC," *Balanced Scorecard Report* (July–August 2003): 5–7.

11. L. Bebchuk and J. Fried, *Pay Without Performance: The Unfulfilled Promise of Executive Compensation* (Cambridge, MA: Harvard University Press, 2004); G. Crystal, *In Search of Excess: The Overcompensation of American Executives* (New York: W.W. Norton, 1991).

12. J. Cohn and R. Khurana, "Strategy Maps for CEO Succession Planning," *Balanced Scorecard Report* (July–August 2003): 8–10.

13. Ibid., 9.

14. M. J. Epstein and M. Roy, *Measuring and Improving the Performance of Corporate Boards*, Management Accounting Guidelines, Society of Management Accountants of Canada (Mississauga, Ontario, 2002).

15. Kaplan, "First Commonwealth Financial Corporation."

16. "Improving Business Reporting—A Customer Focus: Meeting the Information Needs of Investors and Creditors," Report of the Special Committee on Financial Reporting, American Institute of Certified Public Accountants, 1992.

17. "Measures That Matter," Ernst & Young white paper, 1999 (available from Cap Gemini Ernst & Young Center for Business Innovation).

18. M. Epstein and K. Palepu, "What Financial Analysts Want," *Strategic Finance* (April 1999).

19. M. Epstein and B. Birchard, *Counting What Counts: Turning Corporate Accountability into Competitive Advantage* (Reading, MA: Perseus Books, 1999); M. Epstein and P. Wisner, "Increasing Corporate Accountability: The External

Disclosure of Balanced Scorecard Measures," *Balanced Scorecard Report* (July–August 2001): 10–13.

20. One of the few exceptions is Skandia, a Swedish insurance company, which published its Navigator of nonfinancial measurements, for many years, as part of its annual report (see "The Value-Adding Power of External Disclosures: An Interview with Jan Hoffmeister, American Skandia Investment," *Balanced Scorecard Report* (September–October 2001): 10–11.

21. See presentations at http://irco.com/investorrelations/analysts.

22. See Wendy's analyst presentations at http://www.wendys-invest.com/main/pres.php.

23. "The Best-Practice Hamburger: How Wendy's Enhances Performance with Its BSC," *Balanced Scorecard Report* (July–August 2003): 6–7.

CHAPTER EIGHT

ALIGNING EXTERNAL PARTNERS

THE FINAL COMPONENT in an organization alignment program is for the enterprise to build scorecards with strategic external partners, such as key suppliers, customers, and alliances. When an enterprise builds a Balanced Scorecard with a strategic external partner, it enables the senior managers from the two entities to reach a consensus about the objectives for the relationship. The process creates understanding and trust across organizational boundaries, reduces transaction costs, and minimizes misalignment between the two parties.

The scorecard also provides an explicit contract by which interorganizational performance can be measured. Without a Balanced Scorecard, contracting with an external partner focuses only on financial measures, such as price and cost. A Balanced Scorecard provides a much more general contractual mechanism that allows service, timeliness, innovation, quality, and flexibility to be incorporated into the relationship.

SUPPLIER SCORECARDS

Supply-chain management is both interfunctional and interorganizational. It is interfunctional because the effective production and supply of goods require close coordination among marketing, operations, procurement, sales, and logistics. It is interorganizational because the systems and processes among all the supply-chain participants—raw materials provider, manufacturer, distributor, and retailer—must be integrated and coordinated for optimal performance along the entire chain. The Balanced

Scorecard, the ideal alignment mechanism, should provide great benefits for supply-chain management.

In the 1980s, many companies adopted total quality management and just-in-time practices. A natural consequence of these Japanese management tools was that manufacturing companies built stronger relationships with their suppliers so that defect-free components and products could be reliably delivered, just-in-time to plants' production processes. Supplier selection, formerly based on price, now had to incorporate a potential supplier's capability for on-time delivery of zero-defect products.

Metalcraft Supplier Scorecard

Metalcraft Corporation (disguised name) is one of the largest Tier-1 automotive suppliers in the world.[1] It operates an extensive system of its own suppliers and evaluates their performance with an extensive supplier scorecard system. The Metalcraft supplier scorecard classifies performance in three categories: quality, timing, and delivery. Each supplier plant receives a monthly rating from each Metalcraft plant to which it ships. Metalcraft calculates an overall supplier rating by aggregating the scores from all of a supplier's plants.

Quality
The supplier scorecard uses three measures of quality: an overall measure based on the status of the supplier plant's implementation of specific ISO and quality standards, launch quality rejects (QRs), and parts-per-million (PPM) defect rates.

Metalcraft stresses the ability to ramp up production quickly for new products. It therefore highlights a supplier's ability to achieve high-quality production quickly during a new product launch phase. The QR (launch quality reject) score measures the number of problems reported in the production start-up phase of a new component. QRs are tracked from the date that a first prototype was built until fifteen days after the start of full production.

Once high-volume production is under way, Metalcraft measures PPM defect rates by dividing the number of defective parts (returned, scrapped, or reworked) that it receives from a supplier by the total number of parts received, multiplied by one million.

Timing
The timing section of the scorecard tracks the supplier's ability to meet promised dates for certification of new components for production. Met-

alcraft uses a detailed certification process to verify that components made using the final production process adhere to engineering specifications. Like the QR metric, this measure assesses a supplier's ability to bring new components into high-volume production quickly and reliably.

Delivery

Metalcraft operates just-in-time production processes. Any delay in supplier delivery leads to rescheduling costs, overtime production, and expedited delivery costs. Metalcraft scores delivery performance on several dimensions, including under- and overshipment to schedule, communication and record maintenance, and problem resolution and prevention.

Metalcraft's supplier scorecard aggregates a plant's quality, timing, and delivery performance into an aggregate green, yellow, or red score. A green plant qualifies for unrestricted sourcing. A yellow plant can continue to be used for sourcing but only after a "nonpreferred sourcing approval request" has been approved by a senior supplier development engineer. A red plant, considered a "nonpreferred" supplier, requires even higher-level approval to remain as a supplier; if it remains red for three consecutive months, its products may be sourced from an alternative facility.

Other Supplier Scorecards

Dana Corporation, another automotive OEM supplier, operates a Supplier Balanced Scorecard (SBS) system that tracks supplier performance on four dimensions:

1. Quality (25 percent)
   - PPM (0.8)
   - Number of reject occurrences (0.2)
2. On-time delivery (25 percent)
3. Support (25 percent)
   - Supplier's commitment to supporting Dana's goals of minority sourcing and QS-9000/ISO-14000 implementation (criteria reestablished each year based on Dana's priorities for that year)
4. Commercial (25 percent)
   - Supplier's commitment to meeting Dana's productivity (cost-reduction) goals

Like Metalcraft, Dana provides each supplier with Web-based access to its SBS score and uses the score to motivate continuous improvement from its supplier base.

Rolls Royce's supplier scorecard also uses traditional quality and delivery metrics. In November 2003, the company added a cost metric—the cost of nonquality—to measure its prevention, appraisal, and failure costs associated with a supplier's products. Federal Mogul includes, in addition to delivery and quality metrics, a measure of supplier cost-saving suggestions. The full score (100 points) is awarded for suggestions that enable a 5 percent savings in projected annual spending. Zero points are awarded for suggestions that aggregate less than 0.9 percent of annual spending.

These examples indicate that supplier scorecards are being used by many manufacturing companies. But these are not truly Balanced Scorecards. The supplier scorecards are actually key performance indicator (KPI) scorecards, where the company uses nonfinancial measures to motivate suppliers to deliver products better (zero defects), faster (short lead times and just-in-time), and cheaper. At best, one can interpret these supplier scorecards as consistent with a company following a low-total-cost strategy. The scorecards do not stress supplier innovation—helping the company develop entirely new product platforms—nor do they measure how suppliers help provide more complete solutions to customers.

Even with a low-total-cost strategy, a more complete supplier Balanced Scorecard would include objectives for development of human capital and information capital by the supplier that would enhance the relationship, as well as metrics relating to how well the supplier was innovating and partnering with the company to provide value even beyond delivering existing or already designed products with zero defects, on time.

Of course, for companies like Metalcraft, Dana, or Rolls Royce, developing such a customized supplier Balanced Scorecard for each of its thousands of suppliers is unrealistic. Such an effort should be made only for *strategic suppliers*—those with which the company wants a long-term relationship and those to which it looks as a continuing source of new ideas and new processes for revenue growth and cost improvement.

Collaborative Planning, Forecasting, and Replenishment Scorecards

Somewhat more highly developed supply-chain scorecards are being created in the consumer packaged-goods supply and retailing industry. Manufacturers, such as Procter & Gamble, Nestlé, and Kellogg, are working with large retailers, such as Wal-Mart, Sainsbury, and Tesco, to optimize the supply chain from manufacturer to consumer.

The Collaborative Planning, Forecasting, and Replenishment (CPFR) initiative (see www.cpfr.org) strives to link best sales and marketing practices in category management with supply-chain planning and execution; the aim is to increase availability of products while reducing inventory, transportation, and logistics costs. For example, Procter & Gamble's CPFR goal is to achieve 100 percent product availability on retail shore shelves while simultaneously reducing inventory requirements in retail stores, customer distribution centers, and P&G plants. P&G wants to produce and ship in response to a consumer demand signal from a retail point-of-sale terminal.

CPFR involves extensive coordination of processes between supplier and retailer. Creating a scorecard for performance is one of the central features of the initiative. For example, early adopters of CPFR initiatives hope for the following benefits:

- Improved forecast accuracy
- Improved internal communications
- Increased sales
- Improved relationships with channel partners
- Improved service levels
- Reduced out-of-stock conditions
- Decreased inventory
- Better asset utilization
- Better deployment of organization resources

Each of these is measurable and could serve as a component in a comprehensive CPFR scorecard for a manufacturer-retailer trading relationship.

The CPFR effort is perhaps farthest along in Europe, where the program office prepared the template in Figure 8-1 to identify a menu of key performance indicators to describe a particular CPFR relationship.[2]

Procter & Gamble in its CPFR pilots has introduced metrics for nine elements in its supply-chain relationships:

1. Forecast accuracy versus actual orders
2. Distribution center service level and inventory
3. Retail in-stock service level and inventory
4. Manufacturer order fill rate versus original order
5. Manufacturer order fill rate versus advance ship notice (ASN)
6. Delivery punctuality
7. Transportation efficiency

Figure 8-1 Key Performance Indicators for CPFR

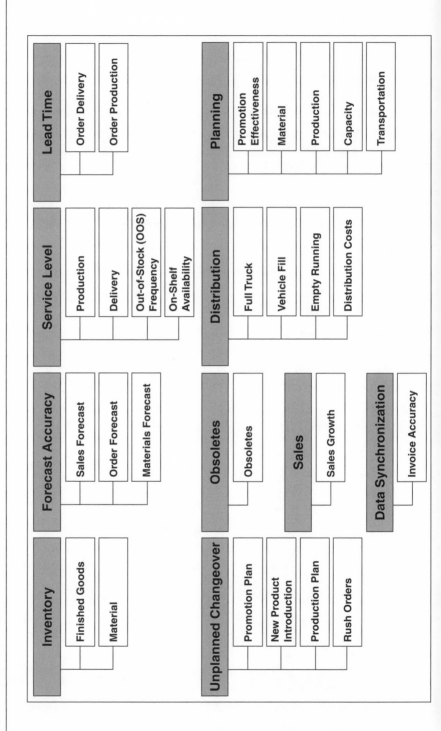

8. Shipment variability by SKU (stock-keeping unit)
9. Profitability or cost reduction

Sainsbury, a U.K. retailer, has been a major force in the Global Commerce Initiative to make the CPFR principles operational.[3] Sainsbury's relationship with a manufacturer starts with an entry-level global scorecard that measures performance on fifty-two self-reported questions in three sections: readiness, consumer focus, and operations.

The readiness section includes questions about the supplier's ability to share insights, to make business decisions, to work in collaborative, multifunctional teams, and to provide and receive feedback with the retailer. The consumer focus section includes questions about the supplier's capacity to support retailer promotions, to introduce new products based on consumer research, and to have a clear understanding of the targeted consumer of the supplier's products. Questions in the operations section explore the manufacturer's capacity to develop a joint supply-chain strategy; its processes for order generation and receipt and electronic ordering and funds transfer; and its replenishment and surge capability. The responses to these entry-level scorecard questions let both parties identify opportunities for reduction in delivery lead times, improved forecast accuracy, mutual reduction in inventory levels, and faster new product launches.

For advanced suppliers, Sainsbury uses an intermediate-level scorecard that measures performance through responses to ninety-five questions organized into three major sections:

1. Demand
   • Demand strategy and capabilities
   • Assortment
   • Promotions
   • New product introductions
   • Consumer value creation
2. Supply management
   • Supply strategy and capabilities
   • Responsive replenishment
   • Operational excellence
   • Integrated demand-driven supply
3. Enablers
   • Common data and communication standards
   • Cost, profit, and value measurements
   • Product safety and quality processes

Here are examples of the questions:

- Is there a detailed analysis of the costs in the total supply chain?
- Is in-store implementation of new product launches actively monitored?
- Are there agreed procedures in place to rectify delivery issues?

Manufacturer responses are chosen from among the following:

- No/never
- Limited
- Progressing
- Yes/always

The supply-chain scorecards being developed through the CPFR and ECR initiatives are more general than the ones we described being used in the automotive transportation equipment industry. They record a supplier's ability to introduce new products rapidly and its capacity for enhanced coordination, such as joint promotions, with the retailer. They also include a learning and growth component that identifies employees having specific responsibilities and capabilities to work in joint project teams; the alignment of information systems for ordering, invoicing, and payment between the two companies; and the sharing of end-use consumer data. Building scorecards to enhance the evolving collaborative relationships in the food and packaged-goods supply chain is a leading example of what is possible in many other supply-chain situations.

A SUPPLY-CHAIN BALANCED SCORECARD

Brewer and Speh propose a more general framework for supply-chain scorecards.[4] They emphasize that one size should not fit all. The supply chain that's designed to reduce the cost of production, delivery, and merchandising of standard commodity products with predictable demand has very different objectives than the supply chain for companies in the unpredictable marketplace of fashion apparel. One stresses low cost and rapid inventory turns; the other requires flexibility, quick response, forecast accuracy, and innovation.

When a supply-chain Balanced Scorecard is constructed, then, the process starts with clearly articulating the supply-chain strategy. This should be a multifunctional, multiorganizational project and, as with any effective scorecard project, should provide an opportunity for individuals in diverse functions and organizations to collaborate to define common, shared objectives. Once the team members agree to the strategy, they can start building the scorecard for the strategy.

The Financial Perspective

The financial measures for a supply-chain scorecard are traditional and generic. A well-functioning supply chain should lead to higher profit margins, reduced unit costs, increased cash flow, growth of revenues, and high return on invested capital for all supply-chain participants. The scorecard can feature specific supply-chain measures, such as the costs of transportation, order processing, order receipt, warehousing, merchandising, obsolescence, and markdowns.

The emphasis placed on specific financial measures depends on the strategy. For the production and distribution of mature products, the dominant measures will be cash flow, unit costs, and return on assets. For differentiation strategies, the measures of revenue growth, increased margins, and reduced obsolescence and markdowns will play a more important role.

The Customer Perspective

The customer perspective should reflect customers within the supply chain as well as the end-use consumer. Benefits to all these customers should include improved quality of products and services, shorter lead times, improved availability (including reduced stock-outs and late deliveries), greater flexibility, and higher value.

The Internal Process Perspective

Improved processes throughout the supply chain should result in the following benefits:

- *Reduced waste:* This includes elimination or reduction of duplicative processes; harmonization of systems and processes; reduced defects, rejects, returns, and rework; and lower inventory levels.
- *Reduced order-to-delivery cycle times and shorter cash-to-cash cycles for all supply-chain participants.*
- *Flexible response:* This means the ability to meet a customer's unique requirements for product variety, volume, packaging, shipping arrangement, and delivery.

- *Reduced unit costs relative to the degree of customization and flexibility expected by the customer:* Suppliers attempt to drive out non-value-added costs by eliminating duplication of inventories, multiple handling of product, unconsolidated shipments, and uncoordinated promotions and deals.
- *Innovation:* Participants monitor new developments in technology, competition, and consumer preferences so as to jointly design and develop new offerings that will continually earn the loyalty of targeted customers.

The Learning and Growth Perspective

Human capital objectives include employees in procurement, operations, marketing, sales, logistics, and finance having the skills and knowledge to collaborate intra- and interorganizationally to enhance supply-chain performance and deliver more value to customers and end-use consumers. Information capital objectives relate to harmonization and linkages of systems across organizational boundaries, standardization of data protocols, sharing and analysis of customer and supplier information, and provision of information that is relevant, accurate, timely, and accessible. The organization culture should support best-practice sharing, continuous improvement, openness and transparency across all supply-chain partners, and a deep commitment to eliminating waste and delay throughout the system while delivering maximum value to end-use consumers.

As a specific application, consider the supply-chain Balanced Scorecard developed for a joint project between a large international producer of chemicals and a strategic partner, ChemTrade, one of its leading distributors.[5] The strategic partnership consisted of a long-term contract with exclusivity for both parties in several national regions. Each company participated in a project to improve all processes, from raw materials acquisition through delivery to the final consumer.

The project team decided to build a Balanced Scorecard to measure the success of the collaboration, to clarify the strategic objectives of the supply-chain partners, to provide a focus on critical performance measures in both organizations, and to identify opportunities for future improvement. We show its Strategy Map (see Figure 8-2) and Balanced Scorecard (see Figure 8-3) of objectives and measures. (At the time of the report, measures for the development [learning and growth] perspective had not yet been determined.)

Figure 8-2 Strategy Map, Chemicals Supply Chain

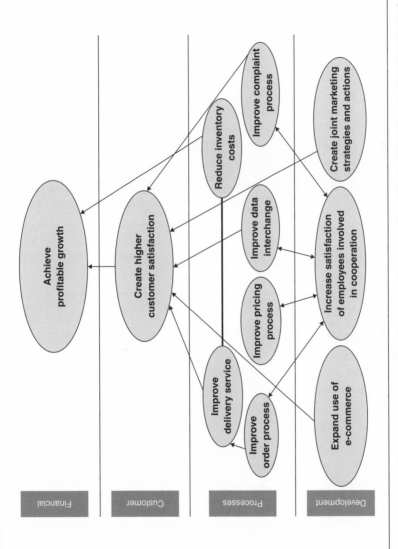

Source: K. Zimmerman, "Using the Balanced Scorecard for Interorganizational Performance Management of Supply Chains: A Case Study," in *Cost Management in Supply Chains* (Heidelberg: Physica-Verlag, 2002).

Figure 8-3 Supply-Chain Balanced Scorecard

Perspective	Strategic Objectives	Performance Measures
Financial	■ Profitable Growth	■ Turnover: product sales through channel
Customer	■ Market Share	■ Channel's market share of customers' purchases
	■ Customer Satisfaction	■ Customer satisfaction index (annual survey) ■ Number of complaints ■ Percentage of orders with complaints
Internal Processes	■ Delivery Reliability	■ Percent on-time delivery
	■ Inventory Management	■ Average inventory held in the two organizations ■ Average inventory divided by monthly sales
	■ Improved Administrative Processes	■ Sales volume in tons
Development	■ Expand e-Commerce	■ TBD
	■ Increased Satisfaction of Employees Involved in Strategic Alliance	■ TBD
	■ Joint Marketing Strategies and Actions	■ TBD

   In summary, supplier scorecards are common in manufacturing and retailing industries. Most of the existing supplier scorecards feature metrics for a low-total-cost strategy of cost reduction, on-time delivery, and consistent, zero-defect quality. These are fine if that is the end customer's strategy, but even for this strategy, KPI scorecards miss opportunities to align suppliers' processes and their human and information capital to enhance supply-chain performance. Additional opportunities exist for constructing more strategy-specific supplier Balanced Scorecards when a company looks to its supplier base for product innovation and to help it provide more complete solutions to its customers.

CUSTOMER SCORECARDS

Supplier and supply-chain scorecards generally look upstream from the company to its most important suppliers. As the company faces the other way, forward and downstream, it sees its strategic customers. The Rockwater Company, the undersea installation division of Brown & Root, provided us with an early example of constructing a scorecard with strategic customers.

Rockwater's new strategy was to nurture long-term, value-adding relationships with its key customers. This strategy was a radical departure from the construction industry norm, where business was almost always awarded to the lowest bidder. Rockwater had identified several of its leading customers that were looking to partner with their suppliers to find innovative ways to lower the total cost of constructing, installing, and operating oil and gas production facilities.

For each customer that expressed an interest in such long-term partnering relationships, Rockwater discussed a list of sixteen attributes that would characterize the working relationship on a project:

Functionality	Safety
	Engineering services
Quality	Minimum revision of submitted procedures
	Quality and awareness of performance
	Standard equipment provided
	Quality of personnel supplied
	Production quality
Price	Hours worked
	Value for money
	Innovation to reduce cost
Timeliness	Meeting schedule
	Timely submission of procedures
Relationship	Transparency of contracting relationship
	Flexibility
	Responsiveness
	Team rapport and spirit

Rockwater asked each customer to select which of these attributes would be most important on the project and then to apply a relative weighting scheme for the most important attributes. Rockwater shared this information with every member of its project team so that all of them knew the factors most important to the customer on this project.

Monthly, each key customer scored Rockwater's performance on the selected attributes. These customer performance scores provided the basis for the monthly meeting between contractor and customer to discuss project performance. Rockwater also aggregated these individual project scores into an overall customer satisfaction index for its own scorecard. This mechanism of constructing a customer- and project-specific index enabled Rockwater to customize its offering to individual customer preferences, to align its project team to deliver the customer's specific value proposition, and to receive feedback on how well it was meeting its customers' expectations.

Tiger Textiles (a disguised name) is the production intermediary between U.S. and European retail apparel chains (such as Gap and The Limited) and low-cost textile factories. Tiger does research to learn about its customers' future apparel manufacturing needs, advises them on fashion trends and new product opportunities, and contracts with factories in low-cost developing nations, such as Sri Lanka, Thailand, and Malaysia, to produce and deliver the desired volume, mix, and quality of clothing in a timely manner.

Tiger, like Rockwater, wanted to be more than a low-cost, reliable supplier of standard products. It wanted to differentiate itself by leveraging its knowledge and capabilities to offer customers more complete solutions. Tiger's strategy incorporated an important "business planning with customer" theme (see Figures 8-4 and 8-5): "Tiger Textiles must have a clear understanding of customers' long- and short-term needs and values in order to jointly develop business plans. Customer-focused planning requires including the customer in our global teams."

Tiger, in its customer perspective, set an objective to deliver high customer intimacy and service and to be recognized by its customers as a source of creativity and fashion ideas. To deliver on this objective, Tiger established an internal process objective: "develop relationships with key customers." It measured performance for this objective by the following:

- The number of (Tiger's) overseas associates that the customer knew.
- Associate turnover. (Tiger wanted associates that could develop long-term relationships with its key customers.)
- Achievement of goals in business plans developed with customers.

Figure 8-4 Tiger Textiles: "Business Planning with Customer" Theme (Strategy Map)

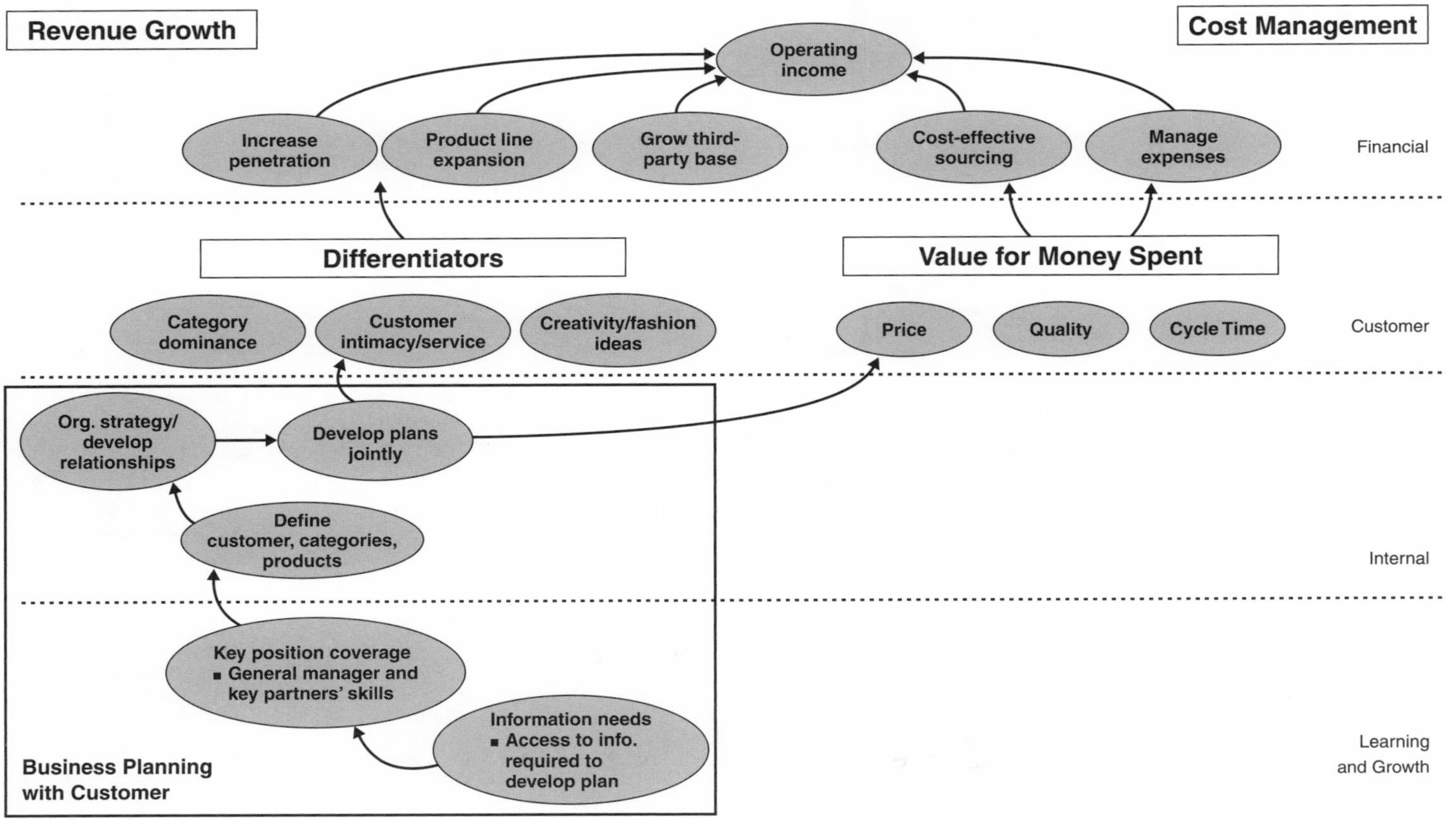

Figure 8-5 Tiger Textiles: "Business Planning with Customer" Theme (Balanced Scorecard)

	Objective Statement	"Do-Wells"	Potential Measures
Internal	**Define Customers, Category, Products** Target customers, categories, products that serve to meet our financial objectives	▪ Extensive knowledge of customer needs ▪ Detailed knowledge of competitive capabilities ▪ Global strategic understanding of sourcing ▪ Detailed planning guidelines ▪ Relative rate of return on product	▪ % of sales growth from new categories and products ▪ Penetration by customer and category ▪ Written business plan (actual vs. plan)

	Organize Strategy
	Develop Relationships
	Create global teams that include the customer to actualize the business planning process
		▪ Define common purpose for the team
		▪ Identify the skills needed to perform the work
		▪ Identify, recruit, train team players
		▪ Provide leadership support
		▪ Provide tools to do job
			▪ **Number of overseas associates that customer knows**
			▪ **Associate turnover**
			  ▪ **Overall**
			  ▪ **Overseas**
			▪ **Achieving the goals of the business plan**

	Joint Customer/Tiger Planning Develop joint customer/Tiger 3-year strategic business plan (reviewed every 6 months) that encompasses sourcing and customer business practices	▪ Convince customer of value of joint planning ▪ Understand workings of customer business processes (current and future) ▪ Develop plan preparation skills ▪ Understand Tiger worldwide capabilities ▪ Develop team leadership skills	▪ Number of objectives shared with a customer ▪ Number of plans developed ▪ % of objectives achieved
Learning and Growth	**Key Position Coverage** **GM and Key Partners (Sales VP, Regional Production Mgr., JV Partner) Skills** Enhance capability to develop the plan, communicate the plan, determine roles, and build the global team for execution of the plan	▪ Training and support of business planning skills ▪ Presentation and communication skills, tools, forums ▪ Train on team building, customer intimacy, leadership skills	▪ **Customer reaction to plan presentation** ▪ **Associate understanding of roles as determined by plan**
	Information Needs Access Develop access to information required to create business plan, including: ▪ Customer business information ▪ External and market (strategic global sourcing) information ▪ Internal (Tiger) business information	▪ Obtain information ▪ Share and distribute information ▪ Analyze information	▪ Availability of information for planning vs. required (timely, appropriate format)

Another key internal process was "joint customer/Tiger planning," with an objective to "develop joint customer/Tiger three-year strategic business plans, reviewed every six months, that encompass sourcing and customer business practices." Tiger measured this objective by the following:

- The number of objectives shared with a customer
- The number of joint business plans developed
- The percentage of objectives achieved

For these two critical internal processes to be implemented effectively, Tiger needed to enhance the skills and capabilities of its associates (employees) who dealt directly with customers. It set a learning and growth objective of strategic job coverage: general managers, sales vice presidents, regional production managers, and joint venture relationship managers had to have the skills to work collaboratively with key customers, including developing the joint business plan, communicating the plan, and building the global team for executing the plan. Tiger measured this objective by the following:

- Customer reaction to presentation of joint business plan
- Associates' understanding of their roles in the joint business plan

In this way, Tiger Textile's scorecard highlighted the objectives in the customer, internal, and learning and growth perspectives that would enable it to grow its business at higher margins by forging long-term, value-adding relationships with its key customers. These customers would supply many of the measures, within this customer intimacy theme, to Tiger.

ALLIANCE SCORECARDS

Increasingly, companies are using alliances to fill gaps in their own capabilities and to grow in new markets and regions. Coordination with alliance partners is not easy; many alliance ventures end in disappointment and failure.

Having a common set of measures from alliance partners is not a natural act. Each party has its own reporting process and measures, and each brings its own perspective of what it wants to contribute to the alliance (probably as little as possible) and what it hopes to gain from the alliance (as much as it can). Transcending these informational and motivational asymmetries, as economists would phrase it, requires an open, transparent process in which both sides clearly articulate their expected contributions and their desired outcomes, resulting in a document that summarizes the theory of the strategic case for the alliance.

Developing an alliance Balanced Scorecard can mitigate the natural conflict between alliance partners. The process of building the alliance Strategy Map and scorecard brings together senior decision makers from both partners to articulate clearly the objectives of the alliance and the strategy for achieving those objectives.

For example, a sales and marketing alliance might highlight the reduced cost of acquiring new customers, the reduced lead time to bring new products to market, and the sales increases resulting from acquiring new customers and leveraging existing customer relationships. A research and development alliance might focus on the quantity and innovativeness of newly developed products, lead times of the alliance's complete "idea-to-product development" cycle, and the incidence and impact of technology transfer to the parent companies. A manufacturing alliance might feature achievements in reducing production costs, improving quality, shortening the time from customer order until delivery, and increasing the reliability of delivery times.[6]

The finished product—a Strategy Map, a Balanced Scorecard of measures and targets, and agreed-upon, funded initiatives—provides a clear road map for the CEO of the alliance, as well as an excellent basis for governance of the venture by the two parent organizations. Yet a McKinsey study reported that fewer than one-fourth of alliances have adequate performance metrics, and this is by McKinsey's definition of "adequate," which may fall quite a bit short of a comprehensive Balanced Scorecard of measures derived from a Strategy Map of linked strategic objectives.[7]

The McKinsey study proposed an alliance Balanced Scorecard with four perspectives: financial, strategic (instead of "customer"), operational, and relationship (instead of "learning and growth"). Figure 8-6 illustrates some key objectives that might be included in such an alliance scorecard.

MERGER INTEGRATION

Of course, the closest integration between two external parties occurs when they merge to become a single entity. Many mergers fail, however, because the new company cannot integrate two management teams,

Figure 8-6 Prototype Alliance Strategic Objectives

Perspective	Objectives
Financial	■ Increase alliance revenues ■ Reduce redundant costs across alliance members ■ Increase parents' revenues through new customer relationships and related product sales ■ Develop growth options for parents from alliance developing new products and new customer relationships
Strategic	■ Develop new technology ■ Increase penetration with targeted customers ■ Increase learning opportunities for parents' employees assigned to alliance
Operational	■ Meet project milestones ■ Reduce costs in manufacturing, sales, or distribution ■ Improve product development and launch processes ■ Enhance coordination between alliance and parents
Relationship	■ Promote fast, effective decision making ■ Communicate effectively within alliance and between alliance partners ■ Build and maintain trust ■ Develop clear roles, responsibilities, objectives, and accountabilities for alliance managers and employees

two cultures, two strategies, two information systems, and two distinct sets of management processes into a single operating entity that can reap the hoped-for synergy benefits. But we have seen several mergers succeed when managers created a Balanced Scorecard to integrate the two companies.

Using the scorecard in this way produces two important benefits. First, developing a Strategy Map and Balanced Scorecard for the new company provides a mechanism by which managers from the two previously independent entities have an opportunity to work together toward a common objective. The intense dialogue and debates about strategy, strategic objectives, and measurements enable managers to learn how their counterparts think, whose opinions they value, and whom they can trust. The opportunities for new friendships and collaborative working relationships emerge organically from the executives' participation in the intensive process to build a Strategy Map and BSC.

The second benefit is that the finished Strategy Map and Balanced Scorecard provide a language executives can use to describe how to capture the intended synergies from the merger. Extensive research shows that most mergers are unsuccessful; the acquiring companies do not earn a competitive return on the amount they spent for the merger. Although some cost savings are realized from consolidation of facilities and administrative staff, in practice it has proven difficult to generate new growth opportunities from the combined organizations. For example, a McKinsey study revealed the following gloomy statistics about mergers in the 1990s:[8]

- Only 11 percent of 193 mergers during 1990–1997 experienced positive earnings growth three quarters after the merger; the typical merger experienced a 12 percent decline in earnings.
- Only 12 percent of acquisitions, 1995–1996, had accelerated earnings growth in the next three years; 42 percent of these had an earnings decline. The median among these mergers was a growth rate four percentage points lower than that of industry peers.
- The primary reasons for the earnings declines were dissatisfied customers and distracted employees.

The principal reason for the poor post-merger performance was an excessive concentration on achieving cost savings and insufficient attention to growing revenues. The few merged companies that succeeded focused on leveraging existing customer relationships for increased revenue, especially by retaining key revenue-generating employees.

These findings provide the rationale for a merged company to develop a Strategy Map and Balanced Scorecard as part of the merger integration process. Managers from the two previously independent companies formulate a specific strategy for leveraging the strengths of each company to create new revenue opportunities beyond what either company could have achieved operating independently. The process also produces a road map for implementing the revenue growth, as well as cost reduction; strategic themes through investment in key processes, employees, and information technology; and a unified corporate culture.

A good example of this process occurred with the merger of two oil companies: Alpha and Beta (disguised names). This merger formed one of the largest marketing and refining companies in the United States. The initial integration of the executive team occurred when the managers built a Balanced Scorecard for the new entity; the first meeting occurred even before the official closure of the deal. Each company had an equal number of representatives on the BSC executive team.

The BSC team built its scorecard on a pyramid (see Figure 8-7) to represent how Alpha-Beta Petroleum would become the best downstream marketing business in the United States. Its scorecard was built on six

Figure 8-7 Alpha-Beta Integration Strategy

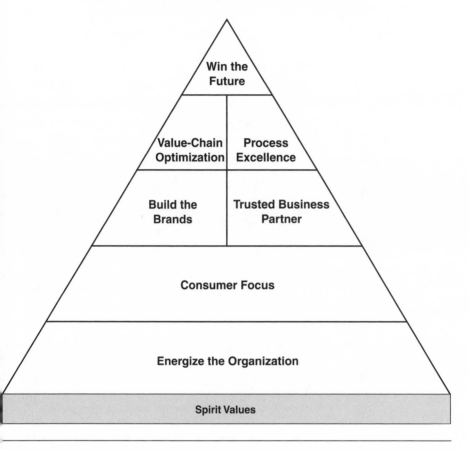

themes (similar to the DuPont Engineering Polymers theme-based score-card described in Chapter 4):

- Consumer focus
- Build the brand(s)
- Trusted business partner
- Value-chain optimization
- Operational excellence
- Energize the organization

The BSC team selected one Alpha and one Beta executive as co-owners of each theme. Each pair oversaw the targets, initiatives, communication, and implementation of its theme.

For each of the six themes, the BSC team selected four to eight strategic key issues and then developed objectives, a Strategy Map, measures, and targets for the theme. For example, Figure 8-8 illustrates a summary of theme 1, consumer focus; Figure 8-9 shows the Strategy Map, scorecard measures, and initiatives developed for this theme.

Alpha-Beta Petroleum used the strategic themes and measures as key elements of its Day One communication, both internally and externally, upon official consummation of the merger. During the next five months it cascaded the scorecard throughout the organization so that local scorecards could be used to set departmental and personal objectives in the new company's performance management system. The process enabled Alpha-Beta to operate as one company, with a coherent, integrated strategy, right from its beginning as a new legal entity.

SUMMARY

Once organizations have aligned internal business and support groups, they can extend their strategic alignment by creating Strategy Maps and Balanced Scorecards with key external partners, including suppliers,

Figure 8-8   Summary of "Consumer Focus" Theme at Alpha-Beta

The consumer focus theme impacts all of our business. The objective is to increase the number of incremental purchases from the targeted customer segments in both gasoline and the convenience store by creating loyalty. In addition, we need to focus our employees and channel partners on the benefits of focusing on the customer.

Key Points and Rationale	High-Level Business Case Description

■ Research-based understanding of consumer buying experience expectations
■ Consistently get the basics right at our branded sites
■ Consistent execution with channel partners
  ■ Build case for consumer focus
  ■ Communication
  ■ Education
  ■ Progams, tools
■ Reward, recognition, consequences
■ Experiment with innovation to differentiate the buying experience (after the basics are right)
	■ Key drivers of growth and profitability are
	  ■ Targeted customer focus
	  ■ Incremental purchases
	  ■ Channel partner and Alpha-Beta (gas margin and convenience retailing)
	■ Gasoline potential
	■ C-store potential
	■ Demonstrates the focus we need to have on convenience retailing

Figure 8-9 Partial Strategy Map for "Consumer Focus" Theme at Alpha-Beta

Customer Focus	Measurements	Initiatives
Innovative experiments around the basics		
Consistently pleasant buying experience		■ Consistent Execution of the Basics Program
Incremental sales per customer	■ Mystery Shopper Index	
Well-defined recognition program to reward and recognize customer service	■ Five Star, Quality Rating, Image Evaluation Program	
Consistent execution of basics	■ Consumer Satisfaction Index	
Consumer-focused employees and channel partners	■ Customer-Focused Organization Employee Survey	■ Consumer Focused Employee and Channel Partners Roadshow and Training Program
Segmented consumer research (fact based)		

customers, and alliances. At present, most supplier, customer, and alliance scorecards tend to be collections of key performance indicators intended to drive improvement in the operational performance metrics of cost, quality, and timeliness.

The opportunity remains for companies to forge deeper and more effective relationships with their external partners through an intense collaborative process focused on producing a Strategy Map and Balanced Scorecard that describes the objectives and strategy of the interorganizational relationship. Such a process builds great consensus and motivation for the relationship, and the jointly developed scorecard serves as the accountability contract for relationship performance.

NOTES

1. S. Kulp and V. G. Narayanan, "Metalcraft Supplier Scorecard," Case 9-102-047 (Boston: Harvard Business School Publishing, 2005).
2. The detailed definitions of each of the measurements, along with a numerical example of a calculation and the respective responsibilities of suppliers, manufacturers, and retailers, can be found at http://www.cpfr.org/documents/pdf/CPFR_Tab_6.pdf.
3. See http://www.globalscorecard.net/download/ecr_related.asp.
4. P. C. Brewer and T. W. Speh, "Using the Balanced Scorecard to Measure Supply Chain Performance," *Journal of Business Logistics* (2000): 75–93; and "Adapting the Balanced Scorecard to Supply Chain Management," *Supply Chain Management Review* (March–April 2001).
5. K. Zimmerman, "Using the Balanced Scorecard for Interorganizational Performance Management of Supply Chains: A Case Study," in *Cost Management in Supply Chains,* eds. S. Seuring and M. Goldbach (Heidelberg: Physica-Verlag, 2002), 399–415.
6. See L. Segil, *Measuring the Value of Partnering* (New York: AMACOM, 2004), 19.
7. J. Bamford and D. Ernst, "Managing an Alliance Portfolio," *McKinsey Quarterly* (Autumn 2002): 6–10.
8. "Why Mergers Fail," *McKinsey Quarterly* (2001): 64–73.

CHAPTER NINE

MANAGING THE ALIGNMENT PROCESS

ALIGNMENT IS NOT a one-time event. The initial project phase of implementing an enterprise-wide Balanced Scorecard program aligns corporate-level strategy with business and support unit strategies. This sets the stage for achieving performance synergies.

Change, however, is constant—in the industry, among competitors, in the regulatory and macroeconomic environment, and in technology, customers, and employees. Strategies and their implementation must therefore continually evolve. An aligned organization at one time will soon become unaligned. The second law of thermodynamics teaches us that entropy (disorder) continually increases. New energy must be continually pumped into a system if it is to remain aligned and coherent. In this chapter, we describe the process of managing and sustaining organizational alignment.

CREATING ALIGNMENT

Sometime in the middle of their fiscal year, almost all enterprises conduct a multiday off-site meeting organized by the strategic planning department. At this meeting the executive leadership team reviews and updates the company's strategy in light of changing circumstances and the new knowledge gained since the last strategy was formulated. The update involves many of the traditional techniques of strategic planning, including environmental scans, SWOT (strengths, weaknesses, opportunities, and threats) analysis, competitive analysis, five-forces models, and scenario planning.

Subsequently, business units and shared-service departments do their own annual strategy planning updates. The strategies of these organizational units, however, are often done in isolation, uninformed by the corporate strategy, and therefore they do not reflect how the units must work together to achieve integration and synergy. These fragmented, unaligned management processes explain why most enterprises encounter great difficulty in implementing their strategies.

A comprehensive and managed alignment process helps the enterprise to achieve synergies through integration. We have identified eight alignment checkpoints (see Figure 9-1) from the practices of successful Balanced Scorecard users. If an organization is aligned at each of the eight checkpoints, all its initiatives and actions are directed toward common strategic priorities:

1. *Enterprise value proposition*: The corporate office defines strategic guidelines to shape strategies at lower levels of the organization, as described in Chapters 3 and 4.

2. *Board and shareholder alignment*: The corporation's board of directors reviews, approves, and monitors the corporate strategy, as described in Chapter 7.

3. *Corporate office to corporate support unit*: The corporate strategy is translated into those corporate policies—such as standardized practices, risk management, and resource sharing—that will be administered by corporate support units, as discussed in Chapter 5.

4. *Corporate office to business units:* The corporate priorities are cascaded into business unit strategies, as discussed in Chapters 3, 4, and 6.

5. *Business units to support units:* The strategic priorities of the business units are incorporated in the strategies of the functional support units, as discussed in Chapter 5.

6. *Business units to customers:* The priorities of the customer value proposition are communicated to targeted customers and are reflected in specific customer feedback and measures, as discussed in Chapter 8.

7. *Business units to suppliers and alliance partners:* The shared priorities for suppliers, outsourcers, and other external partners are reflected in business unit strategies, as discussed in Chapter 8.

8. *Business support units to corporate support:* The strategies of the local business support units reflect the priorities of the corporate support unit, as discussed in Chapter 5.

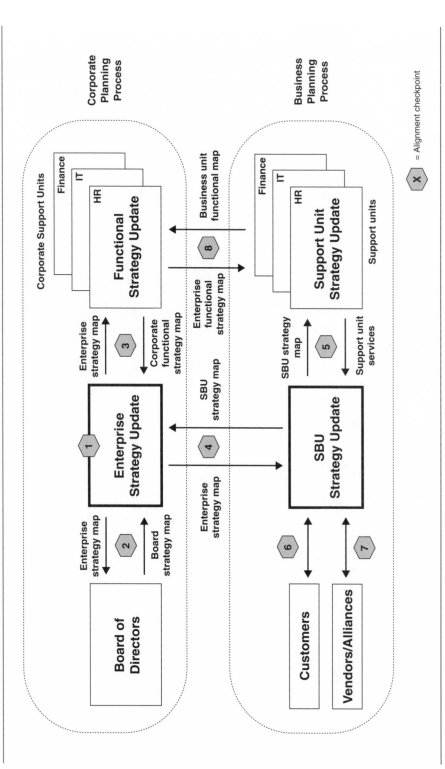

As a specific example of an aligned corporation, let's revisit the Ingersoll-Rand story told in several earlier chapters. Recall that Ingersoll-Rand's new corporate strategy (depicted in Figure 3-4) was to shift from being a holding company of product-centered business units to one providing branded, integrated customer solutions that cut across traditional business unit lines. IR's new enterprise value proposition illustrates fulfillment of checkpoint 1. The strategy shift required a new culture of teamwork and knowledge sharing, new competencies, and new leadership values. The cultural shift was facilitated by the corporate human resources organization, as described in Chapter 5. Figure 5-10 illustrates how Ingersoll fulfilled checkpoint 3 by translating the corporate business strategy into a corporate human resources strategy focused on leadership development, cross-business teamwork, and realignment of personal goals to the new strategy. Once the corporate-level alignment was achieved, Ingersoll's corporate HR group cascaded its template to HR groups in the five major business groups, fulfilling checkpoint 8. This process aligned local HR groups located within business units with corporate HR priorities.

Each of Ingersoll's business groups created a Strategy Map that reflected the dual citizenship theme of achieving local excellence while delivering on corporate-level themes (see Figure 3-4), fulfilling alignment checkpoint 4. Ingersoll also began to communicate the new corporate strategy with its board and shareholders in its annual report (see Figure 7-10), fulfilling alignment checkpoint 2. Thus Ingersoll successfully passed all five corporate planning alignment checkpoints shown in the upper half of Figure 9-1.

The single most important component of the organization alignment occurs at alignment checkpoint 4: the linkage of business unit strategies to the enterprise value proposition. Many organizations take explicit actions to monitor this alignment. At Canon, USA, the corporate planning group creates sticky notes that show every objective from its six main business and support units' Strategy Maps. Then it posts the business and support unit objectives on the corporate map to see how well each corporate objective is supported. Next, it analyzes the results to see why some objectives have strong support and others have weak support. In this way, the planning group not only monitors alignment but also identifies cross-functional and cross-unit links within the strategy so that it can create value-sharing communities across the company.

During the planning process at St. Mary's/Duluth Clinic Health System, the vice president of strategic alignment reviews the Strategy Maps of various divisions and departments to ensure alignment among them and also with the corporate strategy. The Bank of Tokyo-Mitsubishi, discussed in Chapter 4 (Figure 4-1), explicitly identifies objectives on its corporate Strategy Map that are common across all business units. This provides a point of reference for the director of the corporate planning group to ensure that business unit strategies align with corporate themes, such as risk management and cost reduction.

In each of these companies, a corporate-level group managed an explicit process to ensure that business unit strategies were aligned *vertically* with corporate priorities and *horizontally* with the strategies of related business units.

The implementation of business unit strategy has three other alignment checkpoints. In Chapter 5, we describe how to achieve checkpoint 5 by introducing the portfolio of strategic support services, which translates the priorities of a business unit Strategy Map into specific support unit programs and initiatives. Figures 5-3, 5-4, and 5-5 illustrate how Handleman built tight links between business units' strategy and the desired human resources support.

In Chapter 4, we show how IBM Learning (Figure 4-8) developed business unit Strategy Maps to align its training and learning services with business unit strategy. In both the Handleman and the IBM cases, the companies introduced explicit processes to align the strategies of key support units with value creation in business units, as required by alignment checkpoint 5.

Companies can also introduce explicit measures and processes to align with their customers and suppliers (checkpoints 6 and 7). For example, as discussed in Chapter 8, Rockwater developed scorecards jointly with its top ten customers to define explicitly the value proposition desired by each customer. Subsequent quarterly reviews of these scorecards with customers helped to strengthen the bonds and make Rockwater an industry leader. In Chapter 1, Sport-Man, Inc.'s purchasing department (see Figure 1-7) used a similar structure to create strong alignment with the company's suppliers, which manufacture and deliver products to Sport-Man's retail outlets.

In summary, the planning processes at corporate units and in business and support units set priorities, allocate resources, and—the new task—create alignment throughout the enterprise. Organizations create alignment by embedding the eight alignment checkpoints into their planning processes. Having created alignment through the planning process, organizations face the remaining question: how to manage and sustain alignment on an ongoing basis.

MANAGING AND SUSTAINING ALIGNMENT

You can't manage what you don't measure. These are the words we live by.
We developed the Balanced Scorecard so that organizations can measure
and therefore more effectively manage strategic processes such as customer acquisition, customer retention, new product development, and
employee competency development. If we wish to manage the new alignment process, we should—to be consistent with our message—identify
alignment measures.

Figure 9-2 shows the development of alignment measures for each of
the eight alignment checkpoints. Organizations can aggregate these measures into an organization alignment index by choosing weights specific to
their priorities and beliefs about where synergistic benefits are most likely
to arise.

The proposed measures are process—not outcome—measures. The
corresponding outcome measures—such as the percentage of business
units that have achieved six sigma quality levels or the percentage of business units achieving their targets for retention of key customers—should
appear on the corporate scorecard. The process measures monitor the
quality of the alignment process itself. Our theory of alignment predicts
that a superior organization alignment process leads to high achievement
of the corporate outcome measures.

The alignment checkpoint metrics, along with the subprocess measures (see the middle column of Figure 9-2), provide useful feedback
about the performance of the alignment process. We can develop an overall picture of the health of and the issues surrounding alignment by dis-
playing the individual checkpoint measures on an *alignment map,* as
shown in Figure 9-3. Panel A, in the upper-left quadrant, shows the starting point—a blank template that condenses the eight alignment checkpoints into three domains: corporate, business units, and support units.
The three other panels depict situations where organizations typically fall
short in the alignment process.

Panel B, in the upper-right quadrant, illustrates an alignment program
with strong corporate leadership but weak implementation in the business
and support units. The corporate strategy has been defined and translated
into an enterprise value proposition (checkpoint 1), and the strategy has
been reviewed and approved by the board (checkpoint 2). The strategy has
been translated to the corporate staff departments (checkpoint 3), which
in turn have provided guidelines to support departments in the business
units (checkpoint 8). Corporate has made serious efforts to translate its
strategic priorities in the enterprise value proposition to the business units

Figure 9-2 Measuring Organization Alignment

Organization Alignment: Are the various units, departments, and constituents aligned with the enterprise value proposition?

	Alignment Checkpoint	Subprocess Measure		Process Measure
1	Enterprise Value Proposition	■ Enterprise value proposition defined ■ Enterprise scorecard defined	✓ ✓	100%
2	Board/Shareholder Alignment	■ Board responsibilities linked to strategy through corporate scorecard	✓	100%
3	Corporate Office and Corporate Support Unit	■ Percent corporate support units with linked scorecards	✓ HR ✓ IT ✓ Finance ✓ Other	100%
4	Corporate Office and Business Units	■ Percent business units with corporate linkage		100%
5	Business Units and Support Units	■ Percent business units with support unit alignment ■ Linked scorecards ■ Service agreements	40% HR 50% IT 80% Finance	55%
6	Business Units and Customers	■ Percent key customers with BSC or service agreements		40%
7	Business Units and Vendors/Alliances	■ Percent key suppliers with BSC or service agreements		30%
8	Business Support Units and Corporate Support Unit	■ Percent business support units linked with corporate support unit	100% HR 50% IT 80% Finance	80%

Organization Alignment Index

XX%

(Organizations choose weights among the eight alignment checkpoint measures depending on their alignment priorities)

Data are illustrative.

Figure 9-3 Organization Alignment Maps

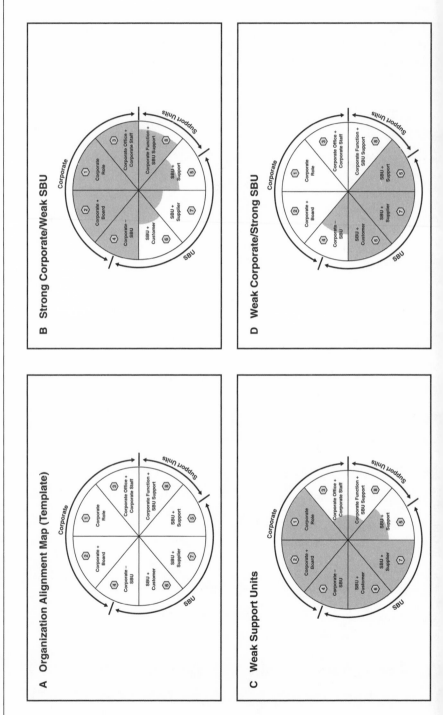

(checkpoint 4), but the business units do not share this passion. Execution at the business unit level (checkpoints 5, 6, and 7) is weak. Many of the potential benefits of the corporate program have yet to be realized.

Panel C, in the lower-left quadrant, describes an alignment process characterized by strong execution at the corporate and business unit levels but weak implementation by the support units. The problem begins with a weak link at the corporate level. Corporate has not emphasized the translation of its priorities to the corporate staff departments (checkpoint 3), and corporate staff has not been able to communicate corporate priorities to the business support units (checkpoint 8). The local support units, therefore, have not been responsive to business unit requirements and therefore cannot support their strategies.

The fourth example, Panel D in the lower-right quadrant, describes a situation that is frequently encountered when the BSC performance management program is initiated in a local business unit. Alignment within the business units is excellent, with strong links to customers (checkpoint 6), suppliers (checkpoint 7), and the local support units (checkpoint 5). The business unit has attempted to integrate its strategy with what it perceives to be corporate strategy and priorities, but without adequate leadership and guidance from the corporate headquarters, it has yet to link with the strategies of other business units and create synergies with them (checkpoint 4). The business unit's support units also suffer from the lack of strategic guidance from their corporate support units (checkpoint 8).

The alignment map provides a simple picture of the current status of organization alignment, and it summarizes the detailed and actionable measures selected by the enterprise to monitor the performance of its alignment processes.

ACCOUNTABILITY

The final building block of managing organization alignment is accountability. Just as the chief financial officer is accountable for running budgeting and the vice president of human resources is accountable for running employee performance management, a senior executive should be responsible for running the alignment process. Unless someone is accountable, alignment will not happen.

Several organizations have started to establish an accountability structure for organization alignment. J. D. Irving, a multibillion-dollar Canadian conglomerate, created a position called *alignment champion* to help business units implement the various change programs in their strategies.

St. Mary's/Duluth Clinic, a health-care provider in northern Minnesota, created a position of *vice president of strategic alignment*. The executive in this position facilitates the execution of the organization's strategy. By placing this position at the vice president level, the CEO sent the message that ensuring organization alignment was a high priority for him. Canadian Blood Services (formerly the Canadian Red Cross) created an *alignment council* at the outset of its Balanced Scorecard program to ensure that the strategies of corporate and various business units would be consistent and integrated.

The Bank of Tokyo-Mitsubishi, Headquarters for the Americas (BTMHQA), discussed in Chapter 6, introduced a sophisticated scheme to create alignment through its governance process. As shown in the first column of Figure 9-4, the bank's strategy was built on six strategic themes: grow revenue, manage risk, improve productivity, align human capital, and enhance financial performance and customer satisfaction.

The bank already had eight committees involved in some aspect of organizational governance, as shown in the column headings in Figure 9-4. The bank asked each committee, in addition to its traditional duties, to monitor the strategy themes within its domain of responsibility. For example, the credit risk committee, at its monthly meeting, discussed and acted on the financial and risk-management strategy themes. At the monthly meeting of the operations control committee, members monitored the customer, risk-management, and productivity themes. On a quarterly basis, the business strategy committee reviewed all six strategy themes. With this formal assignment of responsibilities, BTMHQA embedded alignment and accountability in its core management committees and processes.

The organizations in these examples addressed components of the alignment process by assigning accountability to specific individuals or committees. Although this is a move in the right direction, we believe that alignment and accountability must be built into all the key management processes undertaken throughout the year.

We have recently observed in practice a new role emerging in organizations to manage strategy execution in a comprehensive and integrated way. Examples are the Chrysler Group, Crown Castle, U.S. Army, and St. Mary's/Duluth Clinic. We call this new role the office of strategy management (OSM). The new office is often the successor to the Balanced Scorecard project team. The OSM represents the natural evolution of the Balanced Scorecard from a project to an ongoing alignment and

Figure 9-4 Alignment and Accountability at Bank of Tokyo-Mitsubishi, Americas

Committee / Theme	Business Strategy Committee (Quarterly)	Monthly Profit Review (Monthly)	Operations Control Committee (Monthly)	Bankwide Risk Mgmt Committee (Monthly)	Credit Risk Mgmt Committee (Monthly)	Compliance Committee (Quarterly)	IT Steering Committee (Monthly)	Human Resources Committee (Quarterly)
Financial	■	■		■	■			
Customer	■		■					
Grow Revenues	■	■						
Manage Risk	■					■	■	
Improve Productivity	■		■				■	
Human Capital	■							■

- Major committee meetings are clearly linked to strategic themes and goals of the organization.
- Discussions at all major periodic management meetings focus on relevant areas of the scorecard.
- All areas are reviewed quarterly at the business strategy committee meeting

governance process.[1] One of the key roles for the OSM is to manage the alignment process, with the following job description.

Organization Alignment

The OSM helps the entire enterprise gain a consistent view of strategy, including the identification and realization of corporate synergies. The office of strategy management facilitates the development and cascading of Balanced Scorecards at different hierarchical levels of the organization. Its responsibilities for the alignment process include the following:

- Defining, on the corporate scorecard, the synergies to be created through cross-business integration at lower organization levels
- Linking business unit strategies and scorecards to the corporate strategy
- Linking support unit strategies and scorecards to the strategic objectives of the business units and corporate
- Linking external partners, such as customers, suppliers, joint ventures, and the board of directors, to the organization's strategy
- Organizing the executive leadership team's review and approval of the scorecards produced by the business units, support units, and external partners

Alignment, like the other strategy execution processes, crosses organization boundaries. To be executed effectively, alignment requires the integration and cooperation of individuals from various organizational units. This poses a dilemma because most organizations have no natural home for cross-business processes. Organizations are built on business units or functions that operate in isolation from each other. Those organizations that have instituted an office of strategy management address this problem by creating a small group of individuals to manage the cross-business processes, including alignment, that are critical to successful execution of strategy.

SUMMARY

Any interface where two disparate organizations—corporate, business unit, support unit, customer, or supplier—come together represents a potential source of value creation through alignment. The enterprise value proposition and the cascading process of Strategy Maps and Balanced Scorecards are the mechanisms that unleash and capture this incremental value.

By its very nature, alignment requires cooperation across organizational boundaries, and therefore the process must be managed proactively, preferably by an individual or organizational unit that is accountable for the success of the alignment. Assigning responsibility and accountability for an effective organizational alignment process is a natural task for the new office of strategy management, which can coordinate the multiple planning processes and ensure, at least annually, that all the alignment checkpoints are achieved.

NOTES

1. The office is described in more detail in R. S. Kaplan and D. P. Norton, "The Office of Strategy Management," *Harvard Business Review* (October 2005): 72–80.

CHAPTER 10

TOTAL STRATEGIC ALIGNMENT

THE BALANCED SCORECARD, since its introduction in 1992, has evolved into the centerpiece of a sophisticated system to manage the execution of strategy. The effectiveness of the approach is derived from two simple capabilities: (1) the ability to clearly *describe* strategy (the contribution of Strategy Maps) and (2) the ability to link strategy to the *management system* (the contribution of Balanced Scorecards). The net result is the ability to align all units, processes, and systems of an organization to its strategy.

Figure 10-1 describes a simple management framework for strategy execution. The approach adds several important features to the classic "plan-do-check-act" closed-loop, goal-seeking process introduced by Deming in the quality movement.[1]

- *Strategy* is explicitly identified as the focal point of the management system (as opposed to "quality").
- *Alignment* is identified as an explicit part of the management process. Executing strategy requires the highest level of integration and teamwork among organizational units and processes.
- *Executive leadership* is a necessary condition for successful strategy execution. Managing strategy is synonymous with managing change. Without strong executive leadership, constructive change is not possible.

The core idea is that strategy is at the center of the management system. With the strategy clearly defined, all components of the management

Figure 10-1 The BSC Strategy Execution Framework

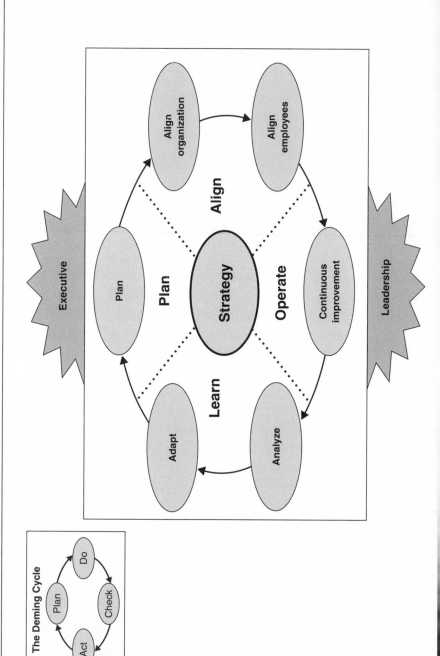

process can be designed to create alignment. As shown in Figure 10-2, alignment has four components: strategic fit, organization alignment, human capital alignment, and alignment of planning and control systems. We look at each of these in turn.

STRATEGIC FIT

Strategy consists of numerous high-impact activities that ultimately must be resourced and coordinated through the management system. A strategy can be described by a detailed set of objectives and initiatives. *Strategic fit,* a concept introduced by Michael Porter, refers to the internal consistency of the activities that implement the differentiating components of the strategy.[2] Strategic fit exists when the network of internal performance drivers is consistent and aligned with the desired customer and financial outcomes. Strategy Maps, extensively described in one of our previous books, provide a mechanism to explicitly identify and measure the internal alignment of processes, people, and technology with the customer value proposition and customer and shareholder objectives.[3]

ORGANIZATION ALIGNMENT

The subject of this book—*organization alignment*—explores how the various component parts of an organization synchronize their activities to create integration and synergy. Strategy Maps and Balanced Scorecards provide executives with a mechanism to describe strategy at each level and to communicate it from one level to the next. They also measure the extent to which goals requiring cross-organization teamwork are being addressed among organizational units.

HUMAN CAPITAL ALIGNMENT

Strategy is formulated at the top, but it must be executed at the bottom—by machine operators, call center personnel, delivery truck drivers, salespeople, and engineers. If employees don't understand the strategy or are not motivated to achieve it, the enterprise's strategy is bound to fail. *Human capital alignment* is achieved when employees' goals, training, and incentives become aligned with business strategy.

Figure 10-2 Creating Total Strategic Alignment

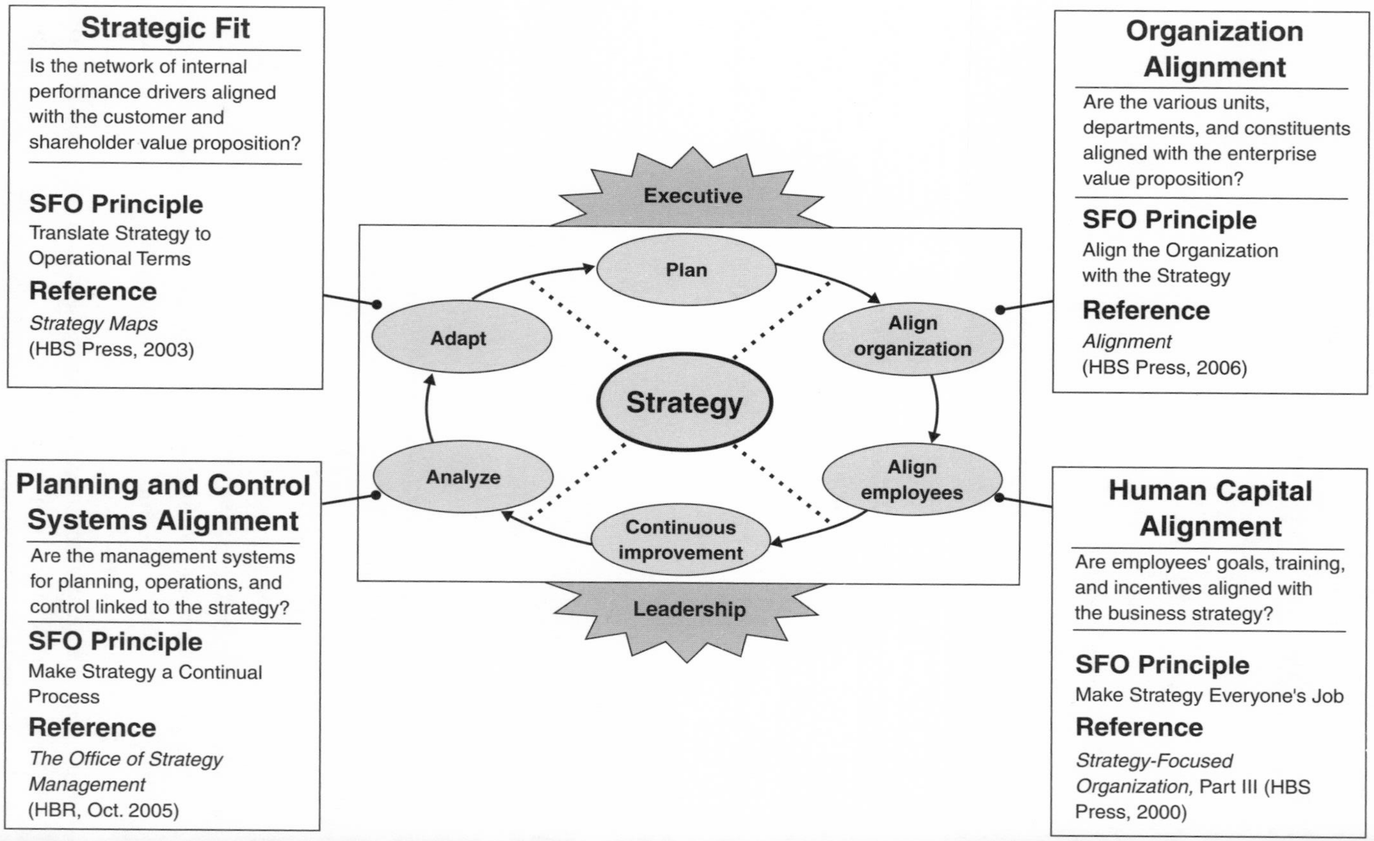

Strategic Fit

Is the network of internal performance drivers aligned with the customer and shareholder value proposition?

SFO Principle
Translate Strategy to Operational Terms

Reference
Strategy Maps
(HBS Press, 2003)

Planning and Control Systems Alignment

Are the management systems for planning, operations, and control linked to the strategy?

SFO Principle
Make Strategy a Continual Process

Reference
The Office of Strategy Management
(HBR, Oct. 2005)

Organization Alignment

Are the various units, departments, and constituents aligned with the enterprise value proposition?

SFO Principle
Align the Organization with the Strategy

Reference
Alignment
(HBS Press, 2006)

Human Capital Alignment

Are employees' goals, training, and incentives aligned with the business strategy?

SFO Principle
Make Strategy Everyone's Job

Reference
Strategy-Focused Organization, Part III (HBS Press, 2000)

Align organization

Align employees

Plan

Strategy

Continuous improvement

Adapt

Analyze

Executive

Leadership

PLANNING AND CONTROL SYSTEMS ALIGNMENT

The organization's planning, operations, and control processes allocate resources, drive action, monitor performance, and adapt the strategy as required. Even if enterprises develop a good strategy and align their organizational units and employees to it, misaligned management systems can inhibit its effective execution. *Planning and control systems alignment* exists when the management systems for planning, operations, and control are linked to the strategy.

Our previous book *Strategy Maps* and this book have dealt in depth with the first two alignment components: strategic fit and organization alignment. To provide a complete alignment picture, we close *Alignment* with brief descriptions of the two remaining components: aligning human capital and aligning management systems.

ALIGNING HUMAN CAPITAL

Alignment programs cannot deliver results unless employees have a personal commitment to help their enterprise and unit achieve strategic objectives. The human capital alignment process must gain the commitment of all employees to the successful implementation of strategy.

Psychologists have identified two forces for motivating people. *Intrinsic motivation* occurs when people engage in an activity for its own sake. They get pleasure from performing the activity; it contributes to their satisfaction and creates outcomes that they value. *Extrinsic motivation* arises from the carrot of external rewards or the stick of avoiding negative consequences. Positive rewards include praise, promotions, and financial incentives. The threat of negative consequences can also motivate; employees will strive to avoid criticism from a supervisor, a loss in prestige from failing to achieve a public target, or a loss of position or employment.

Intrinsic motivation is generally associated with those who engage in more entrepreneurial and creative problem solving; compared with those who are motivated only by extrinsic rewards or consequences, intrinsically motivated employees consider a wider range of possibilities, explore more choices, share more knowledge with coworkers, and pay more attention to complexities, inconsistencies, and the long-term consequences in their environment. Extrinsic motivation focuses employees on actions to achieve a reward or avoid punishment. Extrinsically motivated employees tend not to question the measures used to evaluate their performance. They assume that higher-level managers have gotten the measures correct and that their job is to move the measures in the desired direction and achieve the targets managers have established for the measures.

Although psychologists generally advocate the benefits of intrinsic over extrinsic motivation, companies have found that these two motivating forces are complementary and not competitive. In fact, the best-performing companies use both forces to align employees with organizational success.

Communicate and Educate to Create Intrinsic Motivation

We opened this book with a metaphor of rowers in a shell, attempting to achieve alignment as they row down the Charles River separating Boston and Cambridge. These individuals make huge sacrifices to compete. They wake up early on wintry mornings to exercise and practice. They commit several hours each day to the activity. How much do they get paid for it? Nothing. The athletes sacrifice and work hard because they enjoy preparing for the contest, working with their teammates, and competing to win. Imagine the energy released if a company could get its employees similarly motivated—working hard individually and in teams to help the enterprise be the best in a global competition.

Leaders create intrinsic motivation by appealing to employees' desire to work for a successful organization that makes a positive contribution to the world. Employees want to take pride in the organization in which they spend much of their waking lives. Employees should understand how the success of their organization benefits not only shareholders but also customers, suppliers, and the communities in which it operates. Employees should feel that their organization functions both efficiently and effectively. No one enjoys working for a failing, underperforming enterprise. They should be reassured that the organization does not squander resources in pursuit of its mission. Poorly functioning organizations, bureaucracies that bog down decision making, and turf battles arising from the narrow-mindedness often spawned by functional silos are visible to everyone and demoralizing to all.

Communication of vision, mission, and strategy is the first step in creating intrinsic motivation among employees. Executives can use the Strategy Map and Balanced Scorecard to communicate strategy—both *what* the organization wants to accomplish and *how* it intends to realize its strategic outcomes. Objectives and measures in the financial and customer perspectives of the Balanced Scorecard describe the outcomes the organization seeks with the entities that supply funds: shareholders and customers (donors and constituents, for nonprofit and public-sector organizations). Objectives and measures in the internal and learning and growth perspectives describe how employees, suppliers, and technology are aligned around critical processes that deliver superior value propositions for customers and shareholders while meeting community expectations. Taking all the objectives and measures together provides a comprehensive picture of the organization's value-creating activities.

This new representation of strategy communicates to everyone in the organization what the organization is about: how it intends to create long-term value and where each individual can make a contribution to organizational objectives. Individuals are freed from narrow and restrictive job descriptions, a legacy of the scientific management movement of a century ago. They can now come to work each day energized about doing their job differently and better, helping to advance the organization's success and realize their personal objectives.

New information, ideas, and actions, aligned with organizational objectives, emanate from the organization's front lines and back offices. Employees become truly empowered by understanding what the organization wishes to accomplish and how they can contribute. Organizational units—business units, departments, support units, and shared services—understand where they fit within the overall strategy and how they can create value within their units and by working cooperatively with other units.

Communication by leaders is critical. Employees cannot follow if executives do not lead. Executives at our conferences regularly report that they could not overcommunicate the strategy; effective communication was critical for the success of their BSC implementations. One CEO told us that if he were to write a book describing his successful transformation of a large insurance company, he would definitely include a chapter on the Balanced Scorecard; it played an invaluable role in the turnaround. But he would devote five chapters to communication, because he spent most of his time communicating with business unit heads, frontline and back-office employees, and key suppliers such as insurance brokers and agencies.

Managers report that they must communicate seven times, in seven different ways. They regularly use multiple communication channels to get the message out: speeches, newsletters, brochures, bulletin boards, interactive town hall meetings, intranets, monthly reviews, training programs, and online educational courses.

Reinforce and Reward with Extrinsic Motivation

Extrinsic motivation should reinforce the strategic message. The most successful Balanced Scorecard implementations have occurred when organizations skillfully melded intrinsic and extrinsic motivation. If the organization succeeds because of the efforts of its employees, it should share some of the increase in value with the employees who made it happen.

Quite a few Balanced Scorecard implementations have failed, however, when companies relied only on extrinsic motivation. They changed the compensation system to include nonfinancial measures—organized by customers, processes, and people—as well as traditional financial measures. But the new compensation system was more a checklist of measures, and not a reflection of a new strategy. Executives never communicated the rationale for the measures, nor did they embed the measures in a coherent strategic framework such as a Strategy Map containing linked strategic objectives and measures across the four Balanced Scorecard perspectives.

Companies use two principal tools to create extrinsic motivation. First, they align *employees' personal objectives* and goals with the strategy; some have even created personal scorecards. Setting objectives for individuals, of course, is not new. Management by objectives (MBO) has been around for decades. But MBO is distinctly different from the kind of employee objectives established with the guidance of a Balanced Scorecard. The objectives in a traditional MBO system are established within the structure of the individual's organizational unit, reinforcing narrow, functional thinking. In contrast, when employees, through communication, education, and training, come to understand the strategies of their unit and enterprise, they can develop personal objectives that are cross-functional, longer-term, and strategic. Annually, employees validate their personal strategic objectives with the help of their supervisors and human resources professionals. Several organizations have even encouraged employees to develop personal Balanced Scorecards, with each employee setting targets to improve a cost or revenue figure, boost performance with external or internal customers, improve a process or two that will deliver customer and financial value, and enhance a personal competency to drive process improvement.

The second source of extrinsic motivation is unleashed when companies link *incentive compensation* to targeted scorecard measures. To modify and align behavior as required by the strategy and as defined in the scorecard, an organization must reinforce change through incentive compensation. When Balanced Scorecard measures are linked to an incentive compensation program, managers see a significant increase in employees' level of interest in the details of the strategy.

Incentive plans vary widely across organizations. The plans, however, generally have an individual component and a business unit and enterprise component. Plans that calculate awards only on business unit and enterprise performance signal the importance of teamwork and knowledge sharing, but they also may encourage individual shirking and free rider problems. Plans that reward only individual performance generate strong employee incentives to improve their personal performance measures, but they inhibit teamwork, knowledge sharing, and suggestions to improve performance outside the employee's immediate accountability and control. Typical plans therefore include two or three kinds of awards: (1) an individual award based on achieving targets established annually for each employee's personal objectives, (2) an award based on the employee's business unit, along with, perhaps, (3) an award tier for divisional or enterprise performance.

We often are asked how to *weight the measures* in a Balanced Scorecard. Such a question may be a sign that the organization does not truly understand the Balanced Scorecard management system. It is using the BSC narrowly for extrinsic motivation, by modifying its compensation plan, but has bypassed the more important strategy-setting and communication aspect of the BSC, which creates intrinsically motivated employees. Nevertheless, linking the scorecard to compensation is the time (and the only time) when weights do have to be created so that a multidimensional BSC can be reduced to cash, a single dimension.

Organizations select weights based on the nature of their business and their short-term priorities. When there is little time between improvement in employees and processes and subsequent financial performance, the financial measures can be weighted heavily. Organizations that create value over longer periods of time through innovation, human capital development, and deployment of customer databases should weight these internal process and learning and growth metrics more heavily. If the company has a quality problem, then it can weight process improvement metrics heavily; if it has a customer loyalty problem, then it can weight customer satisfaction and retention more heavily. If the company's strategy requires a rapid installation of new information technology or a major retraining of employees, then those measures can be weighted heavily during the year to highlight the importance of achieving the performance targets during the next twelve months. And if it has an immediate need for cost reduction, then measures related to process improvements and productivity will be highly weighted. Thus, although measures may stay relatively consistent from year to year, the relative weights applied to those measures in the annual compensation plan can vary based on short-term priorities.

We have learned, however, that paying bonuses when financial performance is poor is probably not a good idea even if customer, process, and employee performance are excellent. Financial performance may be disappointing in the short run because of external factors such as an economic or industry slowdown, unexpected changes in macroeconomic variables such as exchange rates, interest rates, and energy prices, or hypercompetition in the industry. Whatever the causes, bonuses must be paid in cash and such payments may not be desirable when the company is hemorrhaging cash during times of financial distress.

This consideration argues for setting a minimal financial hurdle before bonuses are paid. The hurdle might be measured by, say, achieving profits as a targeted percentage of sales, or a minimum return on capital, or achieving breakeven in an economic-value-added calculation. Once the financial hurdle has been exceeded, some portion of the excess is committed to a bonus pool, with actual bonuses based on performance of BSC metrics and a majority of weight on measures in the three nonfinancial perspectives.

Best-Practice Case: Unibanco

Unibanco, with more than $23 billion (USD) in total assets, is the fifth-largest bank in Brazil, and the third-largest in the private sector. Unibanco started its Balanced Scorecard project in 2000 by building a company scorecard and scorecards for its four major business units: insurance and pension, retail, wholesale, and asset (wealth) management.

During 2001, senior executives launched a communication campaign to inform all twenty-seven thousand employees about the new strategy and the method for managing it. Unibanco called on the Schurmann family of Brazil, famous for traveling the world in a sailboat, to give talks to two thousand managers at various bank locations on the topic "We're all in the same boat," emphasizing that each crew member must know the destination to contribute to the objective of the boat reaching it successfully.

Advertisements and articles about the Painel de Gestão (management panel) and the relevant indicators appeared on the corporate intranet portal and the internal TV network, as well as in the internal monthly magazine and in personal e-mails sent to every manager. The "successful sailing" campaign branded the scorecard concept for employees and made all the employees aware that their everyday actions affected the success of the company strategy.

In 2002, Unibanco deployed extrinsic motivation by adapting an existing personnel management tool, the management agreement between each employee and his manager. The first page of the revised management agreement (Figure 10-3) described the unit's and the bank's strategic themes. Then employees, with their supervisors, created their personal management agreements (Figure 10-4), which would now be aligned with the unit's and the bank's strategic themes. The management agreement contained employee objectives in the four BSC perspectives, with each objective derived from one or more unit and corporate strategic themes.

For example, an employee in the marketing department, helping to create a campaign to stimulate new accounts, would have a financial objective related to the estimated lifetime value of new accounts acquired. An employee producing an output used by another bank unit would treat the value delivered to the other unit as a customer objective. For the learning and growth objective in the management agreement, the human resources group helped employees determine the competencies—knowledge, skills, and behavior—they required to reach the objectives in their three other management agreement perspectives.

Unibanco deployed a second extrinsic motivation tool when it imbedded the management agreement in every employee's recognition and bonus plan. Unibanco's previous compensation program had assigned a total compensation pool to each unit based on the unit's financial performance. The bank modified this program (see Figure 10-5) by adding two elements of variable pay. It added (or subtracted) a percentage to the compensation pool based on the leading (nonfinancial) indicators on the unit's Balanced Scorecard; another percentage was added or subtracted based on the company's performance. The company included a corporate bonus component so that employees would think about the total bank's performance, and not just the performance of their decentralized unit.

Then in 2004, Unibanco re-energized intrinsic motivation by launching a new "2-10-20" communications campaign. The company set the following goals to achieve, by its eightieth anniversary year in 2006: R2 billion in income, R10 billion in equity, and a 20 percent return on equity. The communications program promoted the 2-10-20 slogan everywhere, including in elevator displays.

People were encouraged to tell the story of how their actions led to successful outcomes. Each monthly issue of the internal magazine

Figure 10-3 The Management Agreement at Unibanco

Example

Name:	**CIF:**	**Concept:**
Area:	**Period:**	
Function:		**Total (1+2):**
Evaluator:		

Unibanco's Strategic Themes

- Aggressive search for scale
- Continuous efficiency maximization
- Obtain excellence in human capital management
- Effective domain of the credit and collect cycle

Your Unit's Strategic Themes

Your Department's Objectives

Example

Figure 10-4 Personal Goal Setting at Unisance

Work Plan					
	Your Goals for the Year	%	Self-Evaluation	Manager Evaluation	Final Evaluation
Financial					
Customer					
Internal Process					
People and Technology					

Total

Figure 10-5   Unibanco: Employee Compensation System

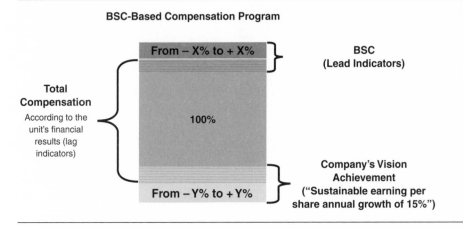

selected the best stories to celebrate the individuals and teams that had achieved significant results on key performance indicators. Annually, Unibanco provided a presidential reward for initiatives that achieved breakthrough results for a strategic theme.

From 1999 to 2004, Unibanco employees' "comprehension of the company's mission and vision" rose from 72 percent to 83 percent. Earnings per share increased from 5.57 in 1999 to 9.45 in 2004, with expectations of continued substantial increases in future years (to reach the 2-10-20 targets).

Develop Employee Competencies

One final stage is required if organizations are to align employees with strategy. Employees must develop the skills, knowledge, and behavior—which we call employee competencies—that enable them to make dramatic improvements in the critical processes that create value for customers and shareholders.

We have described in other work how to identify the strategic job families that have the greatest impact on the critical processes for strategy execution.[6] Significant resources must be devoted to enhancing the employee competencies in the strategic job families. Beyond the strategic job families, employees also have personal objectives that they aspire to achieve. All employees should have accompanying personal development plans that will help them acquire the skills, knowledge, and behavior that make it feasible for them to achieve their personal objectives. In fact, the entire chain of strategy execution starts by equipping all employees with the required competencies to achieve their personal objectives, which link to process improvements, loyal and profitable customer relationships, and, eventually, superior financial performance.

Best-Practice Case: KeyCorp

Cleveland-based KeyCorp is one of the nation's largest bank-based financial services companies, with assets of over $90 billion and more than nineteen thousand employees. The company provides investment management, retail and commercial banking, consumer finance, and investment banking products and services to individuals and companies throughout the United States and, for certain businesses, internationally.

KeyCorp's Balanced Scorecard program followed a classic cascading process (see Figure 10-6). In 2002, under the leadership of newly appointed CEO Henry Meyers, the company created a corporate Strategy Map and BSC containing strategic themes across the four perspectives: "enhance shareholder value (financial) by being the trusted adviser (customer) through excellent execution that brings the full power of Key-Corp's capabilities to all client relationships (internal) and staffed by people proud to be at Key and who live the Key values (employee)."[7]

The BSC team, led by Michele Seyranian, EVP Strategic Planning, cascaded KeyCorp's high-level corporate themes and objectives to scorecards in what, at the time, were its three major business groups: Key Consumer Banking (KCB), Key Corporate and Investment Banking (KCIB), and Key Capital Partners (KCP) (brokerage, investment banking, and asset management). These level II scorecards were then cascaded down to level III (the fifteen lines of business) and to level IV (five corporate support groups: human resources, information technology, finance, marketing, and operations). A further cascading brought strategic objectives to level V, functional or operating groups within each line of business. The project—cascading the Level I corporate scorecard down to Level V functional and operating group scorecards—was completed by the end of 2002.

The final cascading stage to employees, level VI, was accomplished by aligning individual performance objectives and rewards with Key's strategic themes and objectives. A particular alignment challenge arose in KCIB, which had to integrate its traditional corporate banking business with a recently acquired investment banking business. The culture of the corporate bankers was quite different from that of the investment

Figure 10-6 KeyCorp Cascades Corporate and Business Unit Objectives to Employees

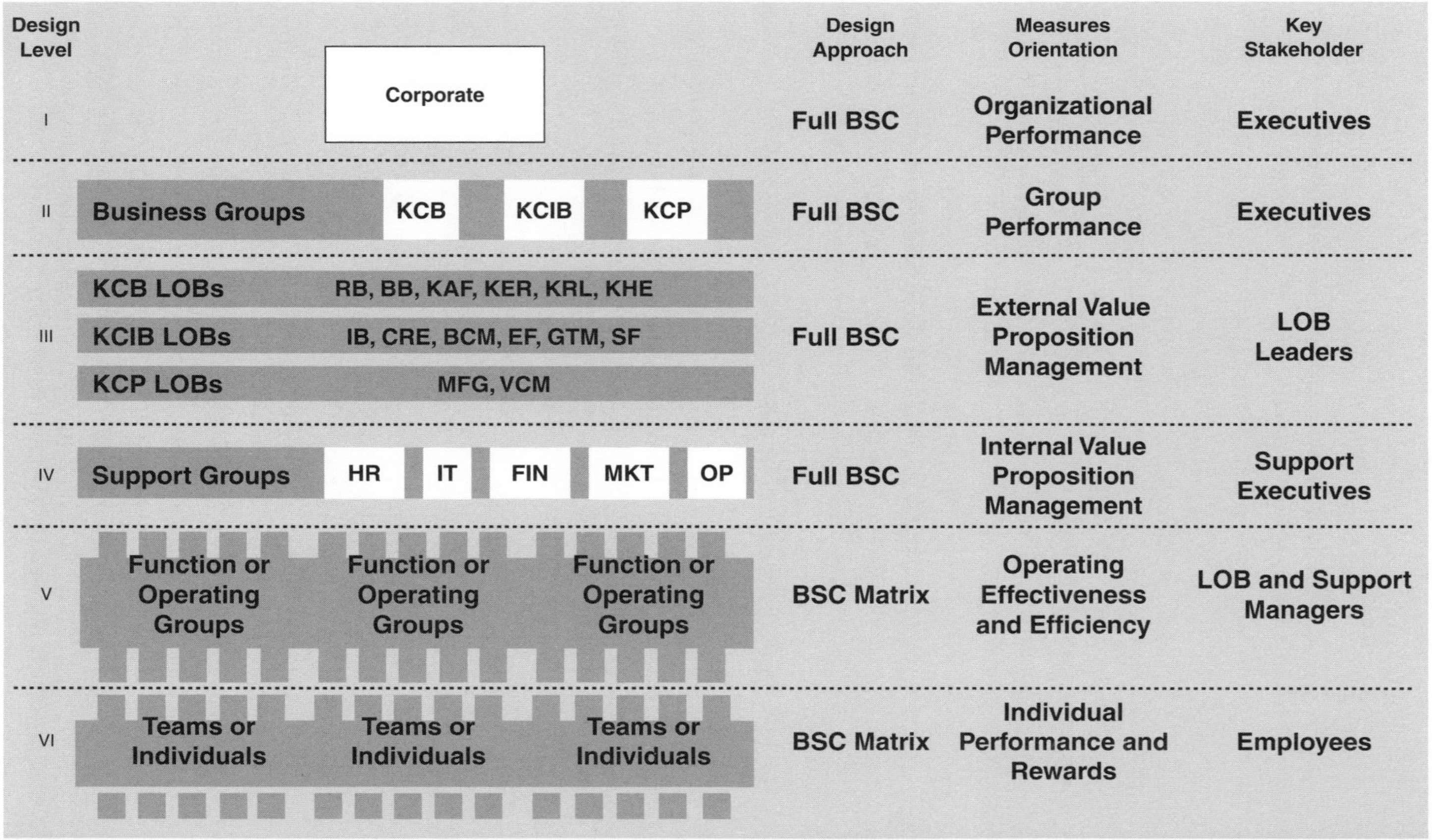
Design Level
Design Approach
Measures Orientation
Key Stakeholder
I
Corporate
Full BSC
Organizational Performance
Executives
II
Business Groups
KCB
KCIB
KCP
Full BSC
Group Performance
Executives
III
KCB LOBs
RB, BB, KAF, KER, KRL, KHE
KCIB LOBs
IB, CRE, BCM, EF, GTM, SF
KCP LOBs
MFG, VCM
Full BSC
External Value Proposition Management
LOB Leaders
IV
Support Groups
HR
IT
FIN
MKT
OP
Full BSC
Internal Value Proposition Management
Support Executives
V
Function or Operating Groups
Function or Operating Groups
Function or Operating Groups
BSC Matrix
Operating Effectiveness and Efficiency
LOB and Support Managers
VI
Teams or Individuals
Teams or Individuals
Teams or Individuals
BSC Matrix
Individual Performance and Rewards
Employees

bankers, and yet individuals from both groups had to learn to work together to sell seamlessly to corporate clients.

Tom Bunn, KCIB President, partnered with Susan Brockett, HR Director for KCIB, to lead a project team to create focus, alignment, and accountability around the KCIB strategy. A critical component of the transformation was the identification and definition of those positions in the newly created KCIB organization that would have the greatest impact on outcomes. The team started by developing a detailed list of the skills and competencies required for each critical job position and the learning needs for each job to close gaps in foundational sales, client management, functional, product, and technology skills. For each position, the team identified the skill levels that were necessary for the employee to make an immediate impact with the new business model, which combined corporate and investment banking functions (see Figure 10-7).

For example, an industry leader and a senior banker needed to be expert—capable of teaching others—in prospect identification, competition assessment, presentation skills, and development of the institutional perspective. A junior banker, in contrast, needed to have working-level skills in these areas but needed expert skills in negotiations to be able to close deals that had been identified and sold by senior bankers and the industry leader.

The project team identified training courses that could bring all individuals up to the required skill levels for their positions. It tracked the enrollment and performance of employees in the various training courses that were offered. KeyCorp soon saw the results of linking its comprehensive competency development program to critical strategic objectives. Unlike earlier training initiatives, KeyCorp's training courses had 100 percent attendance at every session. Employees responded with evaluations such as this one: "The course I just completed is immediately applicable to the work I am now doing . . . When is the next course on [skill xyz] being offered? . . . Finally, training that fits my job."

Lesa Evans, Senior Vice President of Employee Development, led the effort to design the comprehensive competency development program. Line leaders actively participated throughout the needs assessment, program design, and alignment of the curriculum to individual development plans. For this effort Lesa was nominated for and received the Chairman's Award for Outstanding Performance Contribution. When she accepted it, she was greeted with a standing ovation from the 150 top KeyCorp executives.

Since the formation of KCIB in 2002, and its focus of improving its banker's skill sets to create a single point of coordinated contact for its

Figure 10-7 Example: Determining Knowledge Level at KeyCorp

Skill or Competency—Sales	Industry Leader Knowledge Level			Senior Banker Knowledge Level			Junior Banker Knowledge Level			Associate Knowledge Level		
	E	W	L	E	W	L	E	W	L	E	W	L
Negotiation (back-end process)		X			X		X					X
Prospect identification and prequalification	X			X				X				
Prospect identification and prequalification (research)								X			X	
Pricing (process and market knowledge), includes price set and selling it		X			X			X				X
Developing the institutional perspective (external)	X			X				X				X
Competition (understand who else in the game)	X			X				X				X
Presentation (conceptual and delivery)	X			X				X				

KEY	E	Can teach others
	W	Well rounded—can fly alone
	L	Limited—may need support

clients, KCIB's ROE has improved 28.8 percent (16.1 percent in 2005, up from 12.5 percent in 2002). The new business model is delivering results, as revenues have increased and margins have improved. In 2004 KCIB earned $486 million for the year, up nearly 36 percent from $358 million in 2003.

ALIGNING PLANNING, OPERATIONS, AND CONTROL SYSTEMS

The final component of the alignment equation deals with management systems that guide planning, operations, and controls.[8] These management systems assist managers as they clarify direction, allocate resources, guide actions, monitor results, and adjust direction as required. As shown in Figure 10-8, the planning, operations, and control activities complete the closed-loop, goal-seeking process that places organization strategy at the center. Our research into the approaches of successful organizations has identified several best management practices (noted in the figure and described next).

The Planning Process

The Strategy Map allows an organization to clarify the logic of its strategy. Strategic objectives for shareholders, customers, people, and processes are defined and linked to a set of cause-effect relationships. Beyond defining and describing the strategy, executives must plan the supply of resources to execute the strategy. Three management best practices for planning have been observed: initiative planning, integrated HR and IT planning, and budget linkage.

Initiative Planning

Initiatives—special projects with a finite life span—advance the strategy by accomplishing specific changes, creating strategic capabilities, improving processes, or otherwise enhancing organizational performance. Initiatives contribute to closing the gap between actual and targeted performance on a Balanced Scorecard measure. They also generate a stream of strategic benefits that supports future strategic investments.

Initiative planning involves two steps. The first, *rationalization,* entails the review and assessment of the current portfolio of initiatives, maintaining only those that directly support specific strategic performance needs. This step establishes what the organization would like to do. Second, managers periodically create a consolidated resource and *implementation plan*

Figure 10-8 The Strategic Management Process

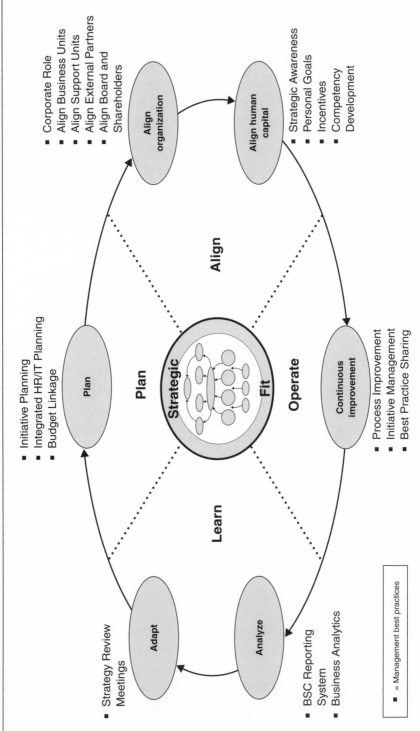

for the initiative portfolio that closes all identified performance gaps. This step addresses the practical constraints of step 1, answering the question, "How many of the rationalized initiatives can we afford?"

Best-Practice Case: The City of Brisbane

The City of Brisbane (Australia) has a rigorous approach to its initiative rationalization. By pinpointing the projects that align most closely with strategy, Brisbane is able to be rigorous about analyzing initiatives and understanding their relationships to strategic outcomes.

Each year, during the planning cycle, cross-functional teams (each with a broad set of capabilities) assess as many as four hundred initiatives to determine whether they fit the city's strategy. This analysis is applied only to projects whose costs exceed a certain threshold beyond what an individual city department could fund from its own budget. The teams use an analytic method to score each project according to its strategic relevance, and then use these scores to set priorities among the many proposed and existing initiatives. Many initiatives, of course, don't make the cut.

Individual teams use initiative-specific criteria in their assessment process. For example, for a proposed $10 million project to install filter beds in area creeks, team members looked at three key criteria, including "increased water quality" and "decreased noxious flora and fauna." They then rated the criteria by their relative importance and the effect of the project in achieving the objective ("healthy rivers and bays") and computed the scores. From these figures, members calculated the degree of fit for the project in achieving the desired outcome.

Using the BSC, executives map every funded initiative and activity aligned to the organization's strategy, establishing an important link between high-level vision and operational activities.

Integrated HR/IT Planning

Intangible assets such as human capital and information capital take on value only in the context of strategy. Therefore, planning for human resources and information technology should be aligned with the strategic plan of the organization. The following three-step process aligns HR and IT plans to the organization's strategy:

1. Identify the intangible assets required to support the strategic internal processes on the organization's Strategy Map.
2. Assess the strategic *readiness* of these assets (how readily deployable the assets are in supporting organizational strategy).

3. Establish measures and targets to track progress in closing any gaps between current readiness levels and what is needed to effectively execute the strategy.

Best-Practice Case: City of Brisbane (IT Planning Alignment)

The City of Brisbane sought to make strategic information available to all of its thousands of employees. It created a customized software program and data warehouse to showcase all scorecards, performance information, and the status of objectives and indicators.

By making available this detailed reporting information, the city enabled tight alignment between IT investments and the city's strategic objectives. IT projects are closely mapped to strategy; those that don't match must be reassessed. Brisbane's IT switched its planning approach from culling (reactive) to preempting (proactive) by identifying line-of-sight links to the strategy. Its goal? To limit the number of IT projects and restrict them to only those that are strategic. Once projects pass strategic muster, the city identifies gaps between IT capability and strategy and determines how technology can be better used to reach strategic objectives.

Budget Linkage

Critics of traditional budgeting argue that it is beyond repair and must be abolished. Admittedly, the budgeting process of most organizations is slow, cumbersome, and expensive, and it hinders effective management during rapid change. But when the BSC is introduced into an organization, an opportunity arises to convert the budget process into a useful means of strategic resource allocation. The BSC makes it possible to transform this deeply ingrained process into one that contributes to both strategic outcomes and operational performance.

Best-Practice Case: Fulton County Schools

The Fulton County school system, based in Atlanta, begins its annual budgeting, planning, and strategy process with the BSC. With annual priorities clearly articulated in the BSC, school officials at Fulton can allocate funding to the most strategic programs. Central office departments refine their strategic plans based on annual priorities represented in the BSC and then develop their budgets.

At planning and budget review sessions with top school administrators, department leaders explain their plans for the upcoming year and justify their requested budgets. School principals, in turn, meet once a year with their area superintendents to propose their use of discretionary resources in alignment with their strategic plans. The public is invited to view budget documents and comment on budgetary decisions during two annual public hearings.

The BSC has helped Fulton County Schools increase its accountability to taxpayers. Using it to justify new projects has also helped boost the school system's credibility in the business community, whose support is necessary if tax increases are needed for new educational initiatives. BSC data clearly shows which programs support the overall strategic mission—boosting overall academic performance—and which ones do not. The BSC thus helps the school board determine which programs to retain or eliminate.

The Operations Management Process

Having developed the plans, committed the resources, informed and aligned the organization with those plans, our best-practice companies typically rely on a variety of operational processes to execute the strategy. These processes tend to fall into three categories: (1) continuous improvement programs like total quality management, (2) initiative management programs that execute one-time change programs, and (3) programs for sharing best practices. Each of these creates value for the enterprise through alignment of program content with the strategy.

Process Improvement

Although more than a century old, quality management has enjoyed a revival in the past twenty-five years, thanks to the success of many Japanese companies. Today, the quality movement encompasses such programs as total quality management (TQM), the Baldrige National Quality Program, the European Foundation for Quality Management (EFQM), and, most recently, six sigma. Reengineering, championed by Michael Hammer and James Champy in the 1990s, is a powerful approach to discontinuous process improvement.[9] Activity-based management stimulates process improvement and management insight, starting from the organization's cost model. Customer management—embodied in customer value management, customer relationship management, and customer life-cycle management—focuses the attention of managers and employees on operational improvements to yield better performance.

These various approaches to process improvement have helped many organizations achieve dramatic gains in the quality, cost, and cycle times of their manufacturing and service-delivery processes. Inevitably, many of the same organizations that adopt the BSC to implement their strategies need to integrate one or more of these management disciplines. But some organizations are confused about the relative roles of these programs and do not understand how to integrate them, especially if one is already in place.

The BSC can be effectively combined with one or more of these approaches to achieve advantages beyond what any one of them could deliver on its own. It imbues each with organization-wide legitimacy, giving it a strategic context and anchoring the program to the overall management system in a holistic way. The scorecard's cause-and-effect links help highlight those process improvements and initiatives that each program identifies as having the greatest impact on the organization's strategic success. As one quality expert remarked at one of our conferences, "six sigma teaches people how to fish; the Balanced Scorecard teaches them where to fish."

Best-Practice Case: Siemens ICM

Siemens Information and Communications Mobile (ICM), the mobile communications unit of Siemens AG, has successfully combined the top-down strategic focus of the BSC with the bottom-up approach of six sigma. ICM combined the two approaches for two reasons: to reach all individuals in the organization, and to equip them with the means to close performance gaps.

ICM uses the BSC to identify strategic gaps in key cross-functional processes: idea to market, problem to solution, and order to cash. Six sigma is then used, at the project level, to drive out defects, wasted time, and non-value-added costs from these processes.

ICM believes that although six sigma may empower small teams to solve concrete problems, it is not by itself a strategic tool. Since integrating these approaches, ICM has seen a change in managers' behavior; meetings are now highly interactive, and the discussions focus on how projects are being used to achieve strategic performance targets. Managers now have a forum in which to fight for their parts of the strategy.

Initiative Management

Initiative management involves monitoring the progress of all strategic initiatives, assessing their relevance in light of strategic changes, and ensuring their timely completion. Effective initiative management begins with clear accountability. A member of the executive team is usually identified as the initiative sponsor. This means that any issues that are blocking progress can be efficiently dealt with by an individual empowered to make changes. A program manager is appointed and becomes responsible for executing the initiative.

These programs can be simple, stand-alone projects, such as a training program, or complex, ongoing projects, like six sigma. The program manager requires a broad set of skills in project management, consulting, relationship management, and change management.

Best-Practice Case: Handleman

When the Handleman Company introduced its BSC program, executives saw the BSC's potential as a strategy-coordinating and management tool throughout the company's many different entities. Handleman created a center for performance management (CPM) to promote strategy execution as a core competency. To be most effective, this new organizational entity was given an overarching set of responsibilities—and the support of executives at the highest levels. Handleman uses initiative management to manage its portfolio of initiatives to ensure coverage of the entire strategy.

CPM devised a four-step initiative management process that it uses with the company's executive team council.

1. *Gating*: council members screen proposed initiatives to determine those meriting formal review.
2. *Presenting*: Once proposals are approved for consideration, CPM presents them to the council for a final go/no go decision.
3. *Tracking progress*: CPM follows a disciplined procedure to monitor initiatives' progress.
4. *Tracking benefits*: CPM follows a disciplined procedure to assess whether promised benefits are realized.

The tracking of progress and benefits is the core process for setting priorities and managing the ongoing strategic initiative portfolio. CPM conducts Balanced Scorecard review meetings to track, discuss, and take action on active, approved initiatives. Once an initiative is completed, the initiative owner conducts periodic lessons-learned analyses to determine whether the promised benefits are being delivered by the initiative and to capture strategic learning for future efforts.

Best-Practice Sharing

The strategic governance process should provide feedback that is used to test whether the strategy is working, and ultimately, whether it is indeed the best means of achieving the organization's mission and vision. When BSC performance information is shared widely throughout the organization, people gain insights into the factors that contribute to performance.

When the organization allows access to performance information, people can easily learn whether their strategy is working and which units, departments, and teams are doing a better job of achieving strategic outcomes.

Although the field of best-practices research is, by now, well developed, how to link specific best practices to strategic outcomes is less well understood. Traditional approaches to leveraging best practices typically are independent of strategy. Many organizations now use their BSC reporting capabilities to identify high-performing teams, departments, or units based on their ability to deliver strategic results. Organizations can then document how the high performance was achieved and disseminate this information broadly throughout the organization. In this way, they educate and train others about how to improve performance.

Best-Practice Case: Crown Castle International (CCI)

Crown Castle's knowledge management system, CCI-Link, is a comprehensive database and library of the company's best practices. This knowledge management tool, which taps BSC-based analysis, is key to centralizing and sharing performance information and best-practice knowledge throughout this global and highly decentralized company.

CCI uses the BSC to benchmark each of its forty district offices on strategic performance measures. Benchmarking helps executives discover which processes and practices work best across the firm, and it aids them in training people in other areas of the organization on these processes and practices so that they can meet the higher performance levels achieved elsewhere. A focus on internal best practices allows Crown Castle to incorporate the lessons learned and help integrate the strategy, scorecard, process improvement, and training activities throughout the organization.

Crown Castle's knowledge management practice has contributed immensely to alignment and operational efficiencies—especially during a period of job cuts. CCI-Link's core architecture is common across diverse geographies. Countries have common traditional functions listed, such as finance, assets, and human capital, but the content is largely local. A detailed analysis helps differentiate between geographic areas so that managers can understand the true basis for performance differences.

The Learning and Control Process

Arguably, the most important part of the closed-loop performance management process is the control process: the ability to detect deviations from target, to determine the cause of these deviations, and to take corrective action as required. When dealing with an organization's strategy, this process is more about learning than about control.

A strategy is nothing more than a set of hypotheses about how the organization expects to achieve its desired results. The hypotheses should be tested continually, as part of a monthly review, analysis, and adjustment process. Two types of processes are found in our best-practice library: BSC reporting systems and strategy review meetings.

BSC Reporting Systems

Most early BSC reporting systems were based on off-the-shelf spreadsheet applications. Today, with more than twenty commercially available Balanced Scorecard software applications, BSC adopters increasingly are considering their automation options from the outset. And those that have already developed a spreadsheet-based reporting system are, by now, planning to migrate to a specialized BSC reporting tool.

What are the advantages of automation? Compared with manual systems, it is much easier to revise and aggregate data across scorecards, and data can be aggregated into "parent" scorecards, with far less time and effort. Analysis and decision making are thus more straightforward. That's particularly important for organizations that have dozens of BSCs.

Best-Practice Case: Royal Norwegian Air Force

The Royal Norwegian Air Force uses an automated system called Cockpit to report the results of all its organization units' scorecards. In addition to presenting data on most measures and initiatives, Cockpit includes executive assessments (interpretations).

This reporting system is based on an underlying enterprise resource planning platform and is accessible to all personnel. Updated information is reported through Cockpit every month, although a paper-based summary is also available. The agendas for strategy meetings are based on specific areas as reported and housed in the Cockpit application. Cockpit also supports management meetings.

Strategy Review Meetings

Just as the BSC is the centerpiece of the strategic management system, so is strategy itself the centerpiece of the new strategic management meeting. As advanced BSC users well understand, it's no longer sufficient to say that the BSC is on the agenda; the BSC *is* the agenda.

These meetings should begin with an overall strategic performance review based on the Strategy Map and the relevant Balanced Scorecard(s). Even if data is not available for each measure (often the case early on), the management team should examine strategic performance in its totality. The owner of each objective leads the discussion about his or her objective(s) and the strategic theme(s) for which she is accountable.

It's important that senior leaders create a supportive culture that encourages honest disclosure and does not punish negative results. Doing so fosters teamwork and motivates managers to reveal problems sooner, before they worsen. Below-target results should be seen as opportunities for improvement, as well as occasions to challenge the validity of the strategy—to understand whether and how it is actually working. Resources may need to be directed to underperforming areas, or executives may need to adjust targets that prove to be too aggressive.

At one organization, top strategic performers were reporting results in the red (under-target) zone. In fact, these units were outperforming other units that had not imposed equally aggressive targets on themselves. This situation arose in an organization that prized truthfulness and showed a great willingness to pursue stretch targets.

Best-Practice Case: Korea Telecommunications (KT)

Since early 2000, KT has used the Balanced Scorecard to drive the agenda of its quarterly executive meetings. Whereas agendas were once merely reports of financial results, today they are discussions of strategy in which participants refer to measurements within the four scorecard perspectives. The heads of KT's twenty-four offices and business groups gather to discuss the performance of the previous quarter, along with overall performance and strategy. At the fourth-quarter meeting, executives evaluate the year's overall strategic performance and plan strategies for the next year.

In addition to ensuring a timely flow and transparency of performance evaluation data, the BSC also profoundly affects the way executives track performance and manage strategy execution. The BSC serves as an organizing framework for discussion and analysis. For example, at one strategy review meeting, division heads identified early on the potentially explosive demands created by a new transmission technology, a result of BSC-related performance monitoring. Thanks to the BSC, management was prepared to quickly readjust the network capacity target to meet the new demands and was able to capture a greater share of this emerging market.

SUMMARY

Balanced Scorecard Hall of Fame companies have shown that strategy can be executed successfully. By allowing us to document their management practices, they have shown that the successful execution of strategy requires the successful alignment of four components: the strategy, the organization, the employees, and the management systems. Underlying this is the guiding hand of executive leadership. Each of these alignment components is a necessary, but not sufficient, condition for success. Taken together, however, they provide a recipe around which a successful management process can be developed (see Figure 10-9).

Chapters 1–9 of this book describe the organization alignment process. This chapter provides a high-level overview of the processes for aligning employees and systems with the strategy. We believe that, taken together—along with our related work on Strategy Maps, Balanced Scorecards, strategy-focused organizations, and the office of strategy management—these processes constitute the foundation for a *new science of strategy management.*

Strategy execution is not a matter of luck. It is the result of conscious attention, combining both leadership and management processes to describe and measure the strategy, to align internal and external organizational units with the strategy, to align employees with the strategy through intrinsic and extrinsic motivation and targeted competency development programs, and, finally, to align existing management processes, reports, and review meetings with the execution, monitoring, and adapting of the strategy.

Figure 10-9 Management Best Practices Underlying Alignment

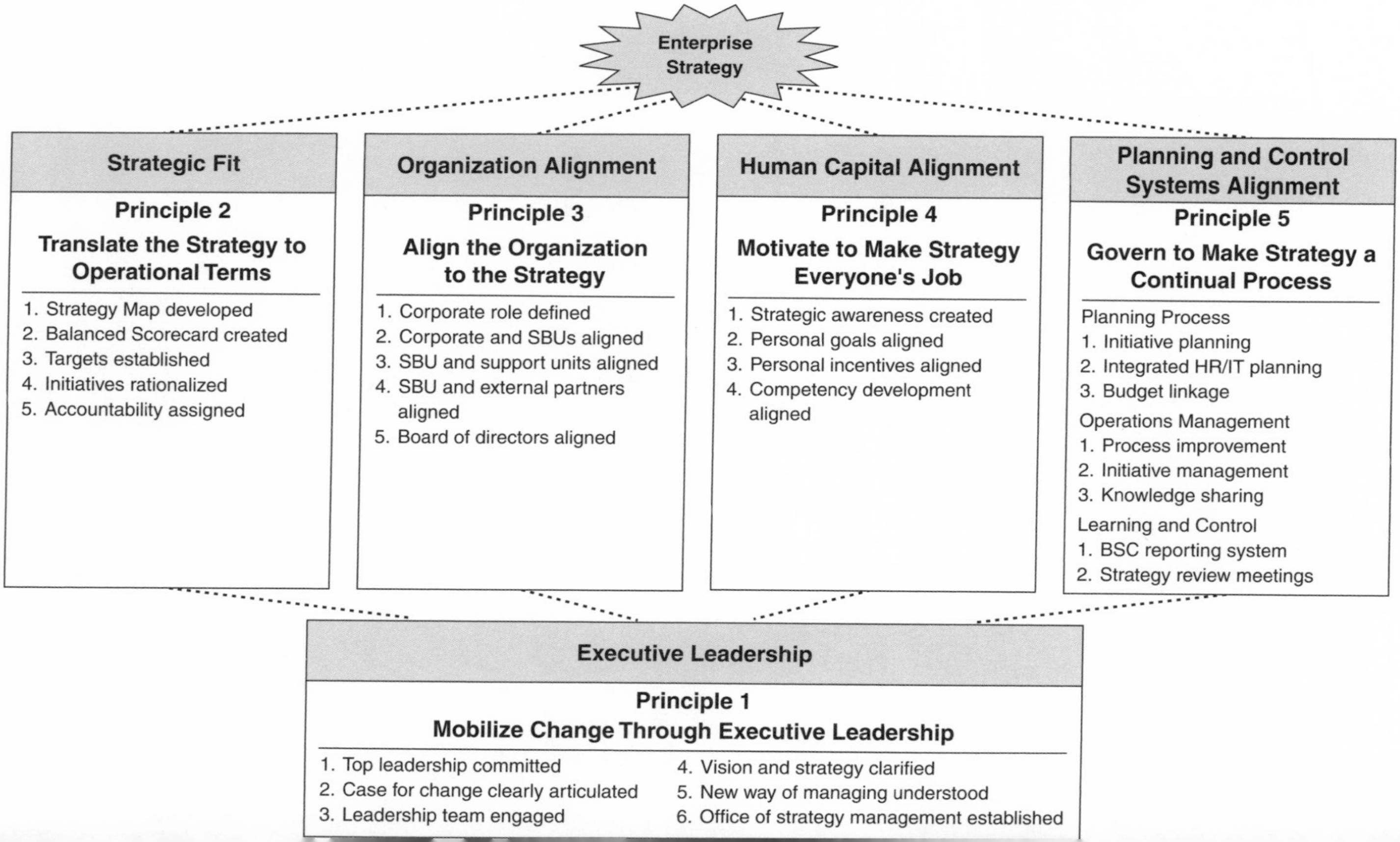

Enterprise Strategy

Strategic Fit

Principle 2

Translate the Strategy to Operational Terms

1. Strategy Map developed
2. Balanced Scorecard created
3. Targets established
4. Initiatives rationalized
5. Accountability assigned

Organization Alignment

Principle 3

Align the Organization to the Strategy

1. Corporate role defined
2. Corporate and SBUs aligned
3. SBU and support units aligned
4. SBU and external partners aligned
5. Board of directors aligned

Human Capital Alignment

Principle 4

Motivate to Make Strategy Everyone's Job

1. Strategic awareness created
2. Personal goals aligned
3. Personal incentives aligned
4. Competency development aligned

Planning and Control Systems Alignment

Principle 5

Govern to Make Strategy a Continual Process

Planning Process
1. Initiative planning
2. Integrated HR/IT planning
3. Budget linkage

Operations Management
1. Process improvement
2. Initiative management
3. Knowledge sharing

Learning and Control
1. BSC reporting system
2. Strategy review meetings

Executive Leadership

Principle 1

Mobilize Change Through Executive Leadership

1. Top leadership committed
2. Case for change clearly articulated
3. Leadership team engaged
4. Vision and strategy clarified
5. New way of managing understood
6. Office of strategy management established

NOTES

1. W. Edwards Deming, *Quality, Productivity, and Competitive Position* (Cambridge, MA: Center for Advanced Engineering Study, MIT, 1982), 101–104.
2. M. E. Porter, "What Is Strategy?" *Harvard Business Review* (November–December 1996).
3. R. S. Kaplan and D. P. Norton, *Strategy Maps: Converting Intangible Assets into Tangible Outcomes* (Boston: Harvard Business School Press, 2004).
4. R. S. Kaplan and D. P. Norton, *The Strategy-Focused Organization: How Balanced Scorecard Companies Thrive in the New Business Environment* (Boston: Harvard Business School Press, 2000).
5. R. S. Kaplan and D. P. Norton, "The Office of Strategy Management," *Harvard Business Review* (October 2005).
6. R. S. Kaplan and D. P. Norton, "Measuring the Strategic Readiness of Intangible Assets," *Harvard Business Review* (February 2004): 52–63; see Chapter 8, "Human Capital Readiness" in Kaplan and Norton, *Strategy Maps*, 225–243.
7. Correspondence with the Balanced Scorecard Collaborative.
8. The content of this section is drawn from "Govern to Make Strategy a Continual Process," *Balanced Scorecard Report* (January–February 2005).
9. M. Hammer and J. Champy, *Re-engineering the Corporation: A Manifesto for Business Revolution* (New York: Harper Business, 1993).

INDEX

ABB, 37–38
accountability, 253–256, 282
  organizational design and, 102
activity-based management, 78, 281
adverse selection problem, 195, 196
Akerlof, G. A., 219n
Aktiva, 46–49
Alexander, M., 27n, 39, 41n
alignment, 1–28
  accountability and, 253–256
  Balanced Scorecard for, 39–40
  board and investor, 193–220
  checkpoints for, 16, 246–247
  creating, 245–249
  external organization, 14–15
  external partner, 221–244
  of headquarters with operating units,
    13
  of human capital, 261, 262, 263–277
  importance of, 2–3
  integrated planning and, 160,
    162–164
  of internal support/service units,
    13–14
  managing, 15–17, 245–257
  as ongoing process, 160–165
  organization, 261, 262
  planning and control systems, 262,
    263
  process of, 15–17, 160–165

relationship managers in, 160, 162
sequence for, 10, 12–15
7-S Model for, 38
strategic fit and, 261, 262
of support functions, 119–167
sustaining, 250–253
total strategic, 259–289
alignment champions, 162, 253
alignment councils, 254
alignment index, 20, 22
alignment maps, 250, 252–253
alliance scorecards, 237–238, 239
Allstate, 78
Alpha-Beta Petroleum, 240–242, 243
Amanco, 55
American Diabetes Association, 6
American Institute of Certified Public
  Accountants, 214
Ann Taylor, 171
Anthony, R., 166n
audit committee, 212
auditors, 197

Balanced Scorecard (BSC). *See also*
  individual organizations
  as alignment tool, 39–40
  alliance, 237–238
  in board governance, 200–213
  for boards of directors, 208–213
  bottom-up approach with, 52

Balanced Scorecard (BSC) (*continued*)
  business unit, 13, 184–186
  cascading, 67, 68, 69–71, 169–192
  collaborative planning, forecasting,
    and replenishment, 224–228
  customer, 232–237
  executive, 203–208
  with external partners, 14–15
  getting started with, 184–186
  Hall of Fame for Strategy Execution,
    2–3, 287
  high-benefit users, 2–3
  human resources organization tem-
    plate for, 140, 142
  interagency, 113, 115–117
  key performance indicator, 224
  line organization, 120–122
  linkage, 138, 140
  low-benefit users, 3
  management links with, 78–82
  reporting systems, 285
  7-S Model compared with, 38
  supplier, 221–228
  supply-chain, 228–232
  support/service unit, 13–14
  support unit, 136, 138–144
  for total strategic alignment, 259–289
  for virtual organizations, 113
  weighting measures in, 267–268
Balanced Scorecard Collaborative, 2,
  96–97
Baldrige National Quality Program, 78,
  281
Bamford, J., 244*n*
Bank of Tokyo-Mitsubishi (HQA),
  79–82, 249
  cascading at, 169–170, 186–192
  governance at, 254, 255
Barker, John, 217
Barnes, Roy, 86, 87
Barney, J., 28*n*
Bebchuk, L., 219*n*
benchmarking, 120
Berkshire Hathaway, 7, 45
Bernard, V. L., 219*n*
best practices
  knowledge sharing and, 96
  sharing, 20, 22, 283–284
  at Sport-Man Inc., 20, 22
best total cost value proposition, 4
Birchard, B., 219*n*

boards of directors, 14–15, 193–220
  alignment of, 16
  in alignment process, 246, 247
  Balanced Scorecard for, 200–213
  CEOs and, 199
  committees in, 212
  enterprise scorecards and, 200–203
  executive scorecards and, 203–208
  executive selection/evaluation and,
    198
  financial decision making and, 198
  governance and, 193–199, 212
  integrity and compliance and,
    197–198
  limitations of, 199–200
  responsibilities of, 197
  scorecards on, 208–213
  strategy monitoring by, 198
  time management for, 200
Bower, J., 28*n*, 41*n*
Brady, Larry, 119, 122
brands
  customer perspective and, 54–55
  enterprise value propositions and,
    52–55
  financial synergies with, 52–62
  internal process perspective and,
    54–55
  leveraging, 35
Brewer, P. C., 228, 244*n*
Brisbane, Australia, 62–63, 279, 280
British Petroleum (BP), 10, 78
Broadbent, M., 166*n*
Brockett, Susan, 275
Bronson, John, 94, 118*n*
Brown, S. L., 28*n*,
Brown & Root Engineering Services, 10,
  83
  Rockwater Company, 232–234, 249
Bryan, J. Stewart, 63–64
BSC. *See* Balanced Scorecard (BSC)
budgets, 280–281
Bunn, Tom, 275
business groups, 34–35, 93. *See also*
  conglomerates
business units
  alignment of, 16
  in alignment process, 246, 247
  enterprise-derived value versus, 3–6
  enterprise value proposition and, 246,
    248–249

headquarters alignment with, 13
increasing shareholder value of, 7
support units compared with, 136, 138
synergies from, 13

Campbell, A., 27n, 39, 41n
Canadian Blood Services, 254
Canon, USA, 122, 248
capital markets
    adverse selection and, 195, 196
    intermediation in, 196–197
    moral hazard and, 195–196
Carr, N., 166n
cascading, 169–192
    at Bank of Tokyo-Mitsubishi, 81, 186–192
    bottom-up, 172–173
    from business units, 184–186
    customer value proposition and, 69
    in franchise operations, 169, 170–171
    in holding companies, 169, 172–173
    hybrid processes for, 173
    at KeyCorp, 273–277
    at MDS Corporation, 178–184
    at Media General, 67, 68
    middle-to-top-down, 186–192
    office of strategy management in, 254, 256
    top-down, 170–171, 174–178
    top-to-middle and middle-to-top, 178–184
    in the U.S. Army, 174–178
case studies
    Aktiva, 46–49
    Bank of Tokyo-Mitsubishi, 79–82, 169–170, 186–192
    Citizen Schools, 71, 73, 74–75
    DuPont Engineering Polymers, 103–109
    Handleman Company, 125–136, 156–160
    Hilton Hotels, 69–71, 73
    IBM, 97–101
    Ingersoll-Rand, 55–62, 144–146
    KeyCorp, 273–277
    Lockheed Martin Corporation, 149–152
    Marriott Vacation Club, 85, 86–87, 88–90
    MDS Corporation, 178–184

Media General, 63–67
New Profit Inc., 49–52
Royal Canadian Mounted Police (RCMP), 109–113, 114
Sport-Man Inc., 17–26
Unibanco, 268–272
U.S. Army, 174–178
Washington State salmon recovery, 113, 115–117
centralized functional organizations, 29–32
chaebols, 34. See also business groups
Champy, James, 281, 289n
Chandler, Alfred, 32, 39, 27n, 40n, 41n
change, constancy of, 245
Charlotte, North Carolina, 62–63
Chemical Retail Bank, 215
ChemTrade, 230–232
chief executive officers (CEOs), 199
    executive scorecards for, 204–208
chief financial officers (CFOs), 153, 185
chief information officers (CIOs), 204
chief knowledge officers (CKOs), 95–96
chief learning officers (CLOs), 94
Chrysler Group, 2, 254
Cigna Property & Casualty, 215
Citizen Schools, 71, 73, 74–75
Cohn, J., 207–208, 219n
collaborative planning, forecasting, and replenishment (CPFR) scorecards, 224–228
Collis, D. J., 27n, 40, 41n
Committee of Sponsoring Organizations (COSO), 79, 81
communication
    at Bank of Tokyo-Mitsubishi, 79, 81
    finance units and, 135–136
    with investors/analysts, 214–218
    motivation and, 264–265
compensation committee, 212. See also boards of directors
compensation systems, 266–268
    at Unibanco, 269–272
competencies
    brands/themes and, 53
    core, 39–40, 128, 174
    education/training programs and, 93–95
    employee, developing, 272–273
    strategic, 94–95, 123, 125

compliance issues, 135–136, 197–198
Conger, J., 219n
conglomerates, 34–35
    brands/themes and, 53
    financial synergies and, 44–45
    movement toward, 44–45
coordination, 102
core competencies, 39–40
    at Handleman, 128
    U.S. Army, 174
Couto, V., 167n
Crown Castle International (CCI), 96,
    254, 284
customer management, 78, 281
customer perspective, 6, 7, 9
    in board scorecards, 209
    branding and, 54–55
    at Citizen Schools, 71, 73
    enterprise-derived value and, 83
    finance function, 153, 155
    at Handleman, 156, 159
    at Hilton Hotels, 69–71
    human resources organizations and,
        140
    IT department and, 146
    at Lockheed Martin, 150
    at MDS Corporation, 181
    at Media General, 66
    shared customer synergies and, 62–67
    at Sport-Man Inc., 20
    in supply-chain scorecards, 229
    support units and, 138–139
    synergies in, 39, 62–73
customer relationships, 35–36
    at Handleman, 125–136
    value-chain integration and, 82–87
customers
    aligning, 14–15
    in alignment process, 246, 247
    feedback from, 160, 164
    finance function, 153–155
    retaining versus acquiring, 83
    satisfaction of, 214
    scorecards on, 232–237
    sharing, 62–67
    support unit, 138
customer solutions value proposition, 4,
    122–123
customer value propositions
    cascading and, 69–71
    enterprise-derived value and, 4–5

synergies from common, 67, 68–69

Dahlmann, David, 212
Dana Corporation, 223
Datex Ohmeda (DO), 62
decision making
    in centralized functional organiza-
        tions, 31
    finance units and, 136, 156
    at Handleman, 159–160
    information technology and, 133
Davis, S., 41n
Defense Logistics Services, 9
Deming, W. Edwards, 259, 289n
Dhingra, Arun, 167n
discretionary expense centers, 13–14,
    120
due diligence processes, 45, 52
DuPont Corporation, 32, 33
    Engineering Polymers, 103–109

economies of knowledge, 78
economies of scale, 9–10, 29, 31
    in multidivisional organizations, 34
    shared processes/services and, 77–78
    strategic themes and, 101–117
education/training programs, 93–95
    employee competency development
        and, 273–277
    executive scorecards and, 208
    at Handleman, 128–129
    at KeyCorp, 273–277
    motivation and, 264–265
Eisenhardt, K. M., 28n
E-Land, 2
Emerson Electric, 52, 53, 54
employees, 263–277
    alignment of, 16–17
    compensation systems and, 266–268
    competency development for,
        272–273
    customer value proposition and, 69
    human capital development and,
        93–95
    information technology, 149
    key staff rotation, 20, 22
    leadership development and, 91–93
    motivating, 3, 263–268
empowerment, 265
enterprise-derived value, 3–10, 43–76
    at Aktiva, 46–49

at Bank of Tokyo-Mitsubishi, 79–82
business-unit value versus, 3–6
at Citizen Schools, 71, 73
corporate brands/themes and, 53–62
corporate strategic themes and,
  101–117
customer synergies and, 62–73
customer value proposition synergies
  and, 67, 68–73
definition of, 5
financial synergies in, 43–62
at Hilton Hotels, 69–71
holding company model and, 43–49
at Ingersoll-Rand, 55–62
intangible assets and, 87, 91–97
at Media General, 63–67
at New Profit Inc., 49–52
shared customer synergies and,
  62–67
shared processes/services synergies
  and, 77–82
value-chain integration and, 82–87
enterprise scorecards
  for boards of directors, 200–203
  four-perspective framework for, 6–10
  Sport-Man Inc., 18, 19
enterprise value propositions, 6–10
  as alignment checkpoint, 246, 247
  alignment process and, 15–17
  brands/themes and, 53–55
  BSC perspectives and, 39–40
  business unit alignment with, 246,
    248–249
enterprise-wide alignment. *See*
  cascading
entropy, 245
Epstein, M. J., 219n
Ernst, J., 244n
ethics, 199
European Foundation for Quality Management (EFQM), 78, 281
Evans, Lesa, 275
executive scorecards, 203–208
extrinsic motivation, 263–264, 266–268

Federal Mogul, 224
feedback, client, 160, 164
finance departments, 29, 31. *See also*
  shared-service units
  aligning, 152–160
  at Handleman, 156–160

strategic services portfolios of,
  135–136
financial perspective, 6, 7
IT department and, 146
at Media General, 66–67
at Sport-Man Inc., 20
in supply-chain scorecards, 229
support units and, 138–139
synergies in, 39
financial synergies, 43–62
  at Aktiva, 46–49
  corporate brands/themes and, 53–62
  holding company model and, 43–52
  at Ingersoll-Rand, 55–62
  at New Profit Inc., 49–52
Finegold, D., 219n
First Commonwealth Financial Corporation, 200
  board scorecard at, 212
  enterprise scorecard at, 201–203
  executive scorecards at, 204, 205–206
FMC Corporation, 7, 52, 53, 119,
  172–173
  governance at, 45–46
forecasting, 224–228
franchises, 169, 170–171
Frangos, Cassandra, 166n
Fried, J., 219n
Fulton County Schools, 280–281

General Electric (GE), 32, 193
  branding at, 52, 53, 54
  human capital development at,
    93–94
Gilmore, T., 41n
Global Chemical Inc., 91, 92
Global Commerce Initiative, 227
global economy, 35
  intangible assets and, 87–101
Gold, Robert S., 148, 167n
Goold, M., 27n, 39, 41n
governance, 3, 193–199. *See also* boards
  of directors
  at Aktiva, 46–49
  financial synergies and, 45–52
  at Sport-Man Inc., 25
governance committee, 212
Govindarajan, V., 166n

Hackett Group, 120
Hammer, Michael, 281, 289n

Handleman Company, 125–136, 249
   finance department, 156–160
   initiative management at, 283
Harris, Bob, 179
Harvard Business School, 214–215
Healy, P. M., 219n
Heinz, I., 167n
Henkel, Herb, 56, 60, 146, 217. See also
   Ingersoll-Rand
Hertzberg, F., 167n
high-benefit users (HBUs), 2–3
Hilton Hotels, 7, 69–71, 73
Hirschhorn, L., 41n
Hoff, Ted, 97, 98, 101
holding companies, 43–46, 172–173
   cascading in, 169
Horvat, Darko, 47, 49
human capital. See also intangible
   assets
   alignment of, 261, 262, 263–277
   developing, 93–95
   HR departments and, 96–97
   in supply-chain scorecards, 230–232
human resources organizations, 96–97.
   See also shared-service units
   aligning, 140–144
   at Handleman, 125–136
   at Ingersoll-Rand, 144–146
   integrated planning for, 279–280
   linkage scorecards for, 138
   strategic services of, 123, 125

IBM, 82, 83
   Learning, 97–101, 162, 249
Immelt, J., 219n
incentive compensation, 266–268
Industrial Revolution, 29
information capital, 230
information technology (IT)
   aligning, 146–152
   at Handleman, 129, 133
   integrated planning for, 279–280
   learning and growth perspective and,
   10
   at Lockheed Martin, 149–152
infrastructure, 133
Ingersoll-Rand, 55–62, 248
   Enterprise Leadership Team, 60
   Global Business Services, 56–58, 60
   human resources at, 144–146

investor/analyst information at,
   215–218
initiatives, 160, 164
   common value propositions and,
   170–171
   financial services portfolios and, 136
   human resources organizations and,
   143–144
   implementation plans, 277, 279
   managing, 282–283
   owners of, 164
   planning, 277, 279
   rationalization, 277
Institutional Investor Research Group,
   217
Instrumentarium Corporation, 62
intangible assets
   human capital development and,
   93–95
   at IBM, 97–101
   knowledge sharing and, 95–96
   leadership development and, 91–93
   support groups and, 120
   synergies from leveraging, 87, 91–101
integrity, 197–198
interagency processes, 113, 115–117
internal capital markets, 43
internal process perspective, 6, 9–10
   in board scorecards, 209, 212
   branding and, 54–55
   customer value proposition and, 69
   enterprise-derived value and, 83
   finance function, 155
   at Handleman, 159–160
   human resources organizations and,
   140, 143
   IT department and, 146, 148–149
   at Lockheed Martin, 150, 152
   at Media General, 66
   at Sport-Man Inc., 20
   in supply-chain scorecards, 229–230
   support units and, 139
   synergies in, 39–40
   at Tiger, 234, 237
   U.S. Army, 174
intrinsic motivation, 263–265
investors, 214–218

J.D. Irving, 162, 253
Jenkins Committee, 214

Johnson & Johnson, 156
joint ventures, 14–15. *See also* alliance
  scorecards; initiatives; partners
just-in-time practices, 222

Kerr, Steve, 93–94
KeyCorp, 273–277
key performance indicator (KPI) score-
  cards, 224
key staff rotation, 20, 22
Khanna, T., 41*n*, 76*n*
Khurana, R., 207–208, 219*n*
Kinnarps, 95
knowledge sharing, 95–96
  with investors and analysts, 214–218
Kolodny, H., 41*n*
Korea Telecommunications, 286
Kulp, S., 244*n*

Lawler, Edward, 199, 219*n*
Lawrence, P., 41*n*
leadership. *See also* intangible assets
  communication and, 264–265
  developing, 91–93
  development programs for, 125
  motivation and, 264–265
  in total strategic alignment, 259
lead indicators, 199
learning and control processes, 284–286
learning and growth perspective, 6, 10
  in board scorecards, 212
  customer value proposition and, 69
  enterprise-derived value and, 83
  finance function, 155–156
  human resources and, 143
  at Media General, 64
  motivation and, 264–265
  at Sport-Man Inc., 20, 22
  in supply-chain scorecards, 230–232
  support units and, 139
  synergies in, 40
  U.S. Army, 174
learning curve effects, 34
Limited, The, 9, 78
linkage scorecards, 138
  human resources organizations and,
    140
Lockheed Martin Corporation,
  149–152
Lorsch, Jay, 200, 219*n*

low-benefit users (LBUs), 3
low-cost strategy, 122–123

management
  activity-based, 78, 281
  alignment of, 16–17
  of alignment process, 15–17
  of the alignment process, 245–257
  BSC excellence and, 3, 4
  buyouts, 36
  customer, 78
  framework for strategy execution,
    259–261
  of matrix organizations, 36–38
  in strategy implementation, 3
management by objectives (MBO), 266
managers
  communication by, 265
  moral hazard and, 195–196, 209
Markides, C., 27*n*, 41*n*
Marriott Vacation Club (MVCI), 85,
  86–87, 88–90
Maslow, A., 167*n*
matrix organizations, 36–38
  ABB, 37
  DuPont, 103–109
Mausner, B., 167*n*
McKinsey & Company, 38, 238, 240
MDS Corporation, 178–184
Media General, 2, 63–67
Meehan, Ed, 149–150, 152
mergers and acquisitions, 43
  failure of, 239–240
  integrating, 238–242
  risk reduction and, 44–45
Metalcraft Corporation, 222–223
metrics
  alignment, 249, 250–253
  customer value proposition and, 69
  financial, 46, 69, 153
  investor/analyst information and,
    214–218
  motivation and, 264–265
  regulatory/social process, 55
  for support departments, 119–120
Meyers, Henry, 273
M-form structure, 32–34
mobilization, 3
Mobil US Marketing & Refining, 215
money managers, 196–197

Montgomery, C. A., 27n, 40, 41n
moral hazard problem, 195–196, 209
Moran, M., 167n
motivation, 3, 263–277
  compensation and, 266–268
  extrinsic, 263–264, 266–268
  intrinsic, 263–264
  at Unibanco, 268–272
multidivisional (M-form) structure,
  32–34

Nagel, Michael, 167n
Narayan, V. G., 244n
Naylor, Craig, 103
New Profit Inc. (NPI), 49–52
  Citizen Schools, 71, 73, 74–75
nonprofit organizations
  enterprise-derived value and, 6
  New Profit Inc., 49–52
Northwestern Mutual, 9

office of strategy management (OSM),
  16, 254, 256
operations management, 281–284
organizational culture
  at Handleman, 160
  information technology and, 149
  leadership development and, 91–93
  supply-chain scorecards and, 230
  in support groups, 120
organization alignment, 261, 262
organizational strategy
  aligning with structure, 36–38
  history of, 29–41
organizational structure
  aligning with strategy, 36–38
  centralized functional, 29–32
  conglomerates, 34–35
  history of, 29–41
  matrix, 36–38
  multidivisional, 32–34
  post-industrial, 38
  strategic themes and, 101–102,
    101–117

Palepu, K., 41n, 76n, 219n
partners, 14–15, 16, 221–244
  in alignment process, 246, 247
  alliance scorecards, 237–238, 239
  customer scorecards and, 232–237
  merger integration and, 238–242

supplier scorecards and, 221–228
supply-chain scorecards and, 228–232
performance indicators, 224. See also
  metrics
performance management processes,
  125
Peters, T. J., 41n
Petrobras, 14
Pettigrew, A., 41n
Phillips, J. R., 41n
Pinus TKI, 47
plan-do-check-act process, 259
planning
  aligning, 277–281
  budget linkage with, 280–281
  building alignment into, 12
  collaborative, 224–228
  finance units and, 136, 156
  for initiatives, 277, 279
  integrated HR/IT, 279–280
  integrated process for, 160, 162–164
planning and control systems, 262,
  263
platforms, leveraging, 36
Porter, Michael, 27n, 39, 289n
post-industrial organizations, 38
process improvement, 281–284
Procter & Gamble, 153, 224, 225, 227
production departments, 29
product leader value proposition, 4,
  122–123
public-sector organizations
  enterprise-derived value and, 6
  financial synergies and, 44
  Royal Canadian Mounted Police
    (RCMP), 109–113, 114
  salmon recovery and, 113, 115–117
  shared customer synergies in, 62–63
  strategic themes and, 102–103

quality movement, 78, 259

Raynor, M., 41n
Red Cross, 6
reengineering, 281
regulatory processes, 55, 199
relationship managers, 160, 162
reporting to investors and analysts,
  214–218, 285
research, leveraging, 36
Retail, Inc., 136, 137

Rice, Don, 144
Rigby, D., 27*n*
risk management, 13–14
  at Bank of Tokyo-Mitsubishi, 79, 81
  boards of directors and, 203
  in conglomerates, 34
  investor/analyst information and, 214–218
  mergers and acquisitions as, 44–45
Rockwater Company, 232–234, 249
Rolls Royce, 224
Ross, J., 219*n*
Roy, M., 219*n*
Royal Canadian Mounted Police (RCMP), 6, 109–113, 114
Royal Norwegian Air Force, 285

Sainsbury, 224, 227–228
sales departments, 29
salmon recovery case study, 113, 115–117
Sarbanes-Oxley Act of 2002, 136, 137, 153, 197, 208
SAS Institute, 10
Segil, L., 244*n*
service agreements, 160, 164
7-S Model, 38
Seyranian, Michele, 273
shared-service units, 13–14. *See also* human resources organizations; information technology (IT); planning
  aligning, 119–167
  as discretionary expense centers, 13–14
  at Sport-Man Inc., 22–24
shareholders
  alignment of, 16
  in alignment process, 246, 247
  disclosure to, 14–15
Siemens Information and Communications Mobile, 282
six sigma programs, 282
  branding and, 54–55
  at DuPont, 106
Smith, Adam, 29, 31, 36
Snyderman, B., 167*n*
Society for Human Resource Management, 96–97
Speh, T. W., 228, 244*n*
Sport-Man Inc., 17–26, 133, 134, 249

enterprise scorecard at, 18, 19
St. Mary's/Duluth Clinic Health System, 248–249, 254
stakeholders, 214–218
strategic competencies, 94–95, 123, 125
strategic fit, 261, 262
strategic job families, 94, 272–273
  at Handleman, 129–133
  at Sport-Man Inc., 22
strategic portfolio approach, 139
  at Handleman, 125–136
  at Sport-Man Inc., 133, 134
Strategic Readiness System, 174–178
strategic themes, 101–117
  at DuPont Engineering Polymers, 103–109
  Royal Canadian Mounted Police (RCMP), 109–113, 114
strategy
  boards of directors and, 198
  communicating, 264–265
  definition of, 259
  historical perspective on, 29–41
  management of, 287
  review meetings on, 285–286
  support unit, 122–123
  translation of, 3
Strategy Maps. *See also individual organizations*
  board, 209, 210
  common value propositions and, 171
  finance function, 153–155
  for human resources organizations, 140, 141
  IT department, 146, 147
  line organization, 120–122
  support unit, 136, 138–144
Strome, Stephen, 125
suppliers
  aligning, 14–15
  at Metalcraft, 222–223
  scorecards for, 221–228
  strategic, 224
supplier scorecards, 221–228
  at Dana Corporation, 223
  delivery, 223
  at Metalcraft, 222–223
  quality, 222
  timing, 222–223

supply-chain management, 221–228
  collaborative planning, forecasting,
    and replenishment scorecards in,
    224–228
  at Handleman, 125–136
  scorecard for, 228–232
support units, 119–167
  aligning, 136, 138–144
  in alignment process, 246, 247
  closing the loop with, 160–165
  costs/benefits of, 165
  extensions of alignment and, 165
  finance, 152–160
  finance portfolio of, 135–136
  at Handleman, 125–136
  human resources, 140–146
  information technology, 146–152
  monitoring and evaluating, 119–120
  processes in, 120–122
  strategic services and, 123–125
  strategies and, 122–123
synergy
  business process, 39–40
  customer, 39, 62–73
  customer value propositions and, 67,
    68–69
  enterprise-derived value and, 5–6
  financial, 39, 43–62
  global economy and, 35
  from intangible assets leveraging, 87,
    91–101
  learning and growth, 40
  from shared processes/services, 77–82
  sources of enterprise-level, 10, 11
  at Sport-Man Inc., 20
  from value-chain integration, 82–87
system platform value proposition, 5

Tata Group, 34, 55, 93

Tesco, 224
Thomas, H., 41n
Tiger Textiles, 234–237
total quality management (TQM), 78,
    214, 222, 281
transaction processing, 133, 135, 155,
    156
Treadway Commission, 79, 81

Unibanco, 268–272
U.S. Army, 14, 174–178, 181, 184, 254

value
  alignment as source of, 1–28
  enterprise-derived, 3–10
  value-chain integration, 9–10
  at Marriott Vacation Club, 85, 86–87
  synergies from, 82–87
value propositions
  cascading from common, 170–171
  customer, 4–5
  enterprise, 6–10
virtual organizations, 113
vision, communicating, 264–265

Wal-Mart, 9, 133, 224
Washington State salmon recovery, 113,
    115–117
Waterman, R. H., 41n
Weill, P., 166n
Wendy's International, 7, 201–203, 217
Wernerfelt, B., 27n
Whittington, R., 41n
Williams-Sonoma, 94
Wisner, P., 219n

Zaccardelli, Giuliano, 109
Zimmerman, K., 244n

ABOUT THE AUTHORS

ROBERT S. KAPLAN is Baker Foundation Professor at Harvard Business School. He is the author or coauthor of sixteen *Harvard Business Review* articles, more than one hundred other papers, and twelve books, including four with David Norton. His research, teaching, consulting, and speaking focus on linking strategy to performance and cost management systems, primarily the Balanced Scorecard and Activity-Based Costing. He has received numerous honors, including the Outstanding Educator Award from the American Accounting Association (AAA), Lifetime Contributions Award from the Management Accounting Section of the AAA, and the Chartered Institute of Management Accountants (UK) Award for "Outstanding Contributions to the Accountancy Profession." He can be reached at rkaplan@hbs.edu.

DAVID P. NORTON is President of Balanced Scorecard Collaborative/Palladium, a professional services firm that facilitates the worldwide use of the Balanced Scorecard approach to strategy execution. Previously he was the President of Renaissance Solutions, Inc., a consulting firm he cofounded in 1992, and of Nolan, Norton & Company, where he spent seventeen years as President. Dr. Norton is a management consultant, researcher, and speaker in the field of strategic performance management. With Robert Kaplan, he is the cocreator of the Balanced Scorecard concept, coauthor of seven *Harvard Business Review* articles, and coauthor of three books—*The Balanced Scorecard: Translating Strategy into Action,*

The Strategy-Focused Organization: How Balanced Scorecard Companies Thrive in the New Business Environment, and *Strategy Maps: Converting Intangible Assets into Tangible Outcomes.* He is a Trustee of Worcester Polytechnic Institute and a former Director of ACME (the Association of Consulting and Management Engineers). He can be reached at dnorton@bscol.com.